Moral Injury and a First World War Chaplain

Moral Injury and a First World War Chaplain

The Life of G. A. Studdert Kennedy

Dayne Edward Nix

LEXINGTON BOOKS
Lanham • Boulder • New York • London

Published by Lexington Books
An imprint of The Rowman & Littlefield Publishing Group, Inc.
4501 Forbes Boulevard, Suite 200, Lanham, Maryland 20706
www.rowman.com

86-90 Paul Street, London EC2A 4NE

British Library Cataloguing in Publication Information Available

Library of Congress Cataloging-in-Publication Data

Names: Nix, Dayne E., author.
Title: Moral injury and a First World War chaplain : the life of G.A. Studdert Kennedy / Dayne Edward Nix.
Other titles: Life of G.A. Studdert Kennedy
Description: Lanham : Lexington Books, [2021] | Includes bibliographical references and index. | Summary: "This study examines Chaplain G. A. Studdert Kennedy, a British chaplain during World War I. The author analyzes Kennedy's poetry, prose, and postwar activities and the impact of moral injury on a combat veteran through the lens of contemporary psychological research"— Provided by publisher.
Identifiers: LCCN 2021046620 (print) | LCCN 2021046621 (ebook) | ISBN 9781666908657 (cloth) | ISBN 9781666908664 (epub)
Subjects: LCSH: Studdert Kennedy, Geoffrey Anketell, 1883-1929. | Church of England—Clergy—Biography. | Pacifists—Great Britain—Biography. | Military chaplains—Anglican Church—Biography. | World War, 1914–1918—Chaplains—Great Britain—Biography. | World War, 1914–1918—Religious aspects—Christianity. | Moral injuries—Great Britain.
Classification: LCC BX5199.S85 N59 2021 (print) | LCC BX5199.S85 (ebook) | DDC 283/.092 [B]—dc23
LC record available at https://lccn.loc.gov/2021046620
LC ebook record available at https://lccn.loc.gov/2021046621

I dedicate this work to Linda Kay on our golden wedding anniversary.
In our more than fifty years of companionship I have been blessed
by your rock-solid faith, your love, and your infinite patience.

Contents

Introduction

My Personal Introduction to Chaplain G. A. Studdert Kennedy

> "This is a fairly faithful and accurate account of an incurably religious man under battle conditions."[1]

> "The dead weigh heavy on the hand, and on the heart."[2]

The year 2018 marked the centenary of the First World War armistice. During the prior four years, Great Britain and Europe held numerous observances and memorials of the Great War on the battlefields of France. Numerous academic conferences focused on various aspects of the war: the events that led up to the war, its conduct, conclusion, and aftermath. I was fortunate and honored to participate in a conference conducted by the International Network for the Study of War and Religion in the Modern World that focused on the religious aspects of the Great War. It was (and continues to be) held at the Armed Forces Chaplaincy Center, Amport House, Hampshire, England, chaired by Michael Snape. The gatherings are held each July and I have had the privilege to attend and present papers in 2014, 2016, and 2017. As a retired U.S. Navy Chaplain and retreaded academic, my own interest and work focuses on religion and war, particularly on the instrumental use of religion to promote war aims.

In 2014, and at subsequent conferences, Reverend Stuart Bell presented papers on the life and writings of the Reverend Chaplain Geoffrey Anketell Studdert Kennedy, who he described as the most famous chaplain of the First World War. Stuart's work has been published in a number of venues and has resulted in at least one book, a critical and annotated edition of Studdert Kennedy's *The Hardest Part*, containing the chaplain's reflections on the war and his combat inspired theology of the Suffering God. I was deeply interested in Chaplain Studdert Kennedy's work, his prose, and his poetry. As a retired military chaplain, I felt a kinship with him and could identify with some of the experiences recounted by Reverend Bell. I purchased *The Hardest Part* and *The Unutterable Beauty* (Studdert Kennedy's collected poetry) and read them for devotional purposes. While his writing was a bit dark at times, I discovered a deeply committed Christian who had served faithfully in war and suffered traumatic psychological and spiritual wounds as a result of his experiences. Even though he lived in a very different culture and time, his writings spoke to me from across the years.

The recent centenary of the First World War has resulted in a reawakening of interest in the war, generally, as well as renewed interest in Studdert Kennedy's life and work. His poetry, essays, and other published works have found a new audience as they provide literary and emotional insight into the living conditions, hopes, and deaths of those who once populated the now deserted trenches and the challenges of postwar Britain. There has also been interest in understanding the impact of war on its combat survivors, how those who fought in the war's terrible conditions survived shell shock and the invisible wounds of war: PTSD, moral injury, and spiritual injury.

Chaplain Studdert Kennedy was never diagnosed with shell shock or "neurasthenia" (the term usually applied to officers who suffered shell shock). But his wartime experiences produced a profound and lasting impact upon him. Numberless images of combat dead and maimed bodies populated his waking and sleeping thoughts and caused him to question the traditional understanding of a sovereign and loving God. The grinding years of dashed hopes for an end to the war caused him to question the wisdom of political and military leaders and moved him from patriotic idealism to pacifism. His natural empathy and wartime longing for his own wife and children raised in him an abiding grief for the mothers, wives, and children of soldiers who would never see their loved ones come marching home or, in so many cases, even to bury their shattered bodies. When he returned home at the completion of his military service in 1919, all agreed that he was not the man who had gone to war, that the war had significantly changed him. He carried with him the physical (damaged lungs), moral, and spiritual injuries of war. But his life also exemplified resilience and post-traumatic growth as he worked tirelessly and sacrificially to transform postwar Britain in spite of, or because of, those scars.

My background is fairly eclectic, with a PhD in the humanities and master's degrees in divinity, religious education, and national security studies. I am not a theologian, historian, or mental health professional, although my treatment of Studdert Kennedy requires that I address each perspective. Personally, I approach him as a chaplain interested in the care of souls; his, mine, and those of the thousands of military men and women to whom we ministered during our military careers. I served in the military for twenty-nine years, and as a chaplain for twenty-four. Either fortunately or unfortunately, I was never directly involved in combat, although I did spend six months in the CENTCOM Theater (Qatar, Kuwait, and Afghanistan) during the U.S. war there. But military deaths don't just happen on the battlefield. Dealing with the human and spiritual dimension of training accidents, car accidents, and suicides was a significant part of my military duties. My introduction to mass carnage was the 1997 KAL 801 airline crash in Guam in which I assisted the sailors of the USS *Frank Cable* (AS-40) (of which I was a crewmember) on the crash site and in the recovery of victim's bodies.[3] I was then responsible, with members of the Navy's Special Psychiatric Rapid Intervention Team (SPRINT), to schedule and conduct debriefs of the three hundred members of our crew[4] who had volunteered on the crash site. The formal debriefs occurred over the next three weeks, but the ship's chaplain department spent many months in formal and informal counseling situations listening to sailors' experiences.[5] The goal of that process was to help the responders deal with their often-horrific memories. The post-9/11 world has introduced an entire generation to death and terror conducted on a massive scale, and to its accompanying and inescapable trauma.

One of my most rewarding duties as a chaplain was assisting in the conduct of returning warrior retreats[6] organized for military members and their spouses. The three-day retreats were intended to provide information and resources for those returning from the wars in Afghanistan and Iraq. Part of the weekend was a roundtable discussion including both warriors and their spouses. The discussions were designed to help the married couples understand the experience of war through their loved ones' eyes. One of the takeaways for me was the ubiquitous comment by our warriors that "only those who had been involved in combat could really understand." As facilitators, we generally agreed, but countered that all of us, working together, could address the problems they were facing.

For me this is the real power of Studdert Kennedy. He experienced the carnage of war and was forced to deal with the myths that we as Christians hold about life, often unintentionally (or intentionally) communicated from the pulpit and in Sunday school classrooms. He was forced to find answers to the dilemmas caused by war, and his answers resonate with those who have experienced the questions and disillusionment that come from the horrific experiences of life. While his answers may not square with the theologians who reflect in their book-lined studies, they do speak to the soldiers and the family members who have faced the realities of war firsthand. I'm afraid that our generation, and succeeding generations, unacquainted with realities of generational slaughter experienced in the First and Second World Wars, will fail to understand Studdert Kennedy's message. Perhaps only his generation, the veterans and families who accepted him as one of their own, could fully understand that message. But I am confident that his struggles and answers carry a timeless message; for today's combat veterans, for survivors of terror, and for the families bereft of loved ones as a result of whatever contemporary horror. That is the rationale behind this book.

There is a greater danger. That contemporary clergy and theologians will (or have already) resurrect the theologies that led to disillusionment with God, faith, and the church, that unintentionally inflict moral and spiritual injury. There will always be "wars and rumors of wars."[7] War continues to serve as an option for twenty-first-century political leaders. Many of those leaders have no experience of war other than their observations of it on news programs and in films. Even those who visit the wounded in military hospitals or attend memorial services have no idea of the intensity and lethality of combat. Inevitably, they will send young men and women to conflicts in far-off lands who will march with their idealisms and sense of indestructibility into the jaws of contemporary and future battle. Those who emerge will ask similar questions, feel similar disillusionment, and risk getting lost in the vast industrial and technological bureaucracy of national security. Unfortunately much of the world is considered "post-Christian," no longer finding value in the message of faith, opting instead for the promises of psychology and mental health. I believe that Studdert Kennedy's message, that of a suffering God who knows and shares our pain, still has application in today's world. I believe it is the responsibility of chaplains, churchmen, and mental health professionals to work together to heal the inescapable wounds that our world inevitably inflicts upon us. As we pursue our responsibility as healers, the insights worked out by Studdert Kennedy in the cauldron of the Great War can assist us in bringing about spiritual and psychological health for today's and future survivors of physical, moral, and spiritual trauma. A welcome by-product of our effort may be the preservation of Studdert Kennedy's message for posterity.[8]

NOTES

1. G. A. Studdert Kennedy, *The Hardest Part* (London: Hodder & Stoughton, 1918), 191.
2. Ibid., 154.
3. I was not present in Guam when the crash occurred but arrived a day later. I subsequently spent a number of days on the crash site, providing a chaplain presence for members of the crew of my ship, the U.S.S. *Frank Cable* (AS40). Those days were intense, with reminders of the crash victims and even bits of bodies stuck in the

mud of the site. On one of those days, the senior person present asked for volunteers to go into the portion of the fuselage that had burned and had been too hot to enter to retrieve victim's bodies. There were very few ship's crew present and as I looked around, I recall thinking, "I really don't want to do this." But I felt bound to assist my crewmates, so we all suited up and spent the next number of hours, as Studdert Kennedy calls it, in hell, although a different hell than he experienced.

4. The full crew of the ship numbered nearly 1,300, but only three hundred actually participated in rescue and recovery at the crash site.

5. I was trained and had experience in the "Mitchell Model" of Critical Incident Stress Debriefing and assisted the Navy's SPRINT team (Special Psychiatric Rapid Intervention Team) deployed to Guam to care for the Navy's personnel who participated in rescue and recovery at the crash site. These included personnel from Naval Station Guam, the Naval Hospital as well as the crew of the USS *Frank Cable* (AS-40).

6. As a member of the Navy's CREDO program, my wife and I participated in forty retreats over three years.

7. Matthew 24:6, the Bible

8. Many of these comments were included in an email, Dayne Nix to Rev. Stuart Bell, dtd. May 16, 2017.

Chapter One

Who Was the Rev. G. A. Studdert Kennedy?

In 1928 the Great War had been over for ten years. But for the Reverend Geoffrey Anketell (G. A.) Studdert Kennedy, a veteran of nearly four years' service as chaplain to the British soldiers who fought in France, memories of the war were as vivid as the many speaking engagements that filled his calendar.[1] In his 1928 book *The Warrior, the Woman and the Christ*, he recalled an early-morning excursion accompanying a sergeant during the 1916 Battle of the Somme.

> I can remember this night much more clearly than any single night last year. . . . Before the dawn broke, the Sergeant was dead, and many other mother's sons with him. But the question remained clearly formulated as a question in my mind and burned all-the-more deeply into it because of the horror of that night. That is the way with war. It shouts and bawls its questions at you. It throws them at you stark, raw, quivering, and all shot through with pain.[2]

Many, if not all, veterans of war can identify with Chaplain Studdert Kennedy's experiences, reporting that the memories and emotions experienced in the heat of battle intrude on their waking and sleeping moments for years after the conclusion of hostilities. Today, we understand more about the impact of combat on the soldiers that serve their nation's interests and have developed means to assist them as they return to everyday life, forever changed by war. Chaplain Studdert Kennedy serves as an excellent case study to help us understand the impact of war on an individual. Not only did he spend four years in the crucible of military combat, but he also thought and reflected deeply on the terrible reality of war and its impact on his beloved soldiers and their families. He wrote extensively of his experiences, illustrating the challenges of combat and its impact on the mind and spirit in both prose and poetry. Before I discuss these issues, I'd like to provide a brief biography of Geoffrey Anketell (G. A.) Studdert Kennedy.

G. A. Studdert Kennedy has been described as the most well-known and popular British chaplain of the more than five thousand British chaplains assigned to the British Expeditionary Force (BEF) during the First World War. His work and life have been the subject of many books and articles, with the British scholar Michael Snape listing him as a "perennial favorite with amateur biographers."[3] His popularity with the troops, and subsequently with the British public, was based on the chaplain's ability to connect with the common people through his engaging and "racy" speaking style and obvious love for the British soldiers and their loved ones back home. During the war, it was also facilitated by the careful management of Assistant Chaplain General Rev. D. F. Carey, who ensured that Studdert Kennedy received his "baptism of fire" in the trenches, serving with fighting troops during three major engagements. But the majority of Studdert Kennedy's assignments during his four years in France were in the rear areas, where his speaking and interpersonal skills were most effectively utilized and where he forged an enduring connection with many of the more than five million members of the BEF.

G. A. Studdert Kennedy was born in 1883 to the Reverend William Studdert Kennedy and his second wife, Jeanette Anketell. Of Irish descent, his father was the Anglican Vicar of St. Mary's, Quarry Hill in Leeds, a major industrial town in North Central England. The parish included working-class neighborhoods, and Studdert Kennedy was introduced to working-class conditions and poverty through his father's ministry there. The seventh son of nine children (his father had five children by his first marriage),[4] Geoffrey Anketell was of relatively small and slight build and was afflicted with asthma throughout his life. His life within this large Irish family was described as harmonious and idyllic, although its harmony was marred by the suicide death of elder brother Robert in 1897[5] and the death of their mother, Jeanette Anketell, in 1908.[6] Geoffrey spoke with an attractive Irish brogue, an attribute that served him well as he followed his father's footsteps into the Anglican ministry. Trained for ministry at Dublin's Trinity College and Rugby, his ministry experience began when he accepted a curacy at Rugby (near Coventry) where he was assigned to "study children from four to nine years old, and to work among the tramps. An infant school, two lodging houses, and a work-house were included in my first charge."[7] Later he moved to Leeds, where he assisted his father at St. Mary's. Upon his father's death, in 1914, the church requested that the young pastor remain as the church's vicar,[8] but the bishop thought the church needed someone more suited to the local population, and Studdert Kennedy was assigned to St. Paul's, Worcester, which became his home until his death. He faithfully served the poverty-stricken working-class neighborhoods there, which "consist(ed) almost wholly of crowded small tenement cottages and slums"[9] He quickly earned the respect and love of those in his parish. His lively and unusual sermons ministered to his flock's spiritual needs while his selfless generosity made a small dent in their poverty, as he often gave his meager earnings to whomever had need. In fact, he was famous for his generosity. It was reported that he often gave small amounts of money to those in need, and, shortly after his wedding in 1914 to Emily Catlow, he even gave his bed and mattress to a family that had none. His young wife obviously shared in his generous spirit, as she assisted him in carrying the mattress to the unfortunate family.[10]

The First World War broke out shortly after Studdert Kennedy's arrival in Worcester. The town was located near a military training camp, and as many as two thousand soldiers attended the required "church parade"[11] at the local cathedral. Studdert Kennedy was invited by the dean of Worcester Cathedral, W. Moore Ede, to preach to the assembled soldiers. What most soldiers considered a tedious part of military life became a welcome Sunday retreat, as the men quickly found Studdert Kennedy's sermons both entertaining and spiritually uplifting.[12] Nearly inevitably, Studdert Kennedy applied for assignment as a military chaplain. His request was granted,[13] and in December 1915, he reported to France, where he served in various assignments: at training camps, as a public speaker traveling throughout the war theater, and as chaplain in three major battles. He was beloved by the troops, who were attracted by his witty sermons and engaging personality. They assigned him the nickname "Woodbine Willy" for the Woodbine cigarettes he distributed as they embarked on transport headed to the trenches. He proudly carried that nickname the rest of his life.[14]

During the war, he published four books: *Rough Talks by a Padre*, *The Hardest Part*, *Rough Rhymes of a Padre*, and *More Rough Rhymes of a Padre*. The first records a series of sermons he preached to the troops in France, while the second is a record of his reflections on God during his combat ministry at the Messines Ridge in 1917. He often "spiced-up" his sermons with personally produced poems, and he discovered a facility of expression in them that touched the hearts of his soldiers, regardless of their religious belief. These are contained in his *Rough Rhymes of a Padre* and *More Rough Rhymes of a Padre*, which became wartime best-sellers both in the war areas and at home. His works reflect intense struggle with theological and spiritual issues relating to his and his soldiers' experiences during the war.

Chaplain Studdert Kennedy returned home from France on March 21, 1919, having become disillusioned with the war and its leadership. He initially returned to St. Paul's Worcester, where he resumed his ministry and instituted some popular innovations, including a parish-hall cinema paid for by the proceeds from one of his publishing efforts.[15] Widely known as "Woodbine Willie" from his wartime publications and interactions with the troops, he quickly gained public attention with his often outrageous comments made at various speaking engagements. One illustration that caught the attention of the local papers occurred when he spoke at a local Worcester theater. The local papers reported on his unusual solution for his parish's housing problems. It was evident that his thinking was influenced by his wartime experiences.

> Known among soldiers as "Woodbine Willy" he is vicar of St. Paul's Worcester, which consists almost wholly of crowded small tenements and slums. He was discussing the housing problem, and in the course of his speech said the only way to deal with his parish would be to put 14 batteries of 5-inch guns on Malvern Hills, clear the people out of the houses, and blow the parish to pieces. Then it might be rebuilt and made fit for men to live in.[16]

Another example occurred the following October at a meeting of the League of the Church Militant, where his outspoken solutions and wartime influence were again evident. As he spoke on the need for the reformation of society through individual commitment and service, he also suggested a solution for the housing problems plaguing his area. He asked, "Why they who had smashed the German army in five years could not build a million houses in six months."[17]

Discontent and disillusion were common in postwar Britain, and Studdert Kennedy's October 1919 publication of his book *Lies* captured the public's emotional state while also mirroring his own. "This postwar world is black with lies. . . . There is a bad smell about, a very bad smell; it is like the smell of the dead—it is the smell of dead souls."[18] In this work, he discussed themes that he would develop throughout the next ten years of his public ministry: the futility of war, the failures of the church, the need for commitment to passionate service, the relationship between men and women, democracy and liberty, class warfare, the popular desire for distractions, the conflict between capital and labor, and the ultimate need for a national commitment to the Suffering God revealed in the Cross of Christ.

Studdert Kennedy's invitations to speak increased, and it appears he rarely rejected an opportunity to address an audience. He obviously enjoyed engaging an audience, and the attraction was apparently mutual, with his venues often filled to overflowing with rapt listeners. The papers reported on his presentations, often describing his speeches as "racy" or "characteristically unorthodox." Sponsored by the YMCA or a local church, Studdert Kennedy began to take as his subject opposition to war and the peace process then ongoing in France. At Rugby, where he had served before the war, he presented an "eloquently outspoken address," where he stated,

> A league of nations in itself and by itself was about as much protection against war as a sheet of tissue paper against five mad bulls. It was not worth the paper it was written on. Mr. Kennedy went on to repudiate the suggestion of the ennobling influence of war. . . . War is the most damnable and degrading evil that ever was.[19]

At Wellington's All Saint's Church, Studdert Kennedy "attracted great congregations . . . where he preached morning and evening and addressed a meeting of men only in the afternoon." These crowds were treated with his "somewhat pronounced Irish brogue, earnestness and wit, as well as "utterances unconventional and not often heard from the pulpit that somewhat startled a few of the staid church members."[20] The content of his addresses was startling as well.

> He said that two years after the war was supposed to have ended he could see no sign of the "New World." In his opinion the world was infinitely worse today than it was before the great struggle was engaged in. The "peace" they had obtained was like the "peace" that prevailed in the prize-ring when the combatants had knocked each other silly . . . the peace conference he described as a ghastly and appalling failure, a "muck up" from start to finish.[21]

The 1920 Rochester Diocesan Conference, which focused on various church reforms, was also blessed with Studdert Kennedy's outspoken rhetoric. He was assigned to present the closing address of the conference. After being introduced by the bishop and congratulated for his recent appointment as chaplain to His Majesty the King, Studdert Kennedy proceeded to condemn the church as outdated and out of touch with the people. He commented that the bishops had opposed any idea of progress, and this was the reason people felt the church had failed. Speaking of theology, he said, "I am prepared to burn every theological book that I read before the war."[22] He proceeded to reject the commonly held view of Almighty God and to expound on his conception of the suffering God, viewed by many as an ancient theological heresy. In responding to the young preacher's charges, the bishop congratulated him on his presentation, but took the opportunity to reject Studdert Kennedy's charges against the church and the bishops. "It was good to have new thoughts put before them. The only criticism he would offer was that the speaker seemed to set up a kind of imaginary Church and to have mistaken the church of his grandmother's time with the Church of today."[23]

Studdert Kennedy had adopted an anti-war attitude as a result of his experiences of the war. In July 1922, he participated in the worldwide "No More War Rally" which included more than two hundred meetings throughout Britain. In London the rally included thousands of marchers who proceeded from all areas of the city, past the Cenotaph (Britain's memorial to the First

World War dead) and ended at Hyde Park. The papers reported that more than fifteen thousand people converged on the park where fifteen platforms were set up for simultaneous speeches by various anti-war speakers. Studdert Kennedy was one of the featured speakers, taking as his subject, "Trade Unions, churches, and the League of Nations Union should band together to make the war attitude impossible."[24] By this time, Studdert Kennedy had become a well-known critic of war and expended a great deal of effort to convince others of his viewpoint.

Studdert Kennedy left St. Paul's Worcester in late 1921[25] and, in 1922, joined the Industrial Christian Fellowship (ICF), headed by the Rev. P. T. R. Kirk, himself an Irishman and former wartime chaplain. The ICF was an organization designed to serve as a bridge between the workplace and organized Christianity.[26] Studdert Kennedy became the organization's Chief Missioner, an assignment that would take advantage of his rhetorical skills as well as his commitment to social and economic reform. The ICF's efforts were supported by the Church of England, and Studdert Kennedy was assigned to London's Church of St. Edmund the Martyr, Lombard Street, on June 14, 1922. The church assignment, located in in downtown London and largely emptied of people on weekends, allowed Studdert Kennedy ample opportunity to engage in ICF activities. His family, consisting of his wife and three sons, continued to live in Worcester, and he took the train into the city on weekends to care for his ecclesiastical duties there. His duties as ICF missioner included traveling the country and speaking in packed churches, theaters, open air parks, Rotary Clubs, men's and women's groups, to queues of the unemployed, and even in prisons. The ICF conducted multiday crusades in England's industrial cities designed to reach the country's working men and women with the Christian message while also supporting wage and labor reform. Studdert Kennedy was supported in this work by an extensive administrative staff and lay missioners, individuals, "drawn from the ranks of industry, specially trained and sent to bear their witness for Christ in factory, on the street corner, and wherever they could find those to listen to them."[27] Studdert Kennedy's travels for the ICF took him throughout the major cities of England, Wales, Scotland and, in 1929, to Belfast, Northern Ireland.

I'll address the details of Studdert Kennedy's efforts for social reform in chapter eight, but it is clear from my research that Studdert Kennedy became a "rock star" of the clerical world in 1920s Britain. His life became the subject of thousands of newspaper articles during that time. The daily and weekly news include reports on his travels and speaking engagements, often devoting multiple columns of newspaper space to detail the content of his speeches. Studdert Kennedy's addresses were also broadcast on the radio,[28] and he ministered regularly at Buckingham Palace in his role as chaplain to H.M.

the King.[29] The papers reported when he departed for the United States for a speaking tour (October, 1923),[30] his return,[31] and his selection for the Moorehead Lectures in Australia in 1928.[32] His personal life was also of interest, and it was reported when he was struck by a "six seater" car in Worcester while on a walk (and was severely bruised),[33] his foot injury while rushing onto a train,[34] and on two separate automobile citations and the fines he was assessed.[35] The weekly journal *John Bull* reported an incident in which a suicidal man had come to their offices seeking help. Unsure what to do, they turned the man over to Studdert Kennedy, who took him under his wing.[36] Studdert Kennedy's popularity also resulted in an early case of identity theft. The incident was reported under the headlines "Cleric's Downfall" and "Derby Escapades" that communicated the possibility of scandal.[37] Further investigation revealed that a wayward clergyman had assumed his identity and was charging hotel rooms and meals in Studdert Kennedy's name. The papers also reported the man's subsequent arrest, trial, and conviction.[38]

Why was Studdert Kennedy so popular? In March 1926, he visited Coventry for a series of meetings at the Cathedral. The local newspaper editor asked, and answered, this important question in a revealing character sketch.

> What is the source behind his undeniable power? What is it that makes people hang feverishly to his words, pay allegiance to his sentiments and regard in him the role of apostle who wakens the country to a realization of the importance and truthfulness of the Gospel? Despite his pseudonym he is no demagogue. He does not rely upon tickling the palate of the masses or ingratiating himself to their good wishes. He is no respecter of persons and he goes from town to town bestirring all sorts of conditions of men and women, hitting hard their weaknesses and selfishness, decrying their pettiness and lashing them into a renewed sense of their responsibilities. Yet they admire him. . . . Why? Surely it is because of his transparent sincerity and earnestness. He speaks what he feels and lives what he speaks, and to listen to him is to feel the glow of his ardour and catch the spirit of his unyielding faith. He is something more than a popular preacher. He is a portent of the new order of things. It is a new order built upon the old Gospel. Mr. Studdert Kennedy preaches Christianity in its oldest and simplest form, but he preaches it in a new way—clothes it with a new speech. . . . He goes straight home with his views in a language all can understand and appreciate because it is the language of beautiful simplicity and power.[39]

His commitment to the work of the ICF and the social ills of the nation drove Studdert Kennedy to fill his schedule with speaking engagements and crusades throughout the country. His friends counseled him to slow down and were concerned for his health. His recurring asthma (complicated by his being gassed during the war[40]) and occasional illnesses did cause concern, but he soldiered on and fulfilled his speaking commitments in spite of the difficulties and long absences from his family. His friends' concerns, unfortunately, proved to be well founded.

In February 1929, Studdert Kennedy conducted meetings in Belfast, Northern Ireland. During the crusade he touched on his favorite subjects: the evils of war, of poverty, and the struggle between capital and labor. He concluded the speech with, "if the Kingdom of God was to grow all must bring their heads to their politics and bring their hearts to God."[41] On the same news page that reported Studdert Kennedy's speech, there appeared a column that discussed the influenza epidemic then afflicting Belfast. Most of Britain was suffering a severe flu epidemic that year. After completing his responsibilities in Ireland, Studdert Kennedy returned home. We don't know if he carried the influenza with him, but when he left home three weeks later to conduct a series of Lenten services in Liverpool, his family was suffering from the flu.[42] It seems certain that Studdert Kennedy was also afflicted, as it was later reported that he was showing signs of the flu as he conducted the Liverpool meetings, although he preached and spoke with his characteristic eloquence. However, Canon Howe, Rector of Liverpool's St. Nicholas Church later reported, "The Rev. Studdert Kennedy was very ill when he preached at the Lenten services, . . . yet he kept to his post until Friday last week."[43] The paper also reported that he had "been ill for some time with influenza" which was complicated by his underlying asthma. The *Birmingham Telegraph* reported the sad outcome of Studdert Kennedy's illness.

> After addressing a large congregation of businessmen, he was stricken with serious illness and had to be assisted to St. Catherine's vicarage, Abercromby Square. . . . Here he was put to bed on the advice of the doctor and his wife was sent for. The crisis was reached on Wednesday and he appeared to be improving until Thursday night when his heart began to fail. He passed away in the early hours of this morning. "The illness was very much on the lines of the King's illness," said the Rev. Edward Harrison to our Liverpool correspondent. "He was unconscious for several days and the end came most peacefully."[44]

Only forty-five years old, G. A. Studdert Kennedy died on March 6, 1929. Many of his friends later commented that they had often cautioned him to slow down, but to no avail.[45] They lamented his death and blamed his rigorous speaking schedule and self-imposed overwork, driven by his own commitment to public service and the needs of Britain's poor, unemployed, and war veterans.

His funeral was conducted in Worcester on March 12, 1929. The dean of Worcester Cathedral, Dr. Moore Ede, who had mentored Studdert Kennedy and assisted with his publishing efforts, conducted the service. "Worcester was a city of mourning, and quite 20,000 people thronged the streets as

'Woodbine Willie' was carried to his last resting place, while there were nearly 5000 people in the historic cathedral where the Dean of Worcester, Dr. Moore Ede, conducted and impressive service prior to interment."[46]

The grief over his untimely death was felt throughout Britain; by the workers in the coal mines who Studdert Kennedy had championed and in Buckingham Palace where he had preached to royalty. The following telegram was sent to his widow by the King's secretary.

> I am desired to assure you of the heartfelt sympathy of the King and Queen in your great sorrow in the death of your husband. The King has lost a valued chaplain and one who frequently and quite recently preached at Buckingham Palace. His work in war and peace will be gratefully remembered.[47]

Perhaps more poignantly, the newspaper report of the funeral concluded with a reference to Studdert Kennedy's wartime service and the many to whom he had ministered who had not returned. "It was a day of deep feeling in Worcester, and it was easy to imagine the spirits of men who died for England present in its ancient streets."[48] There were also reports that many of the thousands of soldiers who attended the funeral adorned the procession's path with packages of Woodbine cigarettes in their final farewell to "Woodbine Willie."

There is an unfortunate postscript that attests to another aspect of Studdert Kennedy's character, his generosity. While his publishing endeavors and speaking engagements earned a substantial income, he dedicated the majority of that income to charity. Evidence of this is found in the front-piece of his volume of wartime poetry, *Rough Rhymes of a Padre.* "All the author's profits on this volume will be given to St. Dunstans Hostel for Blinded Soldiers."[49] The editors of John Bull, in which he published from 1925 until his death, commented, "To mention only one thing, he was one of our highest paid contributors, but not a penny ever went into his own pocket. The cheque was invariably sent to a certain charitable society to which he devoted much time. Woodbine Willie went through life like that. We bare our head."[50] Studdert Kennedy's sacrificial lifestyle unfortunately failed to adequately consider his family's financial needs after his death. This resulted in an appeal for a fund of seven thousand pounds on the behalf of his widow and three young children. The appeal, published throughout Britain, described the unfortunate economic situation of his widow. "'Woodbine Willie,' though he purchased a house and took out life insurance policies which will realize three thousand pounds, spent most of his income on other people."[51] The request was signed by six bishops and various dignitaries. It was announced in 1930 that the fund had accumulated enough contributions to provide Mrs. Studdert Kennedy with five hundred pounds a year, a free house, and an education for their children.[52]

G. A. Studdert Kennedy only survived the First World Way by ten years. His service on behalf of his beloved soldiers and the working men and women of Britain is a testament of sacrificial devotion and love. Those years also provide us with a bounded period in which we may consider the impact of his wartime chaplain experiences as they worked themselves out in his daily life. Before I address those issues, I believe it is important to discuss the role of the military chaplain and how Studdert Kennedy fulfilled that role in war-torn France between 1915 and 1919.

NOTES

1. I am following William Purcell's biography, *Woodbine Willie: A Biography*, for the general outline of Studdert Kennedy's life, supported and supplemented by my own research.
2. G. A. Studdert Kennedy, *The Warrior, The Woman, and the Christ* (London: Hodder & Stoughton, 1928), 17–18.
3. Snape, Michael, *The Royal Army Chaplains' Department: Clergy Under Fire* (Sheffield: Boydell Press, 2008), 5.
4. Linda Parker, *A Seeker After Truths: The Life and Times of G. A. Studdert Kennedy (Woodbine Willie), 1883–1929* (Solihull, West Midlands: Helion and Company Limited, 2017), 17.
5. Ibid., 21.
6. Ibid., 25.
7. "A Preacher's Power: Rev. G. A. Studdert Kennedy's Visit to Coventry," *Midland Daily Telegraph*, March 5, 1926.
8. William Purcell, *Woodbine Willie: A Biography* (London: Hodder & Stoughton, 1962), 76.
9. "Vicar's Remedy for His Parish," *Manchester Evening News,* April 21, 1919, 4.
10. W. Moore Ede, "Studdert Kennedy: His Life in Worcester," in *G. A. Studdert Kennedy by His Friends*, ed. J. K. Mozley (London: Hodder & Stoughton, 1929), 92–93.
11. Church Parade was a "spit-and-polish" Sunday requirement for all soldiers that also included a formal inspection.
12. Purcell, *Woodbine Willie: A Biography*, 95–96.
13. "Another Worcester Vicar as Chaplain," *Birmingham Daily Post,* Dec. 1, 1915, 3.
14. Purcell, *Woodbine Willie: A Biography*, 106.
15. "Broadminded Parson," *The Bioscope*, May 8, 1919, 7.
16. "Vicars Remedy for His Parish," *Manchester Evening News*, April 21, 1919, 4.
17. "League of the Church Militant," *Leicester Daily Post*, Oct. 14, 1919, 1.
18. G. A. Studdert Kennedy, *Lies* (London: Hodder & Stoughton, 1919), ix–x.
19. "Woodbine Willie at Rugby," *Rugby Advertiser*, Feb. 20, 1920, 6.

20. "Woodbine Willie: Famous Parson on the Peace Treaty," *Northampton Mercury*, April 23, 1920, 3

21. Ibid.

22. "Rochester Diocesan Conference," *Tunbridge Wells Courier*, June 4, 1920, 3.

23. Ibid.

24. "World-Wide Demand for No-More War," *Daily Herald*, July 30, 1923, 2.

25. "Rev. G.A. Studdert Kennedy: His Coventry Visit," *Coventry Herald*, March 8, 1926, 12.

26. "Industrial Christian Fellowship: Address by Woodbine Willie," *Hastbourne Chronicle*, April 29, 1922, 6.

27. Purcell, *Woodbine Willie: A Biography*, 190.

28. Daily Radio Schedule, *Shields Daily News*, 17 April 1925.

29. "G. A. Studdert Kennedy Preaches at Palace," *Northern Whig*, 7 May 1928, 8.

30. "Woodbine Wille Departs for U.S." *Birmingham Daily Gazette*, Oct. 31, 1923, 10.

31. "Woodbine Willie: Arrival at Plymouth from America," Western Morning News, March 3, 1924, 5.

32. "Studdert Kennedy Appointed as Moorhouse Lecturer," *Newcastle Journal and North Star*, January 27, 1928, 8.

33. "Woodbine Willie" *Hartlepool Northern Daily Mail*, March 26, 1926, 7.

34. "Woodbine Willie's Accident: Preaches for An Hour With a Badly Damaged Foot," *Liverpool Echo,* March 21, 1924.

35. "Woodbine Willie Fined," *Northampton Mercury*, 22 June 1928, p. 3. The fine was 10s. *Daily Mirror*, October 30, 1926, 2.

36. *John Bull*, November 27, 1926, 14.

37. "Cleric's Downfall, Admits Impersonating Woodbine Willie, Derby Escapades," *The Nottingham Evening Post*, September 17, 1929, 4.

38. "Prison for Cleric: Posed in Derby as Woodbine Willie," *Derby Daily Telegraph,* September 17, 1923.

39. "A Preacher's Power: Rev. G. A. Studdert Kennedy's Visit to Coventry," *Midland Daily Telegraph*, March 5, 1925.

40. Michael Brierly, "Geoffrey Studdert Kennedy: A Brief Life" in Michael W. Brierly and Georgina A. Byrne, *Life after Tragedy: Essays on Faith and the First World Evoked by Geoffrey Studdert Kennedy* (Eugene, Oregon: Cascade Books, 2017), 30.

41. "Problems of Society: Rev. Studdert Kennedy's View," *Belfast Telegraph*, February 2, 1929, 4.

42. Purcell, *Woodbine Willie: A Biography*, 213.

43. "A Famous Padre: Death of Woodbine Willie," *Gloucester Journal*, March 9, 1929, 1.

44. "Woodbine Willie Dead: Famous War Padre," *Belfast Telegraph*, March 8, 1929, 9.

45. H. R. L Sheppard, "Studdert Kennedy: A Friend," in *G. A. Studdert Kennedy by His Friends*, ed. J. K. Mozley (Hodder & Stoughton, 1929), 201.

46. "25,000 Pay Tribute to Dead Padre," *Birmingham Gazette*, March 13, 1929, 4.
47. Ibid.
48. Ibid.
49. G. A. Studdert Kennedy, *Rough Rhymes of a Padre* (London: Hodder & Stoughton, 1918), Frontpiece.
50. "Good-bye Old Friend," *John Bull*, March 16, 1929, 1.
51. "Woodbine Willie Memorial," *Liverpool Echo*, March 25, 1929, 12.
52. "Provision for Rev. G. A. Studdert Kennedy's Widow," *Dundee Evening Telegraph*, Feb, 5, 1930.

Chapter Two

Chaplains, the Military, and the Invisible Wounds of War

"I bet my life on Beauty, Truth, And Love . . ."[1]

ORIGIN OF THE ROLE AND TERM "CHAPLAIN"

"All that such men can do . . . is to touch a few lives with a great love, to open a few eyes to a splendid vision, and often to break his own heart in the process."[2] In these words, Studdert Kennedy biographer William Purcell effectively captured the essence of the famous First World War chaplain's ministry among the soldiers of the British Expeditionary Force in France. But he also communicated the hope, mission, and even heartbreak of the men and women who minister to their nation's soldiers, sailors, and marines as military chaplains. The Reverend G. A. Studdert Kennedy applied for and was approved to become a military chaplain to the British Expeditionary Force (BEF) beginning in December 1915. In doing so, he joined this historic company of spiritual leaders who have served in peace and in war.[3] Members of the clergy or religious representatives have accompanied military units into war for thousands of years. Whether to divine the will of the gods or to seek their favor in battle, they represented the uncertain nature of warfare and the struggle for life and death. The term "chaplain" derives from the act of St. Martin of Tours (c. 361), a Roman soldier and Christian catechumen who is said to have split his cape (*cappellani*) in two with his sword to clothe a naked beggar.[4] Later, his part of the cloak became a relic that was carried into battle by French kings. The priests who carried it were called *cappellani*, the French of which is *chapelains*, and the English, "chaplain." Chaplains provide spiritual cover (ministry) for the military men and women they serve in both peace and war.

RELIGIOUS ORGANIZATIONS SPONSORSHIP OF MILITARY CHAPLAINS

Why do members of the clergy participate in the military and how can these representatives of religion, who are generally viewed as peacemakers, participate in war? Religious denominations who send or endorse members of their clergy to be chaplains usually do so out of a desire to provide religious service to their military members who are often out of reach of the local church due to military responsibilities and deployments. Many religious organizations also view the military as a mission field, with the popular perception that "there are no atheists in foxholes" providing an opportunity for evangelism.

The question of the churches' and clergy's participation in war is an important one, and one with which many chaplains, including Studdert Kennedy, have struggled. Church views on members' participation in war vary across a wide spectrum, with some taking a pacifist viewpoint, others taking a "just war" perspective, while a few even take a completely nationalistic or jingoistic position, supporting their country's war policies fully. Individual chaplains usually mirror the views of the religious bodies that endorse them.[5] Very few chaplains actually promote war or take the "praise God and pass the ammunition" perspective. Most chaplains, along with the majority of military men and women, are the last to desire war, as they are fully aware of the damage that combat inflicts upon soldiers, their families, and the civilian communities caught in the crossfire of opposing armies. As Studdert Kennedy commented to the troops during one of his wartime sermons, "I say, damn all war, and those that make it."[6] Of course, he was not referring to own his own soldiers in this sermon, but to the enemy political leaders who had started the war in the first place.

CHAPLAIN MOTIVATIONS

Chaplain Studdert Kennedy's wartime activities and experiences fully illustrate a chaplain's wartime assignments and motivations. He was an Anglican priest who served the soldiers of the Great War in the trenches and throughout the support areas of France and Belgium. He has been termed the best-known British chaplain of the First World War, a title that he earned through his positive presence, his ability to speak the language of the soldier, and his sacrificial commitment to the Christian ministry. His public speaking and care for the soldiers in the trenches and behind the lines were legendary. His sympathy and empathy for the soldiers and their families back home, communicated through his speeches, poetry, and personal interactions, created a lasting emotional bond. Although he did not consider himself the most attractive of men, he attracted both individuals and multitudes with his wit and Irish brogue. He described himself as a "sensitive spirit" who was immersed in the crucible of the Great War.[7] To that crucible he brought an indomitable spirit that had been trained in the poverty-stricken streets of Rugby and Leeds, where he had ministered to the poor through his church and with his own meager means, making a great difference in the lives of his parishioners there. In that urban parish, he demonstrated sensitivity, love, and care for the common people, and he carried those characteristics with him into the Great War's trenches.

The motivation that energized Studdert Kennedy's service to the soldiers in France is one that informs the ministry of most clergy who join the military. He described that motivation in his poem, "Well," contained in his 1918 book of poetry, *Rough Rhymes of a Padre*. In the poem, the chaplain stood before his God and was struck by his own imperfection in the face of Divinity.

And then at last 'E said one word,
'E just said one word --- "Well?"
And I said in a funny voice,
"Please can I go to 'Ell?"
And 'E stood there and looked at me
And 'E kind o' seemed to grow,
Till 'E shone like the sun above my 'ead,
And then 'E answered, "No,
You can't, that 'Ell is for the blind,
And not for those that see,
You know that you 'ave earned it, lad,
So you must follow me.
Follow Me on the paths o' pain,
Seeking what you 'ave seen,
Until at last you can build the 'Is"
Wi' the brick o' the "might 'ave been.'
That's what 'E said, as I'm alive,
And that there dream were true.
But what 'E meant – I don't quite know,
Though I knows what I 'as to do.
I's got to follow what I's seen,
Till this old carcass dies;
For I daren't face in the land o' grace
The sorrow of those eyes.
There ain't no throne, and there ain't no books,
It's 'Im you've got to see,
It's 'Im, just 'Im, that is the judge
Of blokes like you and me.

And, boys, I'd sooner frizzle up,
I' the flames of burnin' 'Ell,
Than stand and look into 'Is face,
And 'ear 'Is voice say – "Well?"[8]

Self-described as "an incurably religious man under battle conditions,"[9] Studdert Kennedy bore a deep sense of Christian mission and responsibility for the soldiers of the BEF. The poem quoted above communicated the source of his abiding commitment to create the "Is, with the brick of the might 'ave been." He served his God, not as an abstract theory or principle, but as a living reality, an abiding presence in his life. In his prayer and spiritual life, one can imagine him personally regarding the sorrowful eyes of his Lord and promising to faithfully serve the soldiers committed to his care. At times, his mission field consisted of the entire British Expeditionary Force as he was assigned to travel around the war zone and speak on behalf of the Church of England's Mission of Repentance and Hope, ministering in the rear areas and at various training centers throughout France. On three different occasions, his ministry took him to the trenches where he participated in some of the most intense and bloody battles of the war: the Somme in 1916, Ypres (at the Messines Ridge) in 1917, and at the Meuse–Argonne in 1918.[10]

Additional motivations of chaplains for military ministry are varied. Some chaplains are former members of the military who have experienced the spiritual challenges of military life and answered a personal call to address those challenges. Other civilian clergy, like Studdert Kennedy, choose to serve the military in response to a national emergency or a personal connection to the military and their families. In the First World War, the year 1915 saw a national call for soldiers to add to the severely depleted British Expeditionary Force fighting in France. The public enthusiastically supported that call and encouraged their men to do their duty, with the "white feather" being awarded as a badge of cowardice to those who refused. Studdert Kennedy did not need encouragement. An ordained member of the Church of England, he served St. Paul's Church in Worcester, which was located near a military training center. As many as two thousand soldiers and trainees attended the required "church parade" on Sundays at Worcester Cathedral, where he was invited to preach. Instead of a drab and lifeless church service, they discovered a vibrant young Anglican priest who spoke in unconventional ways and who kept their interest while communicating timeless spiritual truths. They were hooked, and so was he. He sought the chaplaincy but was delayed until a replacement for his church could be found. A Birmingham newspaper reported his departure for France in early December 1915 while his wife served as a Red Cross nurse at a hospital in England.[11] The same newspaper page reported the grim toll of the war: the names of hundreds of dead, wounded and those taken prisoner. By Christmas he was serving the troops, conducting a Christmas Eve service in the rain.[12] Throughout the war, he selflessly communicated his care and support to all he encountered: in the trenches, in training camps, or in Sunday services. His passion and service won the appreciation of tens of thousands to whom he ministered in the BEF. An insight into his unconventional approach to the "care of souls" was illustrated in a posthumous book of his previously unpublished essays. His words serve as an example to any chaplain or minister who seeks to serve in religious ministry. He applied this design for effective ministry throughout his service in the war, and after.

> Men are always thinking of a parson as a pious sort of bloke who goes about holding up his hands in horror and cursing people for their sins. But that's not the way I look at it at all. My job is really doctoring people that doctors are no good to, and helping people that nothing on earth but only God can help, and striving all I know to give people faith and hope and power to be happy. . . if by preaching or teaching or talking or just being friends with them I can give them faith and hope and the love of God, then I am doing my job.[13]

CHAPLAIN DUTIES

The official duties of chaplains in the military have evolved over the years. Most descriptions involve conducting religious services, offering prayers, caring for the sick and dying, and conducting christenings, marriages, and burials. Many commanders also expect chaplains to encourage good conduct and to promote religion and morality.[14] These duties are viewed as an essential element contributing to military discipline and morale, with some seeing chaplains as a "combat multiplier," a description that is often unwelcome within the chaplain community. A modern description states that chaplains, "provide spiritual support, pastoral care and moral guidance to all, irrespective of religion or beliefs."[15] The chaplain's role also involves serving as a spiritual counselor who provides a "listening ear" to whomever has a need, regardless of rank.[16] It has often been said that the lower ranks seek out the chaplain during business hours, the mid-ranks in the late afternoon and early evenings, while senior ranks approach the chaplain late at night, when no one else is around. Regardless of the time, chaplains hope to offer an uncritical ear and insightful wisdom. Chaplains also serve as a source of ethical guidance and teaching, often providing training on the ethical conduct of warfare and the Just War Tradition. Many American chaplains share a fabled story of a Marine Corps General's comment during a public event that, "My job is to break things and kill people. Your job, chaplain, is to ensure I don't enjoy it too much."

Contemporary chaplains are fully qualified members of their religious organizations and attend eight to twelve weeks of formal training before assignment to a command. While he was a fully qualified and employed clergyman of the Church of England and was approved to serve as chaplain to the British forces, Studdert Kennedy did not benefit from any formal chaplain training prior to reporting for duty in France. He quickly discovered what all chaplains understand: that his chaplain ministry would consist of whatever his initiative and creativity could make of it. He was initially assigned to a canteen at the Rouen train siding where he conducted a "ministry of presence" among reinforcements heading to the Front. His songs, off-the-cuff addresses, and outgoing personality won him a ready audience with the men. There he discovered the "calling card" by which he would come to be known and loved by the troops of the BEF, "Woodbine Willie." As the soldiers departed for the Front, he gave them the most popular and difficult-to-obtain brand of cigarettes, Woodbines.[17] He also served an important service as he offered to write to their families back home. Many took him up on the offer, sending greetings home as well as money from their pay. One mother's letter, likely written by Studdert Kennedy in Rouen, made it into the press and shared the page with much graver news of the front.

> Mrs. William Penny, of Aryburn Dyce, has received a sympathetic letter from the Rev. G.A. Studdert Kennedy, chaplain to the Forces, in which he gives her news of her son, George Robert Penny, of the Scots Guards, . . . The Chaplain writes Mrs. Penny that he has just had a talk with her son, who was in good spirits and in the best of health. He and his comrades were looking forward to the day when they would see their home folk again, but the home friends would be proud if they could see their cheery faces and hear their merry talk.[18]

During the majority of Studdert Kennedy's time in France he was assigned to training commands, serving at three different Infantry Training Schools. There his duties included ministry to the staff and soldiers engaged in daily training as well as conducting prayers and preaching. He was also assigned to a mobile bayonet training group that traveled throughout the theater providing instruction on the effective use of the bayonet in combat. During this unlikely assignment he often engaged in mock sparring matches with the champion boxer, Jimmy Driscoll, and with the rather large instructor who had killed eighteen German soldiers with the bayonet, his small stature offering a bit of comic relief to the otherwise serious proceedings.[19] During these training events, he usually delivered a twenty-minute address, with his usual wit and effect. The chaplain's duties also included trips to the hospital to visit the wounded. On one such visit, a wounded officer asked him, "What is God like?"[20] The answer would occupy his thinking, writing, and speaking for years to come. I'll discuss that question and Studdert Kennedy's answer in chapter 4.

In common with all military men and women, chaplains are subject to military orders and are often assigned unwelcome duties. In October 1916 Studdert Kennedy was assigned just such a task when he was assigned to preach the Church of England's National Mission of Repentance and Hope, taking him away from his soldiers at the front. The mission, the Church of England's effort to bring religious renewal in the midst of the war, was pursued both on the home front and among the British soldiers in France. In characteristic manner, Chaplain Studdert Kennedy excelled in the assignment, driving home the message with humor and passion. He even transformed the message into a poem that was printed in his *Rough Rhymes of a Padre*.[21] Titled "Sinner and Saint: A Sermon in a Billet," the poem revealed Studdert Kennedy's ability to communicate with the troops in their language as well to touch their heart with his message.

Our Padre, 'E says I'm a sinner,
And John Bull says I'm a saint,
And they're both of 'em bound to be liars,
For neither of them, I ain't.
I'm a man and a man's a mixture,
Right down from 'is very birth,
For part of 'im comes from heaven,
And part of 'im comes from earth . . .
Old England same as us Englishmen,
A mixture o' bad and best.
And that's what I reckon these parsons mean
With their Mission o' 'Pentance and 'Ope
They want us to wash old England's face clean,
Wi' the grace of Gawd for soap . . .
We can't let it be for nothin'
That our pals 'ave fought and bled,
So Lads, let's look to this washin' up
For the sake of Christ--- and our dead.[22]

THE CHAPLAIN IN COMBAT

The role of the chaplain in combat is a matter of some disagreement and discussion. Chaplains are noncombatants and do not carry weapons. Generally, there is broad agreement that chaplains should station themselves at battalion aid stations during ground combat and in the sickbay on naval ships. These locations allow them to assist with the wounded and dying while keeping out of the way of combat troops. No chaplain wants to interfere with or distract soldiers from their combat duties. In the First World War, chaplains were initially barred from accompanying troops to the front lines, the field ambulance (battle dressing station) being viewed as the appropriate location. This policy came directly from the top, with Field Marshall Kitchener being the source of the prohibition.[23] The policy changed in December 1915 when Sir Douglas Haig was appointed Commander in Chief of the BEF. Haig was a firm believer in the benefit of chaplains to the troops and encouraged their presence at the Front to encourage morale and to preach on the goals of the war.[24]

Chaplain Studdert Kennedy arrived in France in December 1915, just as this major change in policy was implemented. He thoroughly agreed with the policy and later informed a newly arriving chaplain (in December 1916) that a chaplain's place, if he was to be of any spiritual benefit, was in the trenches with the troops where "there was the most danger of death."[25] Studdert Kennedy was speaking from experience, having recently participated (June 1916) in the Somme offensive with the 137th Brigade of the 46th division. Later (June 1917) he would serve with the 17th Brigade of the 24th Division, at the Messines Ridge and in the final advance (1918) with the 42nd Division.[26] Studdert Kennedy's duties during those experiences of combat illustrate the role that a chaplain can perform during war.

On June 7, 1917, Studdert Kennedy reported that he "went over the top" with his troops and into "no man's land." He found that the German and British guns had made the land a "howling wilderness." Then he veered to the left into a wooded area in order to set up an Aid Post, where wounded soldiers would be brought before being taken back to a more fully capable medical station. He reported that he was alone, was a bit frightened (had the wind up), and had tripped over a dead German.[27] This event would find its way into many of his later speeches and works and would play a significant role in his musings on the meaning of war and God's role in it.

Death is an ever-present and unwelcome companion on the battlefield, and chaplains play an essential military role that contributes to the morale and well-being of the troops, that of caring for the dying and the dead. This includes providing solace to the dying, providing them prayers or "last rites," and performing burial services. Chaplains are valued as mediators between life and death, an essential role in the psychological and spiritual health of individual soldiers as well as for the morale of the army as a fighting whole. But the role, while necessary, is not welcome. Unfortunately, "There are two rules in warfare, Rule Number One: young men die in war. Rule Number Two: Doctors (and chaplains) can't change rule number one."[28] This adage by the fictional doctor Hawkeye Pierce in the television sitcom *M*A*S*H* captured the reality of combat from a chaplain's perspective perfectly. The impact of combat deaths is tragic for all, but, as Studdert Kennedy would report after the war, "because he sees the boys he loves go down (die) the padre's heart came nearer to breaking in those days than the hearts of other men. . . . Hatred, bitterness and anger were a waste of time.[29]

On June 9, 1917, the Chaplain was alone again, wandering the battlefield in the Ypres Salient seeking out the bodies of British soldiers. He found one, identified only as Pte. Peter ---. Studdert Kennedy mused that he should bury the man ("good thing I brought the shovel") and retrieved the man's identifying papers, paybook, and a photo of his wife and four kids. The chaplain engaged in a one-way conversation with the deceased soldier, reflecting on his own role as a rather "informal and incompetent undertaker, with tears in my eyes and sorrow in my heart."[30] He apologized to the man for his own failures and for those of the church in not serving him more effectively in life and so poorly in death. In the end, he promised he'd strive to do better and would write the soldier's widow.[31]

Chaplain Studdert Kennedy also reported that he conducted communion services in the trenches,[32] helped retrieve the wounded,[33] and endured a terrible German shell barrage with his troops and barely escaped serious injury when their position was struck by a shell. Others were not so fortunate; one individual who had been loudly praying for his own safety was killed.[34] He also reported being in an aid station where a wounded soldier was crying for relief of the pain from his wounds. Studdert Kennedy left the station and ran to the rear for morphine while dodging a heavy artillery barrage both going and coming. He was awarded the Military Cross for this heroic action (and ten days leave!).

Studdert Kennedy's presence in the trenches, his courage, and his willingness to place himself at risk of death or injury for the sake of the troops guaranteed his success and endeared him to the men of the BEF. He serves as a timeless example of effective chaplain ministry. His style of effective ministry has been verified by modern research. "The more a chaplain moved beyond his role and put himself at risk for others, seemingly the more he was accepted, respected and valued, not simply as a man of faith, but as a comrade in service."[35] While effective in terms of winning the acceptance of the troops and the privilege of ministering to their spiritual needs, it also placed the chaplain in great physical and psychological danger. During the First World War, ninety-seven chaplains were killed in action while an additional sixty-nine died as a result of wounds received during their service in the war.[36] Chaplain Studdert Kennedy, like all combat participants, was also exposed to what have come to be called the invisible or "hidden wounds of war."[37]

THE INVISIBLE WOUNDS OF WAR: COMBAT STRESS, PTSD, MORAL INJURY, SPIRITUAL INJURY AND COMPASSION FATIGUE

PTSD and Combat Stress

The world of Studdert Kennedy was unfamiliar with the concepts of combat stress injuries and post-traumatic stress disorder (PTSD). However, that world was too familiar with the effects of industrialized warfare on its troops. "Shell shock" was the diagnosis applied to the psychological casualties resulting from the intense shelling by artillery and mortar batteries on soldiers in the trenches. Later it was noted that even those who had not been subject to artillery barrages experienced shell shock's symptoms. In the final tally, more than eighty thousand soldiers were officially diagnosed with shell shock during the war.[38] So significant were the effects of industrial scale warfare on the troops that the BEF took steps to reduce the impact of extended duty in the front trenches, introducing a rotation system that limited direct exposure to combat to periods of around seven days.[39] Military leaders, however, often had little sympathy for the soldiers thus afflicted, urging them into "no man's land" and its machine guns with calls to glory, and, if need be, threats of death.[40] In spite of the official medical recognition of shell shock, the psychological injuries were often considered nervous reactions or failures of character. After the war, Chaplain Studdert Kennedy commented on the continuing impact of war on the men he had served in France, "There were plenty of men who had served in the war, and they were just frozen inside."[41] He had experienced the conditions that produced "shell shock" firsthand, as he braved combat in the trenches and the constant proximity of death. Although we now have better understanding of the causes of "shell shock" or PTSD, he attributed the ongoing impact of war to fear.

> There never was a time when fear swayed the hearts and minds of men as it did in those days. There are men in asylums now, plenty of them, biting their nails and scratching themselves, shivering at every sound, the men who went mad with fear. There are other men who go about secretly haunted and hunted by fear, and who will go that way to their graves. We bragged and boasted and lied to hide our fear. When war comes in at the door, truth goes out of the window.[42]

Today we know that PTSD is a psychological condition that can be treated, and that lack of treatment can result in long-term disability. We also know that not everyone exposed to combat trauma develops PTSD. There is a great deal of research currently being conducted on the subject and why some service members develop PTSD and others do not.

The American Psychiatric Association lists a number of criteria for diagnosing PTSD in its Statistical Manual of Mental Disorders (DSM-5). While PTSD is widely accepted as a diagnosis resulting from exposure to combat trauma, another approach seeks to avoid the stigma associated with a psychological diagnosis and classifies the psychological response to combat trauma as a stress injury or wound that, similar to other wounds, can be addressed with appropriate intervention and treatment. Charles Figley and William Nash take this approach in their edited work, *Combat Stress Injury*. The United States Marine Corps and Navy have also adopted this approach in the training and care of their combat personnel.[43]

Figley and Nash suggest that combat exposes its participants to physical, cognitive, social, and spiritual stressors that, like all stressors, are cumulative over time. Individuals address these combat stressors through normal coping strategies, consciously or unconsciously adapting to their environment. The cumulative nature of combat stress can, however, overwhelm a service member's coping skills and result in combat stress injuries. Exposure to traumatic events, the danger of one's own death, experience of carnage, and other horrors associated with combat may result in traumatic injury, with resulting psychological symptoms. These symptoms may include hypervigilance, flashbacks, guilt, loss of faith, isolation, emotional numbing, and cognitive dissonance, defined as shattered belief systems.[44] One of the beneficial insights of Figley and Nash's approach is that, with proper training and preparation, the military can assist its members to build resilience as they prepare for combat.

Resilience

Resilience is defined as the ability to "bounce back" from the challenging experiences we face in life. In terms of combat and war, our contemporary military has defined this trait as the ability to experience the multiple stresses of modern warfare and to emerge with psychological health intact and mission ready for further engagement in whatever requirements the national security situation dictates. The recipe for resilience includes intensive physical conditioning coupled with good health, realistic professional training, strong unit cohesion and personal support, and supportive leadership. Individuals are also encouraged to develop positive family support systems and personal spiritual resources. The most important role in this context are the leaders who apply knowledge and experience to develop resilience in the units they lead. These leaders are trained to lead effectively in combat and to work with their units as they return and recover from combat. They are also responsible to identify individuals who bear the invisible wounds of war and to direct them to available healing resources: doctors, mental health professionals, and chaplains. One key perspective is that the mental, moral, and spiritual injuries individuals experience in combat are inevitable injuries of war and that, with proper care, an individual my experience healing and a return to health.[45]

Studdert Kennedy possessed many resources that contributed to his resilience and enabled his continued ministry to British soldiers during his years of military service. Primary among them was his strong faith and commitment to the troops he served. His family life was solid. While it is evident that he did not receive any military training that would prepare him for the human impact of early-twentieth-century industrial warfare, his pastoral ministry in the working-class and poverty-stricken cities of Britain armed him with an awareness of and empathy for extreme human suffering. While Studdert Kennedy's natural resilience did enable him to complete his tour of service with the BEF in France, it is clear that he did not emerge from the war unscathed. His more than three years in the combat theater exposed him to an unending series of personal challenges. As one combat veteran commented to me recently as I described Studdert Kennedy's experiences, it is clear that "every soldier has his limits."[46]

Moral and Spiritual Injury

Researchers note two additional conditions that may afflict those who take part in war: moral injury and spiritual injury. A brief understanding of each is important if we are to understand Chaplain Studdert Kennedy and the impact of his war experiences on his life. Jonathan Shay, a well-known psychologist in the Boston area who treated veterans of the Vietnam war, described the universal and timeless impact of war on combat veterans leading to Post Traumatic Stress Disorder (PTSD). He is also the first to have identified moral injury as a component of PTSD. Shay quoted a Vietnam veteran to illustrate the impact of combat on a soldier in words that are amazingly similar to Studdert Kennedy's experience of the First World War.

> War changes you, changes you. Strips you, strips you of all your beliefs, your religion, takes your dignity away, you become an animal—the animal in the sense of being evil. You know, it's unbelievable what humans can do to each other.[47]

Central to Shay's description of war's impact on soldiers is the role of *themis*. In his 1994 *Achilles in Vietnam* he described *themis* as the understanding of "*what's right*"[48] in a society, its cultural norms. These are the accepted moral principles and normative expectations to which members of a culture are expected to adhere.[49] The violation of *themis*, the betrayal of trust by military and civilian leaders, serves as a source of significant psychiatric injury leading to PTSD in combat veterans. He further stated that the "essential injuries in combat PTSD are moral and social."[50] In his 2002 work, *Odysseus in America*, he further defined this injury as a moral injury and is credited with introducing the term into the psychological literature. When military leaders or politicians violate the trust of those they send into combat, through bad decision making, poor strategy or lack of support, they contribute to the moral injury of their troops. "Powerlessness imposed by those in authority and intentional inflection of violation of "what's right" results in severe psychological injury."[51] This aspect of moral injury "impairs and sometime destroys the capacity for trust. When social trust is destroyed, it is replaced by the settled expectancy of harm, exploitation, and humiliation from others."[52] Moral injury results in a long-term distrust of those in authority and possible disappointment with the individual's commitments that led to the moral injury. For those of a spiritual or religious nature, the authority figure perceived as having violated the individual's trust may include God.

Bret Litz, in his 2009 article "Moral Injury and Moral Repair in War Veterans" expanded the definition of moral injury to include an individual's actions in war. There he defined moral injury as stemming from "events in which a person perpetrates, fails to prevent, bears witness to, or learns about acts that transgress deeply held moral beliefs and expectations."[53] Service members experience moral injury as a result of the very nature of war itself. The taking of a human life, whether combatant or noncombatant, can result in an individual experiencing significant moral impact, especially since society demands respect for all human life. The long-term impact and symptoms of moral injury are often mistaken for PTSD. As Dr. Shay pointed out in his works, moral injury is an important component and may contribute to the development of PTSD, but the two are separate problems. Two experts on Moral Injury, Rita Nakashima Brock and Gabriella Lettini, agree, "moral injury is not PTSD."[54]

> The consequences of violating one's conscience, even if the act was unavoidable or seemed right at the time, can be devastating. Responses include overwhelming depression, guilt, and self-medication through alcohol or drugs. Moral injury can lead to veterans experiencing feelings of worthlessness, remorse, and despair; they may feel as if they lost their souls in combat.[55]

Moral injury is recognized by the U.S. Veterans Administration and is described on its website.

> Like psychological trauma, *moral injury* is a construct that describes extreme and unprecedented life experience including the harmful aftermath of exposure

to such events. Events are considered morally injurious if they "transgress deeply held *moral* beliefs and expectations."[56]

Robert Grant, in his *The Way of the Wound*, highlighted the spiritual dimension in dealing with the human response to trauma. The experience of war trauma, in addition to the symptoms described earlier, may cause individuals to question their faith or the nature of God. War may challenge an individual's preconceived notions of how the world works and their place in it. It may also challenge their understanding of God. These challenges may result in psychological or spiritual dissonance, "a state of psychic tension caused by the simultaneous holding of mutually inconsistent attitudes of the existence of a lack of consonance between attitudes and behavior."[57] Grant addressed this spiritual dimension of trauma and suggested that the resolution of dissonance, through critical reflection and griefwork, may require the reconstruction or transformation of an individual's worldview.

> Trauma initially drives most people either towards or away from the Spirit. Trauma respects nothing. Childhood images of God are often the first to go because they are a mixture of personal hopes, disappointments, and fears. . . . The way of the wound demands that images of God emerge out of personal experience and critical reflection.[58]

These emerging images of God may look very different from the pre-trauma conceptions, an insight that is especially applicable as we consider Chaplain Studdert Kennedy and his response to his soldiers' questions regarding the nature of God

Compassion Fatigue

An additional challenge that afflicts chaplains, and other caregivers, is compassion fatigue. It is a condition experienced by those who care for others but tend not to care for themselves adequately. Continual, uninterrupted exposure to caring situations may overtax an individual's coping ability. Apathy, exhaustion, and a loss or diminished ability to feel compassion for others may result. It is often described as the negative cost of caring.[59] A chaplain's constant exposure to people in need, to combat casualties, and to the requirement to come alongside grieving family members exposes them to risk in this area. We'll see that Studdert Kennedy's wartime experiences, especially the thousands of combat casualties, placed him at risk for this condition. Additionally, the constant exposure to death, experienced by those in morgue units and graves registration units, also contributes to traumatic and moral injury, or worse.[60] After personally dragging the body of a soldier to its burial place,

Studdert Kennedy commented, with tears, that "The dead weigh heavy on the hand, and on the heart."[61] Death was a constant companion of Chaplain Studdert Kennedy during his four years in the war zone. His prose and poetry are filled with images of the dead. No wonder his friends commented that, when he returned home in 1919, "he returned to civilian life embittered, above all conscious of the many, the very many, who did not come back at all."[62]

CONCLUSION

War imposes lasting effects on all its participants: soldiers, support personnel, doctors, medics, and chaplains like Studdert Kennedy. But healing, recovery, and post-traumatic growth are possible with appropriate assistance and guidance. Recovery, however, is not assured. "Healing and coming home from war are difficult, complex and perilous journeys of introspection and understanding."[63] PTSD, defined as a combat stress *illness* by Figley and Nash, is treated with a number of therapeutic interventions, including the administration of appropriate drugs to alleviate symptoms.[64] Combat stress injuries are understood to be similar to other combat injuries; with proper treatment recovery is possible, even likely. Healing from spiritual injury involves addressing cognitive dissonance and reconstructing one's understanding of the spiritual world and one's relationship with the creator, often involving acknowledging one's mistaken beliefs and understanding of the spiritual life. How Studdert Kennedy addressed spiritual injury in his life is the subject of chapter 4. Recovery from moral injury involves acknowledging ownership of one's transgressions and expressing grief over those transgressions while "avoiding denial and forgetting."[65] This aspect of moral injury is treated in chapter 5. The second type of moral injury, when one's trust is violated by those in authority, either military or civilian, is addressed in chapter 6. Jonathan Shay and others remind us that the essential element in the healing process is the participation in a healing community. "Restoration of *thumos* and of the capacity for social trust happens only in community."[66] Shay further stated that this community must be defined as "trust worthy," one where survivors can voice their stories without judgment.[67] Purification through confession and penance are also an important step in the healing process, and Studdert Kennedy choose a surprising community and venue in which to confess his personal and corporate failures. That confession is the subject of chapter 7. An important element that almost always accompanies the healing process and results in post-traumatic growth is public service, either as a self-imposed penance or as a renewed desire to create a better world. Many survivors of moral injury adopt an anti-war mindset and actively promote peace-making. I'll address these last two elements of Studdert Kennedy's life in chapter 8.

Dr. Jonathan Shay, in concert with the experts discussed in this section, asserted that the experiences of war and returning from war are timeless, that soldiers and sailors of all ages have experienced similar psychological and spiritual responses to combat. Whether Achilles in Troy or Chaplain Studdert Kennedy in France, participants in combat throughout history have experienced similar responses to the stresses of war; their responses are universal *human* responses. It is on this basis that I am confident that Studdert Kennedy's life story and war experiences as a chaplain in France during the First World War have application and insights for us one hundred years later. I believe his chaplain service in the First World War also provides an example to modern chaplains as they serve in both peace and war.

The understanding of war's impact on men and women has greatly expanded since the First World War, facilitated by the growth in psychological research, the ongoing experience of war, and efforts to provide aid to the survivors of combat trauma. Studdert Kennedy's experiences and attempts to come to grips with those experiences, examined in these pages, provide insights to both the reality of war and an individual effort to find healing and restoration in its aftermath. We are fortunate that Studdert Kennedy published extensively between 1917 and his death in 1929. His prose writings, poetry, and speeches open a significant window into his struggles and healing efforts, into his soul. His journey, while all too short, is made beautiful by his passion and transparency.

NOTES

1. G. A. Studdert Kennedy, "Faith" in *Peace Rhymes of a Padre* (London: Hodder & Stoughton, 1920), 34.
2. William Purcell, *Woodbine Willie: A Biography* (London: Hodder & Stoughton, 1962), 103.
3. A good deal of this chapter is informed by my experience as a U.S. Navy Chaplain from 1986 to 2009 and the privilege of serving as the Advanced Course Director and Instructor at the U.S. Navy Chaplain's School from 2000 to 2004.
4. Michael Snape, *The Royal Army Chaplains' Department: Clergy Under Fire* (Woodbridge: The Boydell Press, 2008.), 15. St. Martin's part of the cloak was venerated as a holy relic and was carried into battle by French kings. The priests who carried the relic were called *cappellani* (Fr. *Chapelains*, Eng. Chaplain).
5. Clergy who become chaplains are required to be endorsed by a religious body which then supervises and supports the chaplain's ministry in the military. Endorsement requires adherence to the religious body's religious beliefs, usually characterized as a statement of faith and practice. The military also has requirements for an

individual to become a chaplain, and the chaplain must maintain both the military and religious organization's standards to continue in the military.

6. G. A. Studdert Kennedy, *The Hardest Part* (London: Hodder & Stoughton, 1918), 9.

7. G. A. Studdert Kennedy, *Lies* (London: Hodder & Stoughton, 1919), 141.

8. G. A. Studdert Kennedy, *Rough Rhymes of a Padre* (London: Hodder & Stoughton, 1918), 9–16.

9. D. F. Carey, "Studdert Kennedy: War Padre," in *G. A. Studdert Kennedy by His Friends*, ed. J. K. Mozley (Hodder & Stoughton, 1929), 149.

10. Ibid., 125.

11. "Another Worcester Cleric as Chaplain," *Birmingham Daily Post*, Dec. 1, 1915, 3. The article also reported that Mrs. Studdert Kennedy was serving as a Red Cross nurse at Battenhall Mount Red Cross Hospital.

12. Carey, "Studdert Kennedy: War Padre," in *G. A. Studdert Kennedy by His Friends*, ed. J. K. Mozley, 116.

13. G. A. Studdert Kennedy, *The New Man in Christ* (London: Hodder & Stoughton, 1932), 234–235.

14. Michael Snape, *The Royal Army Chaplains' Department: Clergy Under Fire* (Woodbridge: The Boydell Press, 2008), 32.

15. Walker, Simon Herold, "Saving Bodies and Souls: Army Chaplains and Medical care in the First World War." *Postgraduate Journal of Medical Humanities*, 3 (2016), 24.

16. British chaplains are commissioned but do not wear rank insignia and are understood to assume the rank of the individual with whom they are talking.

17. Purcell, *Woodbine Willie: A Biography*, 106.

18. "A Cheery St. Fercus Soldier," *The Buchan Observer*, 15 April 1916, 5.

19. Carey, "Studdert Kennedy: War Padre," 129.

20. G. A. Studdert Kennedy, *Rough Talks by a Padre* (London: Hodder & Stoughton, 1918), 129.

21. Carey, "Studdert Kennedy: War Padre," in *G. A. Studdert Kennedy by His Friends,* 130–131.

22. Studdert Kennedy, *Rough Rhymes of a Padre*, 25–27.

23. Snape, *Clergy Under Fire*, 217. There is currently some disagreement whether Kitchener was the source of the prohibition of chaplains serving at the Front.

24. Ibid., 219–220.

25. David Raw, *Theodore Bayley Hardy* (Yorkshire: Pen and Sword Military, 2018), 50.

26. Purcell, *Woodbine Willie: A Biography*, 108.

27. Studdert Kennedy, *The Hardest Part*, 8–11.

28. Heidi Squier Kraft, *Rule Number Two* (New York: Little, Brown and Co., 2007), 133. This comes from a memorable scene in the television show *M*A*S*H* as Hawkeye Pierce laments the reality of combat deaths.

29. "Fruits of Victory, Woodbine Willie's Analysis for Our Times," *Northampton Mercury*, May 12, 1922, 13.

30. Studdert Kennedy, *The Hardest Part*, 160.

31. Ibid., 143–149.
32. Ibid., 120.
33. Ibid., 15.
34. Ibid., 101 ff.
35. Simon Herold Walker, "Saving Bodies and Souls: Army Chaplains and Medical Care in the First World War," *Postgraduate Journal of Medical Humanities*, 3(2016): 35.
36. Gerald Studdert Kennedy, *Dog Collar Democracy* (London: Macmillan Press, 1982), 53.
37. Rita Nakashima Brock and Gabriella Lettini, *Soul Repair: Recovering from Moral Injury after War* (Boston: Beacon Press, 2012), xv.
38. Wendy Holden, *Shell Shock* (London: Channel 4 Books, 1998), 69. Some current estimates place the true number of shell shock casualties at more than 350,000.
39. British Library, "World War 1: The Daily Life of Soldiers." https://www.bl.uk/world-war-one/articles/the-daily-life-of-soldiers#.
40. Studdert Kennedy, *Lies*, 61–62.
41. "The Center of Unity," *The Advertiser*, May 22, 1926.
42. G. A. Studdert Kennedy, "The Accursed Thing," *John Bull*, Nov. 12, 1927, 24.
43. MCTP 3-30E and NTTP 1-15M Combat and Operational Stress Control (Washington D.C.: Department of the Navy, 2016), Foreword.
44. William P. Nash and Dewleen Baker, "Competing and Complementary Models of Combat Stress Injury" in eds. Charles R. Figley and William P. Nash, *Combat Stress Injury* (New York: Routledge, 2007), 74–76.
45. MCTP 3-30E and NTTP 1-15M Combat and Operational Stress Control (Washington D.C.: Department of the Navy, 2016), 2–11.
46. 1st Baptist Salinas Men's Zoom Meeting, March 5, 2021. During the meeting I described Studdert Kennedy's war service. One gentleman, a former Army Medic and veteran of Desert Storm, made the comment that "Everyone who experiences war has his limits."
47. Jonathan Shay, *Achilles in Vietnam* (New York: Touchstone Books, 1994), 33.
48. Ibid., 5.
49. Ibid., 3–21.
50. Ibid., 187.
51. Jonathan Shay, *Odysseus in America* (New York: Scribner, 2002), 248. See also 206.
52. Jonathan Shay, "Moral Injury," *Psychoanalytic Psychology* (2014) 31, No. 2, 186.
53. Bret T. Litz and Patricia K. Kerig, "Introduction to the Special Issue on Moral Injury: Conceptual Challenges, Methodological Issues, and Clinical Applications." *Journal of Traumatic Stress* (June 2019) 32, 342.
54. Brock and Lettini., *Soul Repair: Recovering from Moral Injury after War*, xiii.
55. Ibid., xv.
56. "Moral Injury," https://www.ptsd.va.gov/professional/co-occurring/moral_injury__at_war.asp, accessed 19 Oct 2018.

57. Barbara Stuart, "Cognitive Dissonance: A Spiritual Perspective," https://www.mediate.com/articles/stuart.cfm accessed 31 Aug 2018.

58. Robert Grant, *The Way of the Wound: A Spirituality of Trauma and Transformation* (Oakland: Robert Grant, 1996), 9.

59. "Compassion Fatigue," www.compassionfatigue.org, accessed 4 Feb 2021.

60. Shay, *Achilles in Vietnam*, 65; Brock and Lettini, *Soul Repair*, xv.

61. Studdert Kennedy, *The Hardest Part*, 154.

62. Purcell, *Woodbine Willie: A Biography*," 152.

63. Brock and Lettini, *Soul Repair: Recovering from Moral Injury after War*, 97.

64. MCTP 3-30E and NTTP 1-15M Combat and Operational Stress Control (Washington D.C.: Department of the Navy, 2016), Appendix A.

65. Shay, *Achilles in Vietnam*, 193. See also Brock and Lettini, *Soul Repair*, 114.

66. Shay, *Odysseus in America*, 162. See also Shay, *Achilles in Vietnam*, 187–189.

67. Shay, *Achilles in Vietnam*, 187–192.

Chapter Three

The Stresses of War

Physical, Cognitive, Social, Spiritual, and Traumatic

"His Mate"

There's a broken, battered village
Somewhere up behind the line,
There's a dug-out and a bunk there
That I used to say were mine.

I remember how I reached them,
Dripping wet and all forlorn,
In the dim and dreary twilight
Of a weeping summer morn.

All that week I'd buried brothers,
In one bitter battle slain,
In one grave I laid two hundred,
God! What sorrow and what rain!

And that night I'd been in trenches,
Seeking out the sodden dead,
And just dropping them in shell holes,
With a service swiftly said.

For the bullets rattled round me,
But I couldn't leave them there,
Water-soaked in flooded shell-holes,
Reft of common Christian prayer.

So I crawled round on my belly,
And I listened to the roar
Of the guns that hammered Thiepval,
Like the breakers on the shore.

Then there spoke a dripping sergeant,
When the time was growing late,
Would you please to bury this one,
'Cause 'e used to be my mate?"

So we groped our way in darkness
To a body lying there,
Just a blacker lump of blackness
With a red blotch on his hair.

Though we turned him gently over
Yet I still can hear the thud,
As the body fell face forward,
And then settled in the mud.

We went down upon our faces,
And I said the service through,
From "I am the resurrection"
To the last great "adieu."

We stood up to give the Blessing,
And commend him to the Lord.
When a sudden light shot soaring
Silver swift and like a sword.

At a stroke it slew the darkness,
Flashed its glory on the mud,
And I saw the sergeant staring
At a crimson clot of blood.

There are many kinds of sorrow
In this world of love and hate.
But there is no sterner sorrow
Than a soldier's for his mate.[1]

COMBAT STRESSES ILLUSTRATED IN "HIS MATE"

In June 1916, Chaplain Studdert Kennedy was assigned to serve with the 137th Brigade of the 46th Division, which fought in the Somme Offensive, which took place between July and November of 1916. His unit, like all units in the offensive, suffered terrible losses. Studdert Kennedy's poem, "His Mate," illustrated the battle conditions they faced and his own chaplain role there. The battle conditions described in the poem capture the essential elements that modern psychiatrists and therapists have come to understand contribute to combat stress and combat stress injury.

The combat environment and its inherent stresses contribute to the possibility of combat stress injury and the development of PTSD, which is termed a combat stress illness. The physical, cognitive, social, and spiritual stresses of combat accumulate over time and can ultimately lead to crisis in the life of those immersed in war: the fighting soldier, combat leaders, medics, physicians, mental health professionals, and chaplains.[2] The danger of traumatic injury and the exposure to other's traumatic injury also has a profound effect on individuals who participate in combat.[3] We are familiar with images of the First World War: muddy trenches, water-filled shell holes and barren battle landscapes. Few today have direct experience of those conditions. Chaplain Studdert Kennedy's poetry and prose paint a graphic and often too-realistic picture of his own experience of those conditions and fully illustrate the various dimensions of combat stress. I'll use his poem "His Mate" to illustrate the environmental conditions that he experienced and were common throughout the battlefields of the First World War.

THE PHYSICAL ENVIRONMENT

The physical environment always contributes to the stressors experienced by our military personnel engaged in battle. Cold, ice, and exposure to the elements compound the challenges they face. In this poem, the environment was characterized by rain and mud, through which the chaplain was forced to slither in order to escape the ever-present enemy fire. Studdert Kennedy never commented upon his own drenched and muddy condition but instead demonstrated great sympathy for the "sodden dead," many of whom were "water-soaked in flooded shell-holes, reft of common Christian prayer." It's probable that the chaplain, earlier in his night rounds in the midst of battle, had dropped at least some of those bodies into those same shell holes to preserve them from the constant shell fire. He now was seeking to retrieve them in order to perform his pastoral duty, to bury them with the thousands he had already placed in the cemetery. The constant rain only served to accentuate the overwhelming emotion, "God, what sorrow and what rain!"[4]

Cognitive Stresses

The cognitive dimension involves our perception of the environment and our beliefs about how we fit and function within it. The impact of the battlefield challenges those perceptions and transforms what had been benign and relatively rare encounters with death into an omnipresent and exceedingly dangerous experience. As Studdert Kennedy recounted in "His Mate," death and the care of mangled corpses had become an all-too-familiar constant in his life. The chaplain grimly described the daily business of collecting the dead for burial while machine-gun bullets chattered around him. There was the very real danger of his own death in the conduct of his duties. He was forced to crawl about on his belly as he performed the normally serene sacramental rites accompanied by the roar of exploding artillery shells. By necessity, his hurried recital of the burial service was delivered as he lay facedown in the mud, accompanied only by the sergeant who had sought his aid. His concluding prayer was punctuated by a German shell that ended the hasty service with the explosive destruction of the body. Miraculously, the chaplain and sergeant emerged unscathed, gazing at a "crimson clot of blood," the body having experienced a sudden, explosive transformation to glory! It is striking how this burial differed from the chaplain's normal peacetime ecclesiastical duties and how he had adapted to the requirements of the battlefield.

The Stress of Social Isolation

The social isolation of the chaplain is a striking element in this poem, although he does not comment on this subject directly. A chaplain is, by the nature of his role, a solitary figure. The military operates in units—fire teams, squads, platoons, companies, etc. A soldier always has a "buddy" or comrade to support him in his duties, someone to "have his back." As is evident in this poem, many of the chaplain's duties are accomplished in a one-to-one relationship; in this case, to the dead soldiers scattered about no-man's-land, where he was isolated by his role and identity.[5] Studdert Kennedy was roaming the battlefield, seeking out the dead in order to transport them to the cemetery. On another battlefield, as he set up an aid station he had mused, "how I hate being alone. It's rotten. One pal makes all the difference."[6] This social isolation and overwhelming sense of duty can contribute to a sense of loneliness and carrying the world's ills on one's solitary shoulders, a malady to which Studdert Kennedy, with his immense sense of empathy and commitment to his soldiers, was evidently prone.

Traumatic Injury

One of the most significant contributions to combat stress on the battlefield is the ubiquity of trauma and death. "His Mate" focused directly on the huge scale in the number of deaths that resulted from First World War battles. The poet reported the reality that, "in one grave I laid two hundred." We can reliably assume that he had ministered at many more similar graves. How many more thousands must he and other chaplains have buried by the time of his writing this poem?[7] The poet reported his dangerous excursion throughout the muddy battlefield, seeking ever more bodies to bury. The numbers are numbing. To personalize the grief that Studdert Kennedy experienced, "His Mate" focused on the loss of just one soldier. A sergeant mourned for a lost buddy and in doing so, we can grieve for all the soldiers and their wives, children, mothers, and fathers of those lost in war. For Studdert Kennedy, the loss was a personal one, as he would also experience the loss of a mate later during this same battle when his chaplain assistant was killed while attempting to escort some wounded soldiers to the rear.

> On the last Sunday in June 1917, the Advanced Dressing Station in which I was working was blown in and everyone in it was killed except the doctor, two stretcher cases, an R.A.M.C.[8] sergeant and myself. Among those killed was Roy Fergusson, my servant, a splendid lad of nineteen years, with whom I was great friends. He went out after the first shell had broken the end of the station to guide some walking wounded to a place of safety and was killed instantly. I found him leaning against a heap of sandbags, his head buried in his hands and a great hole in his back. Poor old Roy, I thought I had saved his life when I sent him on that job.[9]

Studdert Kennedy's poetry and prose recorded the loss of many Soldiers and their mates on the battlefields of the Great War. A brief survey of his writings reveals numerous memories that would accompany him back to England once the war was over, seared into his consciousness. Many years later, he would report that the memories of the Great War were often more real and striking to him than events that had occurred only the day before.[10] In his works, he recorded the following events, any one of which would serve as an effective illustration of combat trauma but, when taken as a whole, communicates the heavy weight of death that effected this chaplain's soul:

- His tripping over the body of a German soldier on 7 June 1917. He was struck by how young, weak, and "non-monstrous" he appeared.[11]
- Reports that he had carried in many wounded and noted that he was drenched in the blood of the wounded men, June 1917.[12]

- Soldier Peter, in a kneeling position facing the front lines with a fatal bullet wound in his forehead, June 1917.[13]
- The death of the soldier he criticized for his selfish prayers, killed in a sudden explosion by friendly fire.[14]
- The death of his own assistant, Roy Fergusson on 24 June 1917.[15]
- His own narrow escape from death in the destruction of the advanced dressing station where he was working. Most present were killed.[16]
- The "Mate" he referred to in the poem of the same title, June 1916.[17]
- The hundreds he had buried in a single grave.[18]
- The thousands killed when the mines at Messines Ridge were exploded, to which his spirit rebelled, June 7, 1917.[19]
- The disemboweled mother and beheaded child he referred to in his poem "Der Tag"[20]

The constant presence and exposure to trauma and the military caregiver's responsibilities in dealing with the wounded and the dead inevitably wear on the spirit. These images remain deep in the memory and often intrude on everyday thoughts, with unwanted flashbacks occurring with even the slightest reminder of war, or with no obvious trigger at all. They show up in dreams and nightmares, often awakening their victims in a cold sweat. For Studdert Kennedy, they also showed up in his poetry, written prose, and public speeches, offering a window into his emotions and thinking process. He was unable and perhaps unwilling to leave the war and its images behind, offering as it did some of the most intense and significant experiences of his life.

Spiritual Stresses and Challenged Belief Systems

Experience reveals that combat also challenges participants' belief systems: one's beliefs about good and evil, one's place in the world, and especially one's place in the grand scheme of life and mortality.[21] In this poem we understand that the chaplain had become all too familiar with traumatic death and had become acclimated to its images, sounds and smells. In the poem, he recalled the repeated requirement to "drop a body into a shell-hole" for its protection and the burial of two hundred in a mass grave as a common occurrence. His prewar innocence has been destroyed by the war and posed very real challenges to his beliefs about life, the war, and God. After his 1917 experiences at the Messines Ridge, he informed a friend, "You know, this business has made me less cocksure of much of which I was cocksure before."[22] After the war, as he reflected on the long-term impact of his war experiences, he reported,

> For me and for a good many others this work of destruction was finally accomplished during the past four years in a brutal, cruel, and merciless fashion. To a sensitive spirit these years of war have been a perpetual torture chamber in which he has often had to have his half-beliefs, which were like parts of his body, torn away from him without even being allowed at the time to utter a cry of pain.[23]

Some of the "half-formed" beliefs that he had torn away were his understanding of God, his understanding of the utility of force to accomplish peace and his trust in the justice of British war aims. I'll return to these issues later.

Ultimately, the real challenge of the war for the chaplain was spiritual as he cried out to the God he understood as loving father. In "His Mate," we hear a cry from his grief-stricken soul as he reflected upon his duties, burying the dead from the recent battle, "God! What sorrow and what rain." There was no time for tears as he performed the rites for each soldier he buried. His only comfort was that the rain might represent God's tearful response to the war's human carnage.

Indeed, of all the challenges discussed in this section, the primary challenge for him was the spiritual one. He had inherited the Christian faith from his family and was thoroughly indoctrinated in the tenets of that faith from childhood. He had followed his father's footsteps into the ministry and had experienced great success. But the war challenged him as the poverty-stricken streets of Rugby, Leeds, and Worcester had not. How would his faith hold up when faced with death dealt on an industrial scale? The chaplain preached to thousands throughout the war zone and felt a deep responsibility for the spiritual well-being of those to whom he ministered, and to their families. He could offer them a stirring message, a prayer, or a pack of Woodbine cigarettes. But was his ministry effective in the face of the war and its accumulated sorrows?

> And I have heard a voice out of the darkness crying, "My God, my God, Why? . . . The woman whose hope of Love was murdered on the battlefields of France crying from her unconscious for the child she will never have. A monotonous, interminable procession, some in anger, some sullen, some scornful, some brokenly submissive, but all in the dark and asking, "Why?" The question no mortal man can answer.[24]

As chaplain Studdert Kennedy accompanied his soldiers into battle and shared their battlefield conditions, he also shared their response to the horrors they experienced. The carnage, the lost mates, the sorrow that he, as a sensitive soul immersed in the horror of war experienced daily shook his spiritual foundations. Looking back on his experiences, he related that his faith was often on the verge of foundering, that the flood of blood and sorrow was like a tidal wave that threatened to overwhelm him. In the last book he personally published, in 1928, he reflected back on his spiritual condition:

> There were times when I could not have helped anyone, because I was forsaken of God. I thought Christ was dead, that He had never lived. . . . I was just sick, sick to death of the sin and wickedness of it all.[25]

In his poem, "Missing, Believed Killed," Studdert Kennedy quoted a Christian scripture that conveys the foundational Christian hope of victory over death through the Easter resurrection of Christ. But he concluded the poem with a paradoxical twist that conveyed his experiences and the experiences of the millions of soldiers that survived the war: the seeming victory of death and the destruction of hope!

> O Grave where is thy victory,
> O death where is they sting?
> Thy victory is everywhere,
> Thy sting's in everything.[26]

Did the chaplain desert his soldiers and deny his faith as a result of these experiences? His faith was certainly challenged, and he asked the hard questions along with the countless soldiers among whom he served. A fearful dark night in the trenches reminded him of an experience on a cloudless night beneath the stars near a booming ocean. In the trenches soldiers often queried unidentified figures approaching them with the question, "who goes there?" What would happen if he asked the same question to the universe?

> Laying in no-man's land at night I watched a dark moving object approach not knowing if it was friend or foe. . . . "Who goes there?" Supposing I cry out to the great-other-than-myself, "Who goes there?" Would there be any answer? . . . Well, I made my cry and I got my answer. I have often doubted it, and never entirely understood it, but it remains. If I lost it I think I would lose my soul. I have been trying to say it ever since. At the time it was only one word, "God." I stood in the presence of God.[27]

This answer certainly dealt with his existential question. But what about the day-to-day challenges he faced? What resources could he find to lighten the burden of the boredom of daily military life punctuated with the horrors of the trenches? He related that the one saving grace for him, and for others, was the occasional glimpse of beauty; of the occasional flower, of a colorful sunset, or the wonder of a dark cloudless night beneath a canopy of stars.

> Again and again in France among the mass of ordinary men whom the bitterness of life was driving every day to the very abyss of despair, that what called them

back to their vague but valid faith in the final goodness of God was the glory of a sunset or dawn; the colour of some wayside flower, or the laughter in the eyes of a peasant child in the village where they went to rest.[28]

There is no question that Studdert Kennedy's faith and spiritual life were tested by his experiences in the war. He questioned his understanding of God's will and goodness, and he hesitantly flung his questions at the universe. But he also received answers to his questions. Ultimately, his faith survived. Indeed, he even found a source of energy to fuel his ministry and offer hope to the soldiers as they faced death across "no-man's land." His vision of Christ crucified over the battlefield empowered him with these scriptural words, "Inasmuch as ye have done it unto the least of these my little ones ye have done it unto me."[29]

I believe the final word regarding Studdert Kennedy's spiritual life and survival was summarized by A. F. London in the preface to Studdert Kennedy's 1925 book, *The Word and the Work*. "No one who has been through what the author has been through during the War and since can help facing it . . . that it shows it to be a possibility, even when you have faced everything, to keep your faith, tremblingly, but still to keep it in a good God."[30]

Chaplain Studdert Kennedy experienced a multitude of combat stresses during his four years in First World War France: physical, cognitive, social, traumatic, and spiritual. His experiences raised great questions, but his deep questioning also discovered answers—his faith was shaken but survived. The accumulated stresses of the battlefield changed him, however, even as they changed all who survived the war. The war created in him both cognitive and spiritual dissonances with which he had to deal if he was to survive spiritually and psychologically. The first dissonance with which the war confronted him was his understanding of God.

NOTES

1. Studdert Kennedy, *Rough Rhymes of a Padre*, pp. 68–71. The reference to Thiepval places the event at the Somme offensive during 1 July–18 Nov 1916. The offensive resulted in over one million dead and wounded.

2. William P. Nash, "The Stressors of War," in *Combat Stress Injury*, eds. Charles R. Figley and William P. Nash (New York: Routledge, 2007), 11–31.

3. William P. Nash, "Combat/Operational Stress Adaptations and Injuries" in *Combat Stress Injury*, eds. Charles R. Figley and William P. Nash (New York: Routledge, 2007), 50.

4. Studdert Kennedy's reports of his experiences in France are characterized by rain and mud. He recorded that his first service upon his arrival in Dec. 1915 had four hundred members of the BEF gathered for Christmas prayers, standing in formation

in the pouring rain, ankle deep in mud (*G. A. Studdert Kennedy by His Friends*, 116). In his *Rough Talks by a Padre*, he reflected on his first experience of battle in the trenches. The rain was unnecessarily and unexpectedly a factor, "Great heavens, how it rained, and just when we did not need it to rain. Fine dry weather would have saved many a British mother's son. It need not have rained either, it was not winter, it was the end of June 1916. Fine weather would have been seasonable and reasonable, and this flood was neither, it was just cussedness." Studdert Kennedy, *Rough Talks by a Padre* (London: Hodder & Stoughton, 1918), 17–18.

5. As a noncombatant, members of the unit may question the chaplain's presence in the front lines since he serves no direct combat role.

6. G. A. Studdert Kennedy, *The Hardest Part* (London: Hodder & Stoughton, 1918), 10.

7. Hew Strachan, *The First World War* (New York: Viking Press, 2003), 195. In the Battle of the Somme, the British and French lost 614,000 men, the Germans between 465,000 and 650,000. Many more chaplains were conducting the same burial services as Studdert Kennedy.

8. Royal Army Medical Corps.

9. Studdert Kennedy, *The Hardest Part*, 154–155.

10. G. A. Studdert Kennedy, *The Warrior, the Woman, and the Christ* (London: Hodder & Stoughton, 1928), 18.

11. Studdert Kennedy, *The Hardest Part*, 11.

12. Ibid.,13.

13. Ibid., 143.

14. Ibid., 101–102.

15. Ibid., 163–190.

16. Ibid., 163.

17. G. A. Studdert Kennedy, *Rough Rhymes of a Padre* (London: Hodder & Stoughton, 1918), 68–71.

18. Ibid., 68–71.

19. Studdert Kennedy, *The Hardest Part*, 4–5.

20. Studdert Kennedy, *Peace Rhymes of a Padre* (London: Hodder & Stoughton, 1920), 17. There is no evidence he actually observed this gruesome scene. It may be a recollection of the reports of German atrocities in Belgium. He also served with a bayonet training team and may have viewed graphic photographs used as training aids depicting bayonet effects and war atrocities. See Studdert Kennedy, *Lies*, 87–88, "The Lie of Lust."

21. Nash, "Combat Stressors," in *Combat Stress Injury*, 24.

22. D. F. Carey, "Studdert Kennedy: War Padre" in *G. A. Studdert Kennedy by His Friends*, ed. J. K. Mozley (London: Hodder & Stoughton, 1929), 154.

23. G. A. Studdert Kennedy, *Lies* (London: Hodder & Stoughton, 1919), 141–143.

24. G. A. Studdert Kennedy, *The Word and the Work* (London: Longmans, Green and Co., 1925), 55–56.

25. Studdert Kennedy, *The Warrior, the Woman and the Christ*, 311.

26. G. A. Studdert Kennedy, *More Rough Rhymes of a Padre* (London: Hodder & Stoughton, 1918), 88. This verse reverses the idea of Christian victory in the Apostle

Paul's I Corinthian's 15:55–56 "Death is swallowed up in victory. O death where is your victory, O death where is thy sting. The sting of death is sin, and the power of sin is the law; but thanks be to God, who gives us victory through our Lord Jesus Christ."

27. Studdert Kennedy, *The Warrior, the Woman, and the Christ*, 203–4.
28. Studdert Kennedy, *The Word and the Work*, 9.
29. Ibid., 57–58.
30. Ibid., v.

Chapter Four

Spiritual Injury

Disappointment with God

"The Sorrow of God"

Yes, I used to believe i' Jesus Christ,
And I used to go to church,
But sin' I left 'ome and came to France,
I've been clean knocked off my perch,
. . .
But it ain't the same out 'ere, ye know.
It's as different as chalk fro' cheese,
For 'arf on it's blood and t'other 'arf's mud,
And I'm damned if I really sees
'Ow the God, who 'as made such a cruel world,
Can 'ave Love in 'Is 'eart for men,
And be deaf to the cries of the men as dies
And never comes home again.
. . .
And the lovin' God 'E looks down on it all,
On the blood and the mud and the smell,
O God, if it's true, 'ow I pities you,
For ye must be livin' I' 'ell.
You must be livin' I' 'ell all day,
And livin' I' 'ell all night.
I'd rather be dead, wiv a 'ole through my 'ead,
I would, by a damn long sight,
Than be livin' wi' you on your 'eavenly throne,
Lookin' down on yon bloody 'eap
That were once a boy full o' life and joy,
And 'earin' 'is mother weep.
The sorrows of God must be 'ard to bear

If 'E really 'as Love in 'Is 'eart,
And the 'ardest part I' the world to play
Must surely be God's part.[1]

Chaplain Studdert Kennedy's poem illustrated the very real challenge that war and combat poses for people of faith. In the beginning of the poem, the soldier related that he had attended church and followed the Christian faith prior to his wartime experience in France. But the death of a comrade had brought that faith into question and the soldier posed the question that so many combat veterans have asked, "How can a loving God allow this to occur?" The rest of the poem recounted the solution that Chaplain Studdert Kennedy suggested for this problem, that of the Suffering God. This solution became a key element of his pastoral care ministry as he worked among the soldiers in France and, indeed, throughout the remaining years of his ministry in Great Britain. It was a solution forged in the crucible of combat that enabled him to minister effectively to his troops.[2] In effect, he became the apostle of the Suffering God, a calling that resulted from the profound spiritual injury he experienced as he faced the suffering he and his beloved soldiers experienced daily in the grind of industrial age warfare.

War has a profound impact upon all its participants. Combatants must face the reality of killing and being killed while innocent noncombatants often face the unwelcome danger of becoming "collateral damage." One of the ever-present dangers of combat is what Psychologist William Nash terms "damage to core beliefs about the world and one's place in it."[3] The violation of one's deeply held values, either intentionally or unintentionally, can result in moral injury, a diagnosis that was not known or imagined during the First World War. But the conditions and effects of moral injury were well known and ubiquitous both during the war and after. Spiritual injury, similar to moral injury, is suffered by those participants in war who believe in God, have a religious faith, and rely on that faith for sustainment during difficult times. Persons of faith subjected to the death and carnage of combat may come to question that faith, and even discover that their belief system contains myths or falsehoods. They may question God's loving nature or even God's existence.[4]

Nash suggests that combat survivors may experience "shattered belief systems"[5] and spiritual or cognitive dissonance, the revelation that experienced reality conflicts with dearly held beliefs. Healing of combat trauma requires that survivors engage a process to address dissonance and reconstruct or repair those belief systems.[6] In chapter 5, I will discuss the evolution of Chaplain Studdert Kennedy's thinking as he came to question the utility of war and his place in it. But the war challenged him on an even more important existential and spiritual level, it challenged his faith and his understanding of God.

Studdert Kennedy, an ordained member of the Church of England, was guided by the church's thirty-nine articles of religion that "contain the true Doctrine of the Church of England agreeable to God's word."[7] The first of those articles, titled "of Faith in the Holy Trinity," states,

> There is but one living and true God, everlasting without body, parts or *passions*; of infinite power, wisdom and goodness; the Maker, and Preserver of all things both visible and invisible. And in unity of the Godhead there be three Persons, of one substance, power and eternity; the Father, the Son, and the Holy Ghost.[8]

The Church of England's statement of faith regarding God's goodness and power and the experienced reality of the trench warfare during the Great War illustrates the existential dissonance encountered by millions of soldiers in France; "if God is all loving and all powerful, how can trench warfare exist." Put in its ancient form, "How can evil exist?" The problem of evil, theodicy, has challenged people of faith for thousands of years.[9] For many, it is a merely a theological or philosophical exercise discussed over a beer at the local pub. On the battlefields of France, the problem took on existential proportions as individuals struggled with their faith even as they battled a mortal human enemy.

The question posed in Studdert Kennedy's poem also suggested a second theological problem. It is also referenced in the Church of England's first article where it describes God as "without passion," in theological terms, "the impassibility of God."[10] The point of this dogma is that God is the "unmoved mover," without emotion and immune to being moved or challenged by human passion.[11] God is therefore "the same yesterday, today and forever." This understanding of God would suggest that God is not moved by human suffering on the battlefield but has plans and intents that humans do not understand. From the human point of view, a loving God would never take this approach, especially in view of the unspeakable suffering experienced on the battlefields of the Great War. For Chaplain Studdert Kennedy, and any chaplain, this doctrine presents a very real problem as he or she encounters the questions of wounded and dying soldiers, "Does God care about our suffering, our pain, our losses?" To respond that "God does not" negates any ministry a chaplain might have among the soldiers. Studdert Kennedy resolved this twofold dissonance by rejecting the traditional view of God and reconstructing his beliefs in a way that enabled him to serve the British Expeditionary Force while also addressing their probing questions. But his solution also violated traditional dogma and risked ecclesiastical censure.

Studdert Kennedy had faced this problem from his earliest days in ministry. His experience of the poverty and suffering in the slums of industrial

England had brought him face-to-face with the problem of evil as it related to his ministry there. Later he would define the evil of poverty as equal to the suffering he had experienced in war-torn France. But he had also faced the challenge of war and God's will prior to his arrival on the battlefields of France. In his 1923 book, *The Wicket Gate*, he recounted a pastoral encounter in which he faced the necessity to reconcile God's will, God's goodness, and the evils of warfare while also ministering to the personal grief and questions of a soldier's mother.

> I can remember, in 1915, before I set out to France, a weeping and distracted mother running into me to tell me that Ronald had been killed—blown to pieces up in Ypres—and asking me if that was God's Will, and I said, "No, ma'am, certainly not, it is the result of evil, it is the result of the concentration of all the evils in hell and earth. It is no more God's Will than the Cross was God's will. . . . Those evils were the cause of the cross and those evils were the cause of this cursed war. Ronald was a good boy, he lived clean and died clean. His courage, his self-sacrifice, his tenderness to you, those were God's will; his death was God's woe, as it is yours.[12]

Studdert Kennedy recalled the traditional theological and pastoral approach to human suffering and evil in his poem, titled "A Sermon," contained in his *More Rough Rhymes of a Padre*, his popular book of poetry that was published in 1919. The doctrines of God's sovereignty and impassibility, that God's will is responsible for all historical events, even war and human suffering, and that God is unmoved by that suffering, seemed completely incomprehensible to those fighting in the trenches of France and offered little peace to those back home. The poem described in painful detail the impact of war on humanity and the unfeeling and unhelpful responses offered by traditionally minded clergy.

> "A Sermon"
>
> My Brethren, the ways of God
> No man can understand,
> We can but wait in awe and watch
> The wonders of his hand . . .
> O Weeping Mother torn with grief,
> Poor stricken heart that cries,
> And rocks a cradle empty now,
> "Tis by God's will he dies,
> His strong young body blown to bits,
> His raw flesh quiv'ring still,
> His comrades' groans of agony,
> They are God's Holy Will.

He measures out our Peace and War
As seemeth to Him best,
His judgments are unknowable,
Remember that—and rest. . . .
He has some hidden purpose sure
For all this blood and tears,
It is His Will—be still—be still,
He is the Lord of years.[13]

Studdert Kennedy addressed the challenge of evil and God's will in his first published work titled, "The Religious Difficulties of the Private Soldier," a chapter in the 1917 book of chaplain's essays titled *The Church in the Furnace* that was distributed to the troops. He later reworked the chapter and published it in a popular pamphlet titled "Why Aren't all the Best Chaps Christians?" In the article, Studdert Kennedy did not shy from the tough questions and immediately tackled the problem of evil. "The first great difficulty of the private soldier is war. Why does not God stop it? Any decent man would stop it tomorrow if he could, and if God is almighty and can do anything, they why does He allow it to go on?"[14] In the article, he also engaged the problem in relation to the Church of England's articles of religion.

> Too often in the past this first clause of our Creed has been interpreted and preached in such a way as to force men to lay upon God the responsibility for evil as though it were in some mysterious way His Will. God has been represented as sending and willing plague, pestilence, famine, disease and war. All these have been represented as the visitation of God. This has led to a very popular fatalism which is a pernicious travesty of Christian truth.[15]

Later, in his postwar book, *Lies*, he passionately engaged the same question in the context of his war experiences. It is evident that the passage of time and experience had only reinforced his disdain for the traditional approach to God's sovereignty.[16]

> What is God Like?—What is He like? What do you mean when you say he is Almighty? What does the first of the thirty-nine articles mean when it says that "There is one God without body, parts or passions, of infinite wisdom and power." What do all those wonderful pictures in the Revelation mean—of God sitting on a throne. . . .—While a German soldier spears a Belgian baby, rapes its mother, and keeps her alive to see the father shot? In God's name, what is Almighty God like?[17]

Studdert Kennedy answered his rhetorical and all-too-practical question with a strong denunciation of the traditional view of God. Instead of the mighty potentate seated on a throne, Studdert Kennedy presented an image of God as a suffering servant, dying on a cross. "God rules because he serves, is supreme because he suffers, is strong because He is weak. The Bible tells the story of how that usurper was cast down, and the true King of Calvary took his place. The King of Calvary must be the God of the world that is to be."[18]

When Studdert Kennedy first arrived in France to assume his duties as chaplain he reported that he had adhered to church dogma and taught and preached the traditional understanding of God as he ministered in the rear areas. After his experiences at the Battle of the Somme, in 1916, he had also preached in the National Mission of Repentance and Hope, an attempt by the Anglican Church to uplift the morale of England's population through spiritual revival.[19] He preached to thousands of troops and fully endorsed the Church of England's efforts and his country's political and military goals. Much of this content was later included in his first book, *Rough Talks by a Padre*. But he later came to regret the content of some of those sermons, understanding that his traditional view of God was a destructive myth.

> At the time, staggered by the immensity of the evil, I simply did not think; I submitted. Now, after three years of it, I believe that this teaching is liable to be utterly misunderstood and does but give occasion to the enemies of the Lord to blaspheme. Never again, I believe, will men bow down and worship this majestic tyrant who sits upon a throne and wields as weapons pestilence, disease, and war. Such a vision of God rouses in the best of men, not reverence, but revolt; not loyalty, but contempt; not love but bitter hatred.[20]

In his book reflecting on his experiences in the war, *The Hardest Part*, Studdert Kennedy reported that his journey to his new understanding of God had been initiated with a question by a wounded officer he had visited in the hospital. The officer had simply asked, "What is God like?" The chaplain had pointed to the crucifix that hung on the wall. But the man had replied that he knew all about Christ, but "What was God like, and how could a loving God will the horror of trench warfare? How could God remain unmoved by the sheer magnitude of human carnage and suffering visited upon the soldiers in this war?"[21] Studdert Kennedy was moved to deep reflection by this question. His answer, forged in the crucible of war and his desire to provide effective pastoral care to his beloved soldiers, caused him to question his own and his church's theological foundations.

For a chaplain teaching God's love and attempting to bring a measure of peace and hope to the Soldiers under his care, the impact was devastating. He acquitted himself honorably during his experiences of combat, with his faith in God and the assurance of heaven sustaining him as he accompanied his men "over the top" into no man's land to establish aid stations for the wounded.[22]

While he survived his three direct experiences of combat, his spirit was wounded by the reality of war and the utter cruelty of modern weapons. The two engagements his units fought in 1916 and 1917 were characterized by all the evils of trench warfare. His unit at Gommecourt during the Battle of the Somme (1916) experienced heavy casualties.[23] His experiences at the Messines Ridge (1917), recorded in *The Hardest Part*, were likewise bloody and nearly resulted in his own death. His faith in God and commitment to Christ provided him the resources to survive both psychologically and spiritually, but his experiences were to have a lasting spiritual impact.

The path by which he came to his conclusion, by which he reconciled the brutality of war with a loving Eternal Father, involved a process that occurred between 1915 and 1917 as he served both in the trenches and behind the lines. The reconciliation of his spiritual dissonance resulted in a revolutionary view of God that would answer his questions and enable him to minister God's compassion to those he served.[24] Studdert Kennedy came to understand and argue that there were two ideas of God in history, the first being a false viewpoint, that of a Darwinian God who created the principle of survival of the fittest. This was the God of the Prussians and their militaristic view of power, that "might makes right."[25] This vision of God, in his view, was also promulgated by the British church hierarchy, which considered the Great War and its mayhem a judgment upon humanity for its failure to obey God and to love one another. This was the God who willed war, as well as the suffering that accompanied it. Studdert Kennedy's experiences of war moved him to reject this Darwinian concept with the deepest possible conviction. In his speaking and writing, he clearly articulated the hatred he felt for what he believed was a false concept of God.

> War is evil. It is a cruel and insane waste of energy and life. If God wills war, then I am morally mad and life has no meaning. I hate war, and if God wills it I hate God, and I am a better man for hating Him; that is the pass it brings me to. In that case, the first and great commandment is, "Thou shalt hate the Lord thy God with all thy heart, and Him only shalt thou detest and despise."[26]

Studdert Kennedy's faith was challenged by his experiences in battle: the carnage, the lost friends and mates, the sorrow that filled his emotions and soul. He reported that he stuffed his feelings in the interest of encouraging the morale of his soldiers. Looking back on his experiences he related that his faith was often on the verge of foundering, that the flood of blood and sorrow was like a tidal wave that threatened to overwhelm his belief in God. The questions posed by the soldiers he served also dogged him. A sudden revelation in the midst of battle brought the light required to answer his and his soldiers' questions.

In *The Hardest Part*, he recounted many of his experiences at the Messines Ridge in 1917 and briefly mentioned tripping over the body of a young German soldier as he searched for a position in which to establish an aid station. The dead German soldier appeared young and weak, hardly the image of a deadly enemy.[27] Later, in his 1925 book *The Word and the Work*, he recalled that the event had a much greater meaning for his faith and played a significant role in resolving the spiritual dissonance he faced regarding his understanding of God and the war.

> On June 7th, 1917, I was running to our lines half mad with fright, though running in the right direction, thank God, through what had been once a wooded copse. It was being heavily shelled. As I ran I stumbled and fell over something. I stopped to see what it was. It was an undersized, underfed German boy, with a wound in his stomach and a hole in his head. I remember muttering, "You poor little devil, what had you got to do with it? Not much great blonde Prussian about you." Then there came light. It may have been pure imagination, but that does not mean that it was not also reality, for what is called imagination is often the road to reality. It seemed to me that the boy disappeared and in his place there lay the Christ upon His Cross, and cried, *"Inasmuch as ye have done it unto the least of these my little ones ye have done it unto me."* From that moment on I never saw a battlefield as anything but a Crucifix.[28]

In addressing the emotional, spiritual, and intellectual challenges he and the Soldiers of the BEF faced on the battlefields of France and Belgium, Studdert Kennedy advanced a resolution that challenged a number of accepted theological formulations. He came to view God as the Suffering God who experienced His own trauma resulting from the suffering of His Son, Jesus Christ, on the cross. God had suffered personal pain as a result of His son's death, and He could therefore identify with the pain of the men and women immersed in the shock and trauma of war.

> Man's history is one long bloody war, with burning homes, dishonored women, tortured children, and all war's usual atrocities repeated like a filthy tale. That fact must be faced, and Christianity faces it in the tortured figure of God incarnate in whom all history is summed up. . . . There is an agony in God's history but again I would stress that it is a victorious agony.[29]

The chaplain who accompanied his flock into combat, who tended to their wounds and prayed over their mangled bodies strengthened their spirits with these words, "For every wound a man receives there's a wound in the heart of God, and every cry of agony finds echo in God's soul."[30] This understanding of God enabled this caring chaplain to provide words of comfort to the wounded and dying he encountered on the battlefield and in the military hospitals he visited. It also enabled him to provide authentic pastoral care to their families: widows, wives, mothers, fathers, and children.

Studdert Kennedy also addressed the theological question posed by the war in reference to God's omnipotence and sovereignty, "Why doesn't God stop the war?" The chaplain's answer flew in the face of official dogma. "The truth is, that history drives one to the knowledge that God cannot be absolutely Almighty."[31] Instead he suggested that God is the God of progress, and that progress is the result of the Suffering God who chooses to work within history alongside imperfect human beings. "It has been a broken, slow, and painful progress marked by many failures, a *Via Dolorosa* wet with blood and tears."[32] Instead of a triumphant all powerful sovereign God who drives history and the wills of men according to His own transcendent plan, the chaplain suggested that God walks with men along a path that meanders between success and failure, that is marked by suffering and love. "If the Christian religion means anything, it means that God is suffering love, and that all real progress is caused by the working of suffering love in the world."[33] He concluded that the human response must be to believe in and support the work of God's suffering love by faithful and sacrificial service.

> War is the crucifixion of God, not the working of His will. The Cross is not past but present. Ever and always I can see set up above this world of ours a huge and towering Cross, with great arms stretched out east and west from the rising to the setting sun, and on that Cross my God still hangs and calls on all brave men to come out and fight with evil, and by their sufferings endured with Him help lift the world from darkness into light.[34]

Studdert Kennedy's theological ruminations enabled him to resolve the spiritual and cognitive dissonance that had plagued him since the beginning of the war. His understanding of the Suffering God enabled him to authentically offer comfort and guidance to his military flock. As they experienced the horrors of trench warfare, the torrent of blood and loss, God also suffered alongside them, experiencing and feeling their losses and pain.

> "The Suffering God"
>
> . . .
> Father, if He, the Christ, were Thy Revealer,
> Truly the First Begotten of the Lord,
> Then must thou be a Suff'rer and a Healer,
> Pierced to the heart by the sorrow of the sword.[35]

Studdert Kennedy's understanding of God energized his ministry both in France and in postwar Britain as he sought to minister to his beloved soldiers, their families and the working men and women of industrial England. His formulation is contained in every one of his books of poetry and in nearly all of his books.[36] His understanding that he was a coworker with the Suffering God in His efforts to minister to a wounded humanity served as a reconstructed foundation for all his ministry.

Studdert Kennedy's theological and pastoral formulation did not meet with universal approval. In fact, it was condemned as a heresy by some. The charge that his approach amounted to the ancient heresy of *patripassianism* is hard to ignore. *Partipassianism* reduces the distinction between the members of the Trinity (Father, Son, and Holy Spirit) and views them simply as differing modes within the Godhead.[37] In this formulation, it is suggested that God (as Father) literally sacrificed himself on the cross. The similarity to Studdert Kennedy's approach is clear, although Studdert Kennedy never confused or merged the separate personalities of the Trinity.

Studdert Kennedy was confronted with the charge of heresy during a wartime discussion with another chaplain in which Studdert Kennedy expounded on his understanding of the suffering God. The Chaplain countered, probably in expectation of a good debate, that Studdert Kennedy's approach was "merely reviving the heresy of the early days of Christianity." Studdert Kennedy's response was passionate and direct.

> To hell with your metaphysics! I have to show God to 'Ole Bill in the trenches in a way he can understand. I have to show him a God who can command his respect and win his love. And why, may I ask, should a doctrine which was considered a heresy in the fourth century necessarily be heresy still in the twentieth?"[38]

Studdert Kennedy understood that his conception of God flew in the face of convention and could cause some hard feelings. His wartime book, *The Hardest Part*, presented his view of God and God's role in ministering to the soldiers and their families of the war. In the postscript, titled, "A reply to some Criticism and a Few Words to any Readers who may Be Hurt by What I Have Written," Studdert Kennedy offered an explanation for his thinking and how it had evolved.

> This is a fairly faithful and accurate record of the inner ruminations of an incurably religious man under battle conditions. I think this accounts for many things. It accounts for what my critics have called a lack of balance which runs through it, the predominance of the one idea (the Suffering God). Battles do not make for carefully balanced thought. There is one main idea in what I have written, but I believe it is a true idea.[39]

A few pages later, he explained that his idea of a suffering God first presented itself to him during his ministry in England but had been fully revealed in the war-torn years in France.

> The vision of the Suffering God revealed in Jesus Christ and the necessary Truth of it, first began to dawn upon me in the narrow streets and shadowed homes of an English slum. All that war has done is to batter the essential truth of it deeper in, and cast a fiercer light upon the Cross. A battlefield is more striking, but scarcely more really crude and brutal than a slum.[40]

Studdert Kennedy's spiritual injury, dissonance and its resolution evolved through the cauldron of four years of warfare, suffering, and loss. His friends and family members reported that he emerged from the war a changed man, subject to nightmares and haunted by memories of carnage in the Valley of the Somme, a memory which, for him, came to symbolize and sum up all the evils of the war. But he also emerged from the war with a reformulated understanding of God that would energize his ministry to the men and women who had served in the war and who would inhabit the postwar slums and industrial wastelands that dominated Britain. While his understanding of the Suffering God addressed his spiritual dissonance, his participation in the war exposed him to a moral injury that would require years of existential struggle and turmoil.

NOTES

1. G. A. Studdert Kennedy, *More Rough Rhymes of a Padre* (London: Hodder & Stoughton, 1918), 17–24.
2. Ibid.,17.
3. William P. Nash, "Combat Operational Stress Adaptations and Injuries," in *Combat Stress Injury*, eds. Charles R. Figley and William P. Nash (New York: Routledge, 2007), 53.
4. Robert Grant, *The Way of the Wound* (Oakland: Robert Grant, 1996), 11.
5. Nash, "Combat Operational Stress Adaptations and Injuries," in *Combat Stress Injury*, 54.
6. William P. Nash and Dewleen Baker, "Competing and Complementary Models of Combat Stress Injury" in *Combat Stress Injury*, eds. Charles R. Figley and William P. Nash (New York: Routledge, 2007), 76.
7. Church of England, Articles of Religion. www.churchofengland.org/p accessed 13 January 2021.
8. Ibid.
9. "Theodicy—The part of theology concerned with defending the goodness and omnipotence of God in the face of suffering and evil in the world." *Oxford Refer-*

ence oxfordreference.com/view/10.1093/oi/authority.20110803103805212 accessed March 24, 2021. Studdert Kennedy is struggling with theodicy, otherwise known as the problem of evil. If God is both perfectly good and all powerful, he would eliminate evil. But since evil exists, either He is not all good or He is not all powerful. Studdert Kennedy opts for the latter, as will be discussed in later pages.

10. Studdert Kennedy's boyhood friend and theological sounding board J. K. Mozley was clear about his disagreement with Studdert Kennedy's views on passibility and God's suffering. He commented in his contribution to the volume he edited, *G. A. Studdert Kennedy by His Friends*, that "As he well knew, I could not agree with him in his reading back of suffering into the life of God" (246). Mozley participated in the Church of England's Commission on Christian Doctrine (1922–1932) and produced a volume titled *The Impassibility of God: A Survey of Christian Thought* (Cambridge: The University Press, 1926). In the volume, while he did not come to agreement with Studdert Kennedy, he did seem to treat the idea with more sympathy, suggesting that the subject required more study in the context of Christian theology.

11. Alister E. McGrath, ed., "Can God Suffer" in *The Christian Theology Reader* (West Sussex: John Wiley and Sons Ltd., 2017), 152. Impassibility—in early Christian thought focused on the God's perfection, and implied changelessness, that change was seen as a marker of either decay or imperfection. Early Christian writers thus tended to interpret the suffering of Christ, as God incarnate, as affecting his human nature and not his divinity. God might know about suffering; God, however, did not experience suffering." God does not experience emotion and is therefore independent, not causally dependent of other beings.

12. G. A. Studdert Kennedy, *The Wicket Gate* (London: Hodder & Stoughton, 1923), 131–132.

13. Studdert Kennedy, *More Rough Rhymes of a Padre*, 32–37.

14. G. A. Studdert Kennedy, "The Religious Difficulties of the Private Soldier," in *The Church in the Furnace*, ed. F. B. MacNutt (London: Macmillan and Co., 1917), 379.

15. Ibid., 385.

16. Alister E. McGrath, ed., *The Christian Theology Reader,* 186. God's Sovereignty suggests that "God is to be seen as our governor and preserver, who sustains all things, inanimate and living. Nothing acts independently of God, in that God's governance lies behind physical events in the world of nature."

17. G. A. Studdert Kennedy, *Lies* (London: Hodder & Stoughton, 1919), 144.

18. Ibid., 224.

19. G. A. Studdert Kennedy, *The Hardest Part* (London: Hodder & Stoughton, 1918), 93–94. The National Mission of Repentance and Hope was initiated by the Archbishop of Canterbury in 1916 and was designed to bring about a revival of religion within England. The main goals were to bring repentance for failure to love God and man as well as to provide hope in the midst of war. It was first conducted in England and then taught to the troops in France. Studdert Kennedy was assigned to assist this effort beginning in the Fall of 1916. See also William Purcell, *Woodbine Willie* (London: Hodder & Stoughton, 1962), 124.

20. Studdert Kennedy, *The Hardest Part*, 93–94.

21. Ibid., xi, xiv.
22. Ibid., 8–14.
23. James E. Edmonds, *History of the Great War: Military Operations 1916 Vol. I* (London: Macmillan, 1932), 465–471. Two battalions of the 137th Brigade attacked Gommecourt Wood at 0730, experiencing the loss of 27 officers and 497 soldiers. The two battalions they attacked with (the 1/5 and 1/7 Sherwood Forest) experienced 80 percent casualties. Edmonds commented, "Ill luck attended the attack of the 137th Brigade from beginning to end."
24. Michael Brierley, in his essay "There Ain't No Throne": Geoffrey Studdert Kennedy and the Doctrine of God" in *Life After Tragedy: Essays on Faith and the First World War Evoked by Geoffrey Studdert Kennedy* (Eugene Oregon, 2017) and Linda Parker, in *Seeker After Truths: The Life and Times of G.A. Studdert Kennedy (Woodbine Willie)*, 1883–1929, relate Studdert Kennedy's early theological training that introduced him to the strains of theology that he eventually adopted and championed.
25. Ibid., 39.
26. Ibid., 35.
27. Ibid., 11–12.
28. G. A. Studdert Kennedy, *The Word and the Work* (London: Hodder & Stoughton, 1925), 57–58.
29. Studdert Kennedy, "The Religious Difficulties of the Private Soldier," 384.
30. G. A. Studdert Kennedy, *Rough Talks of a Padre* (London: Hodder & Stoughton, 1918), 245.
31. Studdert Kennedy, *The Hardest Part*, 40.
32. Ibid., 42.
33. Ibid., 44.
34. Ibid., 44–45.
35. G. A. Studdert Kennedy, *Rough Rhymes of a Padre*, 58–63.
36. See Studdert Kennedy, *Peace Rhymes of a Padre*, 33–36, 80–87, 92–94; *Lies*, 141; *Food for the Fed Up*, 35–36, 53–59, 186–187; *Democracy and the Dog Collar*, 92–99; *The Wicket Gate*, 128–147; *Songs of Faith and Doubt*, 38.
37. McGrath, ed.,*The Christian Theology Reader*, 227. "Patripassianism centered on the belief that the Father suffered as the Son . . . the only distinction within the Godhead was a succession of modes or operations. In other words, Father, Son, and Spirit were just different modes of being, or expressions, of the same divine entity." Also known as Sabellianism.
38. D. F. Carey, "Studdert Kennedy: War Padre," in *G. A. Studdert Kennedy by His Friends*, ed. J. K. Mozley (London: Hodder & Stoughton, 1929), 152–153.
39. Studdert Kennedy, *The Hardest Part*, 191–192.
40. Ibid., 195–196.

Chapter Five

"A Perpetual Torture Chamber"

Studdert Kennedy's Changing Attitude to War

Before the outbreak of the First World War, Chaplain Studdert Kennedy, as a Church of England cleric and young Christian, had not really considered the possibility or ramifications of war. Like most civilians, he was concerned with the daily affairs of his new married life and the problems of his parish. War, as he later commented, was something one read about in the newspapers and, if it occurred, might even be of some benefit to the national character.[1] He was certainly opposed to killing and favored peace. When war did break out, he admitted to some hours of moral struggle as he considered applying for a chaplain's position with the British Army but chose to do so out of a sense of duty.[2] After his experiences at the Somme and the Messines Ridge, however, he began to doubt his decision, and had realized the full horror of war.[3] He began to suffer from what we now know to be a moral injury.

Moral injury occurs when individuals are faced with morally challenging situations and are forced, due to the nature of the situation, to make decisions or to act in ways that transgress deeply held beliefs or values. The conduct of war, by its very nature, inevitably places combatants in danger of moral injury. Military members join the military for a multitude of reasons: a job with decent pay and benefits, the promise of medical care for families, education, or even adventure. Few enlist for the specific purpose of killing another human being. Many who join the military have never fully considered the ramifications of their choice and don't fully understand the requirements of military members during war. When faced with the grim reality of war, of killing an enemy combatant or taking part in actions that result in the deaths or wounding of innocent noncombatants, military members may experience psychological, spiritual, or even physical trauma. Chaplains, even though they are noncombatants, are subject to the same or similar challenges as a result of their supporting role in the conduct of combat actions. Cognitive or moral (and spiritual) dissonance occurs when individuals recognize that their conduct or responsibilities differ substantially from beliefs or values that they hold dear. Dissonance requires resolution,[4] either through an adjustment of values or a change of responsibility. If the violation of values is severe and resolution is not possible, the individual may suffer lasting consequences of grief or guilt, resulting in what has been identified as moral injury.

STUDDERT KENNEDY'S INITIAL SUPPORT FOR THE WAR

When war broke out in 1914, Studdert Kennedy, like many other Englishmen, was convinced of the rightness of Great Britain's entry into the war. The Germans were certainly conducting a brutal and unjust war, characterized by the "rape" of Belgium and endangering Britain's ally, France.[5] Like other members of the clergy in 1914, he exhorted his parishioners to pray for the war effort and encouraged eligible men to enlist in the military. He signed on to support the war effort as a chaplain in 1915 and did so in the full and complete belief that Great Britain was fighting a just war against a foe that meant to do great harm to all of Europe, including England. At some point in their personal journey, chaplains must address questions regarding peace and war and their place in the military; "how can a person dedicated to the peace of God serve in an organization dedicated to war." We often rationalize this problem by explaining that chaplains are there to serve the needs of the soldiers who must fight and are deprived of their access to religious services when deployed in the service of their country. Most understand, however, that the chaplain's presence in the military presents a very real conflict in the minds of many.[6]

Studdert Kennedy admitted that he wrestled with this problem when he considered his calling to serve the troops in France. In his 1921 work, *Democracy and the Dog Collar*, he responded to an imaginary challenger regarding his, and other members of the clergy's, participation in the war. In his answer, he acknowledged that he had joined the military only after much prayer and moral struggle.[7]

> When I went into my study in August 1914 to decide what I as a Christian minister was to do about this business, I went into one of those horrible hours of my life. I believed then as I believe now, only not so clearly or completely, that war was a disaster. I did not believe it quite so clearly and completely then because I, like many others, had a kind of hope and faith that war would have a purifying and uplifting effect upon the character of the nation as a whole, and that out of this valley of the shadow of death we should come a nobler and a purer people. I know now that this was a delusion, and that war is not merely a waste of life,

> but is degrading and brutalizing to the spirit of man. But I decided to play my part in the war rather than protest against it, because I believed that, disastrous as it was, it was forced upon us, and that if we refused to accept the challenge a greater and more awful disaster would fall upon us-not merely upon us as a nation, but upon the world as a whole.[8]

Studdert Kennedy's early chaplain duties included encouraging the troops in a Rouen train-siding canteen, serving at the Battle of the Somme, and then embarking on the Mission of Repentance and Hope as he preached the Christian message to the troops. He preached to thousands of British Soldiers to boost their morale and encouraged them to fight bravely for victory. He did so because he understood the war to be a divinely directed crusade to defeat evil. His message throughout this period, recorded in his *Rough Talks by a Padre*, was of complete support for the war and a belief that God not only supported British efforts but had called England to defeat Germany.

> In August 1914 God called in a voice like thunder. He called to England across the narrow stretch of sea, "Come out, Come out! Come out from home and comfort. Come out to right the wrong. Come out and share my sorrow and help save the world. God called and England answered. Thank God England answered and simply said, I come.[9]

While he did support Britain's participation in the war, he was not a believer in war for the sake of war but saw it as a necessary evil to counter the threat of a belligerent nation intent on harming all of Europe, of the world. In his views on war, he adopted the language of necessity, that the First World War was a Just War.[10]

> War may be a necessary evil at the present stage of our development, but all the allied nations are agreed that it is an evil, and that we must not sit down under its necessity, but must work, plan and scheme to eliminate it. To us it is an axiom of life that peace is a blessing, and war a curse. . . . We want a lasting Peace, and mean to get it. It is a War against War. . . . You may ask what we are fighting for, and I say: the Freedom of the Peoples, the Honour of the Nations and the Peace of the World.[11]

The chaplain served with this understanding of the righteousness of the British cause and support for the war effort. He doesn't seem to have been seriously bothered by even the most difficult aspects of warfare and supported infantry training efforts, including traveling with a mobile training team that instructed soldiers in the correct and effective use of the bayonet, used in hand-to-hand fighting. His messages at the time record a self-assured confidence in his own actions and the actions of the British Expeditionary

Force as it executed the strategic goals of the British government and its allies. Studdert Kennedy served in the *Gommecourt* section of the trenches during the 1916 Somme Offensive and assisted with the wounded and ministry to the dead and knew full well the horrors of trench warfare. Rather than being spiritually devastated by the blood and death he witnessed; he seems to have been energized. Shortly after emerging from the trenches, he was asked to provide guidance to a new chaplain who had just reported to the Front, Chaplain Theodore Hardy. Studdert Kennedy told him, while walking up and down and speaking "very fiercely, because I was full of it."

> Your place is in the Front. The line is the key to the whole business; work in the very front, and they will listen to you when they come out to rest, but if you only preach and teach behind you're wasting your time. . . . The more padres who died in battle doing Christ-like deeds, the better for the church. Most of us would be more use dead than alive![12]

STUDDERT KENNEDY'S CHANGING ATTITUDE TOWARD THE WAR

Studdert Kennedy's attitude began to change after his experience at the Messines Ridge. In June 1917, the Chaplain was assigned to the 17th Brigade of the 24th Division assembled as part of the Second Army posted at the Messines Ridge in preparation for the third battle of Ypres. This was his second assignment in the trenches. The British had tunneled under the German lines and placed nineteen mines totaling 454 tons of explosive. These mines were detonated at 0310 on June 7th, with the blasts causing nearly 10,000 German deaths with 7,500 missing, most killed and buried by the mines.[13] In *The Hardest Part*, Studdert Kennedy recorded his mixed response to the explosions, observed from his position in the British trenches.

> We're all laughing. We're enjoying it. That's the stuff to give 'em. It is a glorious sight, one silver sheet of leaping flame against the blackness of the trees. But it's damnable, it's a disgrace to civilization. It's murder, wholesale murder . . . damn all war! They have wives and kiddies like my Patrick, and they are all being torn to bits and tortured. It's damnable. What's that Lad? Shout a bit louder. It is, you're right, it is the stuff to give 'em.[14]

The dissonance he felt is summed up in a concluding sentence to this reflection. As he and the troops awaited the order to "go over the top" in their trench, he noticed the birds and the beauty of God's creation. . . . "God's fruits, singing birds and splendid beauty, flowers and fair summer skies, golden mists and—bloody slaughter! What is a man to make of it?"[15]

It was probably here that Studdert Kennedy began to doubt the morality of the war, his contribution and part in it, and to suffer moral injury. In his question, "What is a man to make of it?" we hear the cry of a Christian clergyman who realized that the "Huns" they had just slaughtered, accompanied by cheers, were also human beings with homes, wives and children just like him and his countrymen. In his question we see a morally responsible man beginning to question his role in that slaughter.

Caring for the Wounded, Dying and Dead: "The Dead Weigh Heavy on the Hand, and on the Heart"[16]

Comrades Mine
To Six Heroes of Ligny Thilloy, August 1918

Oh I saw ye lying still,
So crumpled and so still,
At the bottom of the hill,
Comrades mine

In the twilight of the dawn,
Of the rose and silver dawn,
That brought in the battle morn,
Comrades mine,

All together in a row,
In a ghastly, gallant row,
With your faces to the foe,
Comrades mine.

And ye taught me how to die,
How a soldier ought to die
Duty done without a sigh,
Comrades mine

God of courage grant me grace
Grant me His especial grace
With you boys to see His face,
Comrades mine.[17]

Another characteristic of chaplain ministry that contributes to the possibility of moral injury is the chaplain's responsibility to the dying and the dead. This is one of the essential roles that chaplains perform for the military, to help their soldiers negotiate the space between life and death. Some clergy enjoy the benefit of performing sacramental last rites, while others offer personal prayers with and over the dead. But this responsibility, over time, inevitably wears on the emotions, mental health, and spirit of a chaplain. In his 1927 novel, *I Pronounce Them*, Studdert Kennedy's semi-autobiographical character Father Jim, also an Irishman and First World War chaplain, recalled his response to the remnants of his unit after the June 1916 Battle of the Somme.

> Once before he had seen Jim weep. . . . It was while they stood together to watch the remnant of the 137th Brigade march down the road from Fonquevilliers to Souastre after the show on July 1st, 1916.[18]

Studdert Kennedy later commented that the continuous and inevitable deaths of his soldiers came close to breaking his heart.[19] A more recent survivor of war agrees with the chaplain and emphasizes the impact of the constant exposure to death inflicts upon the war's participants, "What spills blood spills spirit."[20] The battlefield, with all its physical reality, the "mud, blood and smells,"[21] the bodies, and the cries of the wounded, makes a lasting imprint upon the memory. Chance encounters with an odor or odd sound elicit unwanted memories and "flashbacks" years after a soldier's return home. But the chaplain's (or any caregiver's) empathy for the dead and dying, and their loved ones back home, accumulates over time and may cause questions regarding the morality of the war and the chaplain's part in it. Jonathan Shay, in his *Achilles in Vietnam*, reports that constant and prolonged exposure to combat deaths and personal danger almost certainly results in the development of PTSD and moral injury.[22]

One of the endearing and enduring characteristics of Chaplain Studdert Kennedy was the empathy he felt for the soldiers he served. Yet that empathy placed him at great risk of psychological and spiritual injury, as he experienced deep and abiding grief over the deaths of the soldiers he ministered to and identified with in the trenches. In his wartime book of battlefield musings, *The Hardest Part*, Studdert Kennedy reported his emotional response to finding the body of one his soldiers, identified only as Peter by his identity tag and the documents in his pocket. Studdert Kennedy accomplished his religious duties for the man's body, obtained his identification papers and promised the deceased soldier that that he would write to his wife. In his musing, he compared this average-looking soldier to the Apostle Peter, another average man called to accomplish a monumental task. The chaplain apologized to the dead soldier for the failures of the church, and for his own failures, reduced by the exigencies of battle to a role he did not relish, that of an undertaker and burial detail. But the chaplain did not conduct his duties with the cool detachment of a professional undertaker, but with the tears of one who really cared for the man's soul and awareness of the grief yet to be borne by his family.

> The church of Christ has ceased to be the pillar of cloud and fire which leads the pilgrim Peter along the way of social righteousness and has become a weak and inefficient ambulance brigade which picks up the wreck and ruin of a cruel and mechanical civilization. That's all I am, Peter, an informal and incompetent undertaker, with tears in my eyes and sorrow in my heart.[23]

Later, Chaplain Studdert Kennedy again reflected on his role as an amateur undertaker, but this time sympathized with the mothers back home who would grieve over the loss of their children, and whose loss would be compounded by the grim reality that so many of the bodies, often reduced by artillery shells to "scraps of flesh and bits of clothing," had been buried in unmarked graves in the middle of the battlefield. The ferocity and explosive cruelty of the modern weapons of war paid no respect to the dead or their mothers back home.

> A padre out here has got to be an amateur undertaker. So ghastly amateur, that is the worst of it. We cannot hope to bury half the dead. Many a mother's aching heart must go uncomforted because we know not where we have laid him. No one knows. Some are not buried, because there is nothing to bury but scraps of flesh and clothing. Some are buried, and then blown to pieces out of their graves. There is an enormous crater in the middle of the cemetery, and the bodies are not; that's all that can be said. But where Christian burial can be given, it must be given, if only for pity's sake.[24]

The Requirement to "Stuff" One's Feelings

Studdert Kennedy identified closely with the suffering of those to whom he ministered. But the immensity of suffering experienced by the soldiers of the Great War and his grief over their loss could easily have overwhelmed the chaplain, who it appears was constantly on the verge of tears. Soldiers in war often must "wall off" their emotions in order to maintain their combat effectiveness while many wartime caregivers experience what we now call "compassion fatigue." This malady results in depression and a desensitization to the pain by which they are surrounded. Studdert Kennedy, in order to survive the accumulated grief he experienced, chose instead to frame the war in the context of his faith. In the bodies of the many killed and the unending parade of wounded and gassed, the chaplain chose to see the suffering God and the wounds of the crucified Christ.

> In the days of peace the Broken Body and the Blood outpoured seemed to have so little do with ordinary things in life. But here, broken bodies and pools of blood are the most ordinary things in life. So ghastly ordinary, always bodies, broken battered bodies, and always blood. Is it wrong to see in them His Body

> and His Blood—God's Body, God's Blood. . . . God suffers in man's suffering, and man, if he be man, suffers with God, and the world is saved by the suffering of God in man. The Cross, the Sacrament, the battlefield, there is the vision of God in them all.[25]

As noted above, soldiers often become callous to the realities of war once they've been exposed to it, unconsciously (or consciously) recognizing that they must do so in order to survive emotionally and operate effectively in that harsh environment. Chaplains (and other caregivers) are subject to the same response but must guard against the temptation to become callous and insensitive to pain. Insensitivity will hinder their ability to accomplish their caregiving responsibilities.

Studdert Kennedy, either as a result of having "stuffed his feelings" or due to the overwhelming accumulation of death and grief, experienced this insensitivity toward some of the failures of his soldiers. During an artillery barrage directed at his unit's position, he reported hearing two opposing voices: one the voice of a seasoned sergeant cursing the Germans, the other the voice of a young soldier praying in a frightened way for God's protection. The chaplain, hearing both occurring simultaneously, mused that the sergeant's curses were the more effective prayer, and that so many Christian prayers were offered, like the frightened soldier's, for selfish reasons. In his musing, the chaplain recognized his own insensitivity and reminded himself to pray for the soldier.

> I musn't curse this poor beggar. He's just gone under. He's lost the spirit. I was nearly as bad, for I had nearly lost it too. I must not curse him. I must pray for him. Probably I'd better begin with a fag. Have a fag, lad? I think it's dying down now. Yes, I've got a light. Christ the God—the only God come down into his soul, and make him brave. God Almighty, what is that? Are you there, Sergeant? Well, pull me out, will you. That chap's got it bad; I'll go for stretcher-bearers. This lad's dead, and he never lit that fag. The cup could not pass. I hope he had braced himself to stand before the Christ. . . . It must have been one of our own trench mortars.[26]

Later, during the same battle, the chaplain's overwhelmed emotional state was even more obvious as it drove him to undertake a mission through a dangerous artillery barrage to escape the moans of a wounded soldier. As the wounded soldier lay suffering in agony with no pain-relieving medication, Studdert Kennedy dashed to the rear under intense shellfire to obtain morphine to treat the man. He also demonstrated other acts of heroism that day, retrieving wounded soldiers from the field while exposed to enemy and, unfortunately, friendly fire. For his actions, he was awarded the Military Cross, which was accompanied by ten days of leave back home. The citation reads,

> For conspicuous gallantry and devotion to duty. He showed the greatest courage and disregard for his own safety in attending to the wounded under heavy fire. He searched shell holes for our own, and enemy wounded, assisting them to the dressing station, and his cheerfulness and endurance had a splendid effect upon all ranks in the front-line trenches, which he constantly visited.[27]

Later, when his attitude toward the war had soured completely, the chaplain reported the motivation behind his award-winning actions that day was anything but heroic or altruistic. He had endured near-fatal shell fire because he could no longer bear the moaning of the wounded soldier, that the "hell outside was less awful than the hell within" the aid station.[28]

> The pain—the pain—my Gawd—the pain. For Gawd's sake gimme somefing to stop the pain." There was no morphia. That was the horror. Someone must go for it. I went. I went because the hell outside was less awful than the hell within. I didn't go to do an heroic deed or perform a Christian service; I went because I couldn't bear that moaning any longer. I ran, and as I ran, and cowered down in shell-holes waiting for a chance to run again, I thought—thought like lightening—whole trains of thought came tearing through my mind like non-stop expresses to God knows where. I thought: poor devil, I couldn't have stood that a minute longer. I wasn't doing any good either. If I get through and bring the morphia back, it will be like bringing heaven to him. That is the only heaven he wants right now, dead-drunk sleep. If I bring it back, I will be to him a savior from hell. I'd like that. It's worth-while. I'm glad I thought of that. I can't pretend that it was that I came for. It wasn't.[29]

It is instructive that, even as he raced from shell hole to shell hole, he was processing his emotions and actions, attempting to find a positive rationale for what would turn out to be an award-winning act. In spite of downplaying his rationale for his actions that day, he often wore his medal on his clerical garb after the war.

The Accumulated Impact of Death and Sorrow

In spite of his strong faith and usually positive attitude Chaplain Studdert Kennedy was not immune to experiencing darkness in the face of the immense and accumulated losses the British were suffering. During a normal rotation between assignments in the front trenches, he and his men enjoyed a brief respite in the rear areas, reported in *The Hardest Part.* At parade, the men had sung "God Save the King" and their chaplain was moved emotionally by their song. He reflected that "hell is bad for the nerves." When one is surrounded by death, it is not unusual to begin to see death everywhere. His musing descended into the dark and macabre, imagining that his soldiers were marching on the road to death.

> I never was thrilled by "God save the King" before. As a rule it leaves me cold; today it sent a tingling down my spine and gave me a lump in my throat. I wonder why. I suppose I am a bit upset really; hell is bad for the nerves. The parade was pretty awful too, so many splendid chaps absentees; it gets on one's nerves. I suppose I am a bit windy. We are all in for it again the day after tomorrow, and there will be more absentees. . . . It sounded like the song of a thousand martyrs on their road to death.[30]

Studdert Kennedy didn't just empathize with pain of his soldiers as they suffered and died in the war. He also commiserated with their wives, children, mothers, and fathers just a few miles away, across the English Channel, who missed their soldiers and worried for their well-being. One of his duties was writing to the families of the soldiers he cared for, sending a few lines to report their health and welfare after a short visit at the Rouen café or as he encountered them in the trenches. As we saw in his commentary on the soldier Peter, he also wrote the families of the soldiers killed in the line of duty. As he did so, he understood their deep grief at the loss of their loved ones.

In an emotion-packed poem titled, "I Know Not Where They Have Laid Him," he empathized with the grief of the mother of a soldier killed in battle. What would compound her loss was the probability that she wouldn't know where he was buried and, perhaps, would never know. In his poem, Studdert Kennedy expressed the heartache of a mother whose son has been killed in one of *men's* wars.

> But even a father never knows,
> The ache in a mother's 'eart,
> When she and the body 'er body bore
> Are severed and torn apart.
> The men wouldn't make these cursed wars
> If they knowed a body's worth,
> They wouldn't be blowin' 'em all to bits
> If they 'ad the pains of birth.[31]

Chaplain Studdert Kennedy's summation and commentary on the emotional toll of his war experiences reveal the depth of the personal struggles he faced. He summarized the war as brutal, cruel, and merciless (like all wars) and his own experience as a "perpetual torture chamber" in which he was not even allowed to utter a cry of pain, to express the tidal wave of emotions resulting from the death, loss, pain, and suffering that afflicted his beloved soldiers and himself.[32] This characterization applies to more than just chaplains, but also to most of the soldiers, sailors, airmen, marines, and military caregivers who have experienced war. The emotional toll is huge, and over the last century has been recognized as one of the unfortunate side effects of war. But Studdert Kennedy and his comrades blocked off their feelings and proceeded with the grim work of war; to do otherwise would lead only to desolation, or worse. He recognized, however, that the forgetting could not go on indefinitely, that at some point the chaplain and his soldier comrades would have to remember and face the inescapable experiences of the war.

> A soldier must forget facts if he is to fight, . . . I know something of the methods used to keep up fighting morale. They consisted very largely in helping men to forget, in distracting their thoughts, in amusing, deluding, and drugging them. Our horror was, lest we remember—lest we remember. They were necessary methods; these things had to be. I did my share of it, singing comic songs when I had just taken a hundred funerals, talking nonsense with a dead pal huddled beside me with a lump of shrapnel in his stomach and wild agony in his still wide-open eyes, going over the top on a rum ration and the hope of a blighty.[33] It had to be. I don't cry out against any of it, not even the rum ration; I've had it myself. We had to stop mad dogs that ran amuck. It was necessary, then, this drugging of ourselves. It was necessary then, but it is fatal now. We cannot live on drugs. That was not life, it was bedlam—the world was mad. We stood at the altar of death with the wine cup in our hands and cried to our comrades in hell; 'the world is mad and meaningless, and all the gods are dead; your brothers lie around you crying in their agony, but heaven does not heed; your duty is to kill and kill, to carry flaming death and dire destruction with you as you go, to wipe your bloody bayonet clean, then make it red again; kindness is cruelty and mercy is madness; drink—drink—drink deep—lest you remember that you are still men, and so your strong hands falter and your great hearts fail.' That was very largely the Gospel of military morale—it had to be—and will have to be so long as War continues. But it is not a gospel for life.[34]

Studdert Kennedy's own soul was in a sad condition by the last year of the war. He had endured three years of war and ministered faithfully to his soldiers, offering them what hope and solace he could. In a long poem titled, "Come unto Me," published in his *More Rough Rhymes of a Padre*, he pictured himself in a shell hole in no-man's-land trying to lead others to God as they answered Jesus's biblical call, "Come unto me and I will give you rest." He reflected that his frail body had failed him as he sought to fulfill his spiritual responsibilities and that he also desired the rest that "gives men strength to suffer and endure the length of endless misery that war entails." Instead, he noted the evidence that hate was stronger than love, that instead of rest, "men stagger on to die and where they fall must lie, unburied for the maggots and the flies."[35] His life seemed like that of a soldier wandering in no-man's-land at night, lost and traveling in never-ending circles. He felt that he was only a "blind leader of the blind . . . searching across the bloody battlefields of life." Finally, he saw his efforts as a failure and called out to God in despair, "We cannot come, we are but men, Come to us, O Lord." Finally Christ answered, as if He had been awaiting that desperate cry all along, "I come."[36] He summed up his emotional state in another poem, "A Song of the Desert: On the Hindenburg Line, 1918."

An exile in a weary land,
My soul sighs for release,
It wanders in war's wilderness
And cries for Peace—for Peace.[37]

STUDDERT KENNEDY'S EVOLVING OPPOSITION TO WAR

I noted earlier that sufferers of moral injury experience moral dissonance, a conflict of personal values with one's responsibilities, and that dissonance must be eventually faced and resolved. By 1918, Studdert Kennedy had come to this point in his commitment to his military service. Studdert Kennedy recognized that the "gospel of war" that enabled the soldiers to depart the last trench into no-man's-land to claw for the feet and yards of muddy earth that would lead to victory over the German military machine was no "gospel for life." He served because of his commitment to his soldiers, his idealistic patriotism, and the steady gaze of his crucified God. An idealist, he hoped that his and his soldiers' efforts would produce a new world of peace and justice. But their high calling and devotion did not insulate them from the grim realities of war or the emotions that accompanied the death and destruction they experienced. Like his comrades in arms, Studdert Kennedy put on a grim face and proceeded about his duty. But this "gospel of war" and the environmental conditions he and his comrades encountered on the battlefield multiplied the certainty that they would experience what we now understand to be combat stress injury and moral injury.

Later, after he had received his "baptism of fire" and had spent time in the trenches and knew the bloody reality of the industrial warfare the idealism that he had carried into France disappeared, replaced by a new wisdom. But that wisdom had not come to him easily, for it required that he face the grim conditions of war and to have his own lack of experience and innocence violently excised. He went to the war completely unprepared for the "mud, the blood, and the smells"[38] of early-twentieth-century warfare, warfare waged on an industrial scale. In a postwar chapter, published in 1919, he reflected on his lack of readiness for what he was to face in France.

> I carried the facts—the dry facts of history—out to France in 1915. I was always interested in military history. Yes, that's the word, interested. I was just interested because I knew nothing. Battles were just the movements on the chess board of the world to me. I was as innocent, as fatuously, idiotically innocent as most young men of my generation. I carried the interesting facts into my first battle, and there they came to life, they roared and thundered, they dripped with blood, they cursed, mocked, blasphemed, and cried like a child for mercy. They stood up before me like obscene specters, beckoning with bloody hands, laughing like fiends at my little parochial religion, and my silly parochial God.[39]

Later, he revised his estimate and evaluation of the war and of war in general. Writing in *The Hardest Part*, in 1918, he concluded that war appeals only to those who have no experience of it.

> War is only glorious when you buy it in the Daily Mail and enjoy it at breakfast table. It goes splendidly with bacon and eggs. Real war is the final limit of damnable brutality, and that's all there is to it. It's about the silliest, filthiest, most inhumanly fatuous thing that ever happened. It makes the whole universe seem like a mad muddle. One feels that all talk of order and meaning in life is insane sentimentality.[40]

Studdert Kennedy continued to serve honorably in France and Belgium until November 1918 and the armistice. After the armistice, he remained in France until March 1919, serving the soldiers who remained to guard the peace after the conclusion of hostilities. The war had challenged him psychologically and spiritually, creating dissonances in his mind and spirit that demanded resolution. His religious convictions were tested by the war, but it also facilitated life-changing insights that would energize his postwar ministry. His support for the war and British war-aims had also been challenged, and he came to oppose all war and rejected the utility of force to attain peace. He clearly communicated this newfound pacificism when he published his first postwar book, *Lies*, in October 1919.

> Why be blind any longer? Has not the light of the last four years been strong enough? I have seen it in the ruined villages, in dead men's faces and their staring eyes; I have read it in the misery of that weird wasted land of wire and lonely graves beside the Somme—the Truth. No good can come of any war except the end of war.[41]

In his book of poems, *More Rough Rhymes of a Padre*, published in 1919 after the war had ended in the armistice, Studdert Kennedy summarized his view of war succinctly.

"Waste"

Waste of Muscle, waste of Brain,
Waste of Patience, Waste of Pain,
Waste of Manhood, waste of Health,
Waste of Beauty, waste of Wealth,
Waste of Blood, Waste of Tears,
Waste of Youths most precious years.
Waste of ways the saints have trod,
Waste of Glory, Waste of God.
War![42]

By the armistice, Chaplain Studdert Kennedy had definitely come to hate war. I've described the evolution of his thinking as he faithfully served his country and the soldiers in the BEF. He had committed to the war in spite of his misgivings and Christian doubts about the efficacy of war. He had believed he had no real options and had volunteered in order to do his duty. But by the end of the war, he had come to passionate hatred for war and his role in it. Studdert Kennedy was morally injured and would carry a sense of guilt and loss for years, a sense of his own moral failure burdened by the weight of thousands of British dead. In the next chapter, we'll see that he also experienced a second form of moral injury in the violation of trust that led to the death of his own hopes for Britain's postwar world.

NOTES

1. G. A. Studdert Kennedy, *Democracy and the Dog Collar* (London: Hodder & Stoughton, 1921, 41–49.
2. Ibid.
3. G. A. Studdert Kennedy, *The Hardest Part* (London: Hodder & Stoughton, 1918), 6.
4. Kent Drescher, Mark W. Smith, and David W. Foy, "Spirituality and Readjustment following War Zone Experiences," in *Combat Stress Injury*, eds. Charles R. Figley and William P. Nash (New York: Routledge, 2007), 305.
5. Discussed in chapter 2.
6. The existence of U.S. chaplains has been litigated in court with their presence accepted due to the rationale presented above. But there are many within the church that do not accept the chaplaincy as legitimate. When I attended Duke University in 1993 as a U.S. Navy Chaplain, there was a poster circulated around campus by an antiwar element that asked the question, "How are chaplains and prostitutes different?" The poster answered, "They aren't."
7. D. F. Carey, "Studdert Kennedy: War Padre," in *G .A. Studdert Kennedy by His Friends*, ed. J. K. Mozley (London: Hodder & Stoughton, 1929), 99, 116.

8. Studdert Kennedy, *Democracy and The Dog Collar*, 47–49.

9. G. A. Studdert Kennedy, *Rough Talks by a Padre* (London: Hodder & Stoughton, 1918), 130–131.

10. The just war tradition was originated with the Catholic theologian Augustine and evolved over the centuries to include a rationale for nations to engage in war and their conduct within war. *Jus ad bellum* (reasons to go to war) include: a just cause, comparative justice, competent authority, a right intention, the probability of success, the last resort, and proportionality. *Jus in bello* (right conduct in war) includes distinction and proportionality. Contemporary laws of war, including the Geneva Conventions, have evolved out of the Just War Tradition. I had the opportunity to teach this subject in a class at the U.S. Navy War College.

11. Studdert Kennedy, *The Hardest Part*, 62–66.

12. David Raw, *Theodore Bayle Hardy* (Yorkshire: Pen and Sword Books, 2018), 50–51.

13. Wendy Holden, *Shell Shock* (London: Channel 4 Books, 1998), 42.

14. Studdert Kennedy, *The Hardest Part*, 4–5.

15. Ibid., 6.

16. Ibid., 154.

17. G. A. Studdert Kennedy, *More Rough Rhymes of a Padre* (London: Hodder & Stoughton, 1919), 58–59.

18. G. A. Studdert Kennedy, *I Pronounce Them* (New York: George H. Doran Company, 1927), 21.

19. "Fruits of Victory, Woodbine Willie's Analysis of our Times." *Northampton Mercury*, May 12, 1922, 13.

20. Jonathan Shay, *Odysseus in America* (New York: Scribner, 2002), 209.

21. G. A. Studdert Kennedy, *Lies* (London: Hodder & Stoughton, 1919), 143. See also Studdert Kennedy, *Rough Rhymes of a Padre*, 17.

22. Shay, *Odysseus in America*, 209.

23. Studdert Kennedy, *The Hardest Part*, 160.

24. Ibid., 165–166.

25. Ibid., 136–137.

26. Ibid., 118–119.

27. Carey, "Studdert Kennedy: War Padre," in *G. A. Studdert Kennedy by His Friends*, ed. J. K. Mozley, 143

28. G. A. Studdert Kennedy, *Lies* (London: Hodder & Stoughton, 1919), 225.

29. Ibid., 226–227

30. Studdert Kennedy, *The Hardest Part*, 75–76.

31. G. A. Studdert Kennedy, *More Rough Rhymes of a Padre* (London: Hodder & Stoughton, 1918), 19.

32. Studdert Kennedy, *Lies*, 141–143.

33. A blighty was a wound that was serious enough to send the soldier home, but not so serious as to cause severe damage or death.

34. Studdert Kennedy, *Lies*, 119–120. Rita Brock and Gabriella Lettini note a similar requirement to not forget but to remember and confront war memories and failures as a requirement for recovery from moral injury. See Rita Nakashima Brock

and Gabriela Lettini, *Soul Repair: Recovery from Moral Injury after War* (Boston: Beacon Press, 2012), 114.

35. Studdert Kennedy, *More Rough Rhymes of a Padre*, 62–71.
36. Ibid.
37. Ibid., 87.
38. Studdert Kennedy, *Lies*, 143. See also Studdert Kennedy, *Rough Rhymes of a Padre*, 17.
39. Studdert Kennedy, *Lies*, 5–6.
40. Studdert Kennedy, *The Hardest Part*, 32.
41. Studdert Kennedy, *Lies*, 39.
42. Studdert Kennedy, *More Rough Rhymes of a Padre*, 80.

Chapter Six

"Fed Up!"

Moral Injury, Disillusionment, and Unmet Postwar Expectations

"Jerusalem"

And did those feet in ancient time
Walk upon England's mountains green?
And was the holy lamb of God
On England's pleasant pastures seen?
And did the countenance divine
Shine forth upon our clouded hills?
And as Jerusalem builded here
Among those dark satanic mills?
Bring my bow of burning gold!
Bring me my arrows of desire
Bring me my spear: O clouds unfold
Bring me my chariots of fire.
I will not cease from mental flight;
Nor shall my sword sleep in my hand
Till we have built Jerusalem
In England's green and pleasant land.[1]

WARTIME TRANSITIONS AND THE BETRAYAL OF TRUST

William Blake's poem Jerusalem, set to stirring music by Sir Hubert Parry, brought hope and inspiration to Britain's war-weary soldiers and citizens in 1916 as the full impact of the war, conscription, and the growing lists of missing, dead, and wounded impacted the nation. Chaplain Studdert Kennedy, serving in France with the British Expeditionary Force, shared the poet's lofty sentiment, hoping that the war would result in transformative change in Britain's social and economic life. As the war dragged on into 1917 and 1918 and then transitioned into the postwar years of 1919 and 1920, his lofty hopes gave way to despair and disillusionment. Studdert Kennedy suffered a second experience of moral injury, that caused by the violation of trust by those in moral authority.

In earlier chapters, I discussed moral injury relating to one's acts that violate deeply held moral values and the spiritual injury that occurs when one's trust in the character of the supreme authority, God, is found to be misplaced or misunderstood. Another important source of moral injury occurs when one's trust in leadership is betrayed. Jonathan Shay, in his *Achilles in Vietnam*, ascribed the root cause of combat trauma to the betrayal of trust. He linked the foundational importance of trust to the fact that soldiers exist in a "moral order" that is a "social construction defined by shared expectations and values."[2] "When a leader destroys the legitimacy of the army's moral order by betraying 'what's right,' he inflicts manifold injuries on his men."[3] This concept applies directly to military leadership at all levels, whether the captain who leads a company into battle or the general responsible for operational planning. It also applies to the civilian leadership at the national level responsible for strategic direction. We understand today that war is "the continuation of politics by other means."[4] Political leaders are ultimately responsible for conducting war and guiding the outcomes of that war. Shay suggested that there exists a fiduciary relationship between soldiers and the society that sends them to war. "The vast and distant military and civilian structure that provides a modern soldier with his orders, arms, ammunition, food, water, information, training, and fire support is a fiduciary, a trustee holding the life and safety of that soldier."[5] If those leaders and the civilian society violate this trusting relationship between the nation and its soldiers, wide-ranging moral injury may result. When leaders fail in the accomplishment of their fiduciary duty to their military men and women, often resulting in the death or wounding of comrades in arms, trust in that leadership is compromised or lost completely. "Both flavors of moral injury impair and sometimes destroy the capacity for trust. When social trust is destroyed, it is replaced by the settled expectancy of harm, exploitation, and humiliation from others."[6]

The transition from war to peace is a particularly vulnerable time for members of the military, as they have borne the brunt of the effects of war and have expectations relating to the war's outcome. Civilian and military leaders may have made promises, both implicit and explicit, to the soldiers who shouldered the burdens of war. Military members expect that leaders will lead them to victory in the conflict, applying military expertise to accomplish national objectives with a minimum of spilled blood. They expect that political leaders and the nation they represent will appreciate and honor their wartime sacrifices. There may also be an expectation that they will experience some reward for their labor. When these expectations are violated through poor strategic planning or ineffective and/or duplicitous political leadership, disappointment in that leadership and moral injury is the inevitable result. Symptoms include the loss of trust for that leadership, distrust of authority figures in general, and possible disappointment in the original decision to serve, a sense of having been duped. The experience of Vietnam War veterans as they returned home from that unpopular war is an example of a nation's failure of leadership that caused injury, as their rejection and vilification by the U.S. public served to drive deeper the invisible wounds of the war: PTSD, moral, and spiritual injury.

Although Chaplain Studdert Kennedy was unacquainted with the modern concept of moral injury, he was aware of the importance of trust and the implications of its betrayal. In a sermon he preached to the troops in France in 1916, he expounded on the importance of trust as an essential element of a soldier's character and the bitterness that ensues when trust is betrayed.

> Men are, and must be, left in a position of trust. Life and all it brings with it is a trust which men are given to use or abuse at will. That is the terrible and yet glorious meaning of manhood. You are men just so far as you can be trusted. You fail as men just so far as you prove yourselves unworthy of trust; but you must be trusted before you can prove yourselves worthy of trust, and you must learn from experience the bitterness of sorrow which follows the betrayal of trust.[7]

Studdert Kennedy and the soldiers of the British Expeditionary Force had placed their trust in the British nation, its political leaders, and its people to support them in their fight against the Germans. They shared with the church the hope that a postwar Britain would emerge from the dark days of the war transformed into a new Britain that would provide economic security for all, that would accomplish William Blake's idyllic dream, a new "Jerusalem in England's green and pleasant land."[8] Studdert Kennedy, thoroughly aware of the social and economic challenges of prewar Britain, hoped fervently that transformational change would result from the experiences and lessons of the war. Unfortunately, Britain's soldiers experienced the bitterness of the betrayal of their trust and dashed dreams regarding the future.

Broken Political Promises: "England a Country Fit for Heroes"

Strategic war goals and war termination are the responsibility of the political and military leadership. During the First World War, the political leadership made implicit and explicit promises and raised expectations regarding the outcome of the war. Most important, the government promised peace with honor, a goal of every military man and woman. The government also established national political and military strategic objectives that evolved as the war progressed. In 1914, Prime Minister Asquith stated that the Allies' goals were: the freedom of the smaller states of Europe, defeat of German aggression, and the winning of an honorable peace.[9] In December 1915, Asquith stated that his government was committed to "pursue the war to a victorious conclusion with every resource of men and material."[10]

Studdert Kennedy and his soldiers lacked confidence in British political leadership. In one of the sermons he preached at Rouen in 1916, recorded in his *Rough Talks by a Padre*, he poked fun at Prime Minister Asquith's nickname, "Old Wait and See."[11] Referring to his own series of sermon titles, "What are we fighting for, What Stands in the Way, and Are we going to Get it," a soldier mockingly related that the answers were obvious; "Why, to beat the Germans of course!" and, "These 'ere Germans 'ave got an Army." To the third question, whether they would actually defeat the German military machine, he stated, "Ask Mr. Asquith; 'e gave the only answer to that question years ago: Wait and See."[12]

In 1916 Lloyd George replaced Asquith as prime minister and was more forthcoming about Britain's goals for the war, including restoration of territories taken by Germany and implementation of a "great international peace conference."[13] In 1918, with the armistice signed, the government also included consideration of the soldiers in its goals for the postwar world. The government's program included:

1. Punish the Kaiser
2. Make Germany pay for the costs of the war.
3. Get British soldiers home as quickly as possible.
4. The fair treatment of returned soldiers and sailors.
5. Better housing and social conditions.[14]

In November 1918, the Prime Minister called a general election to elect a coalition government to oversee the peace negotiations and pursue economic and social revitalization at home. The BEF soldiers in France were promised a vote in the election, and Lloyd George made specific promises concerning their future in his Wolverhampton speech.

> The war has improved us all if we had the quality for improvement. It is bad metal that is not better when it is hammered. The hammering of the last four years has made us better . . . after having won through the greatest struggle for human progress that the world has ever seen. . . . Let us rather determine, one

> and all, with one heart, one purpose, one resolve, to see that this England is lifted to conditions and a level to which she has ever before attained.[15]

Lloyd George also suggested that the "wretched" British slums should be defeated even as Britain had defeated the German fleet, that they "were not fit for the men who had won the war." As part of a great agrarian reform program, he proposed that returning soldiers and sailors be provided land and small holdings as well as training and loans to assist them in establishing successful and self-sufficient farms. Most famously, he promised, "Our task is to make England a country fit for heroes to live in."[16]

The phrase, "A land fit for heroes to live in" became a clarion call for the nation and resulted in the election of the coalition government under Lloyd George. But it also raised the expectations of the soldiers who had fought in the war and were now anticipating their return home. Their votes contributed to the massive win for Lloyd George's coalition government. Unfortunately, the Prime Minister's idealistic call to make "England a land fit for heroes," and its attendant social reform was frustrated by long-term postwar economic conditions that resulted in massive unemployment for both the returning soldiers and the working classes of England. The promise of an "England Fit for Heroes to live in" became a broken promise and a term of abuse that was used to criticize the government. Unfortunately, it also became a symbol of dashed hopes for the future and the betrayal of trust for Britain's demobilized soldiers and their chaplain, G. A. Studdert Kennedy.[17]

APOCALYPTIC PROMISES: REPENTANCE, HOPE, AND A NEW JERUSALEM

> Bring my bow of burning gold!
> Bring me my arrows of desire
> Bring me my spear: O clouds unfold
> Bring me my chariots of fire.
> I will not cease from mental flight;
> Nor shall my sword sleep in my hand
> Till we have built Jerusalem
> In England's green and pleasant land.[18]

As I noted at the beginning of this chapter, Great Britain's morale was at a serious ebb in 1916. The home front was reeling from the long casualty lists and the imposition of conscription. The church sought to encourage the morale of the nation through its good offices. The "Fight for Right Movement," a multidenominational organization, "with the object to oppose a premature peace and induce a spirit of cheerful sacrifice in the nation until victory is secured for the cause of humanity"[19] was very popular and sought to encourage the nation's morale. Its program included an apocalyptic hope for the future, that once the victory was secured, "it would usher in a new heaven and a new earth after the struggle."[20] To support their mass meetings, Sir Hubert Parry was commissioned to put William Blake's poem "Jerusalem" to music. The resulting hymn captured this movement's hopes for the future, conveying in William Blake's beautiful poetry and Parry's soaring music the nation's hopes for a transformed future, an England characterized by the heavenly city. The song was presented in a Fight for Right Movement crusade on March 28, 1916, and was a popular success, capturing the imagination of England's people.[21]

The Church of England, concerned by the same conditions that motivated the Fight for Right Movement, launched the National Mission of Repentance and Hope in the fall of 1916 to address the nation's flagging war morale and to revive the church both at home and among the troops in France. Conducted along the lines of D. L. Moody's great revivals in the United States, a great deal of time, effort, and money were expended to design, purchase, and distribute religious pamphlets, posters, and liturgical resources throughout England. Between September and December of 1916, bishop's messengers preached in local churches and conducted weeklong crusades in open-air venues.[22] The National Mission also couched its goals in apocalyptic hopes for the future, similar to the "Fight for Right Movement" and William Blake's poem.

> We look forward to a new England, to a new world. Our repentance will open the way for the Holy Spirit to show us how we can help to make that new England, that new world.[23]

In the fall of 1916, Studdert Kennedy was withdrawn from the front lines to support the mission. The Chaplain preached the mission's message to thousands of troops in his own effective style, even translating the mission's goals into a poetic form the soldiers would love as he encouraged them to victory.

> "A Sermon in a Billet"
>
> And that's what I reckon these parsons mean
> Wi' their Mission o' 'Pentance and 'Ope,
> They want us to wash old England's face clean,
> Wi' the grace of Gawd for soap.
> We can't let it be for nothin'
> That our pals 'ave fought and died,

So, lads, let's look to this washin' up
For the sake o' Christ—and our dead.[24]

The final evaluation of the National Mission of Repentance and Hope was not positive. It has been panned by some historians as a failure and suffered from a number of challenges. But the mission's focus effectively captured the pulse of the nation and provided a vision of hope, of a "new England," for its citizens and soldiers fighting abroad.

Studdert Kennedy made this same connection to the heavenly city in the sermons he preached to the troops in France, applying Christ's Gospel lament over the city of Jerusalem to England. "He (Christ) is crying no to us as He cried years ago to the Holy City that he loved. O England, England that stonest the prophets and killest them that are sent unto thee."[25] In agreement with the lofty goals of the National Mission, Studdert Kennedy also hoped for a changed world after the fighting and dying were over. But Studdert Kennedy understood that England's economic and social problems were deep, and he addressed those problems as he preached to the soldiers in France.

STUDDERT KENNEDY'S ASPIRATIONS FOR A TRANSFORMED ENGLAND

Chaplain Studdert Kennedy was blessed with a hopeful vision for the future and "the gift of the gab,"[26] as his chaplain supervisor and mentor Deputy Chaplain General Gwynn described him. Chaplain Gwynn utilized Studdert Kennedy's unique gifts and provided him the opportunity to speak to the troops throughout the war zone. In 1916, At Rouen, he delivered a series of sermons that were later published in his popular book, *Rough Talks by a Padre*. In these published sermons, Studdert Kennedy spoke on a wide range of issues, including his support for the war, the defeat of Germany, and his passionate hatred for prostitution. In speaking of the war, he clearly articulated and supported the political leadership's war aims. "You ask me what we are fighting for—I give it to you in three words: Freedom, Honour, and Peace." Then the chaplain added an additional, religious purpose. "You ask me what we are fighting for, and I give it to you in one word: Christ."[27] The chaplain also ventured into some surprising areas for a chaplain in the war zone; the social and economic problems back home!

Studdert Kennedy sermons were filled with passion regarding the social issues he had experienced before the war. He hoped the lessons learned in the war would transfer to a postwar peace, that Britain would address and correct its social and economic inequities: slums, poverty, and class warfare.

If Britain neglected these problems, he suggested it would face defeat, not at the hands of the Germans, but because of its failures on the home front.

> If the empire does not solve its social questions, its social questions will dissolve the Empire. We must solve them or they will dissolve us. There will be no guns to blow Great Britain's greatness into dust, but there will be just as deadly and more hidden force to sap it all away. If reaction does not lead to relapse and the old class hatred and party strife is revived.[28]

One stands in awe at the subject matter this wartime chaplain delivered to the assembled troops. Their daily efforts focused on trench warfare, the proper use of the bayonet, and the German enemy just beyond the British front lines. His subject matter served to focus their minds on the problems back home and their hopes for a postwar world. While he did communicate hope for the future, he realistically suggested that the outcome looked grim considering the enormous amounts of British money and blood being plowed into the fields of France and Belgium.

> This much is certain: we shall be poorer, much poorer, than we have been in years. All classes will be poorer. And this fact implies another. We can be sure of this too. Our social problems, which were very complicated and difficult before the war, will be ten times as complicated and ten times as difficult after it. These are two broad certainties on which we can count.[29]

In these sermons, Studdert Kennedy blamed the social and economic problems faced by the country on "the idolatry of wealth." He suggested that the wealthy had failed to understand the true meaning of their resources and misused them in the pursuit of the materialism that characterized much of English social life. He blamed Britain's materialism for the war and linked it to British capitalism and a failure to reckon wealth, "not in money, but in strong men and true, with pure and healthy women and innocent children."[30] British wealth and capitalism had created a stratified society and a class warfare that Studdert Kennedy suggested was the root cause of the country's social and economic problems. He hoped the experience of the war, that threw all classes into the cauldron of "mud, blood, and smells"[31] would break down those class divisions, that Englishmen would learn to appreciate and cooperate with one another through their experiences in the war.

> The men who employ you will be largely the men who have led you in this strife. Surely you will learn from this struggle mutual forbearance and respect. The master cannot, after this, regard the hero of the trenches as a mere machine, and the man cannot look upon his officer as a money grabbing engine. We must learn to lead and be led.[32]

Ultimately, Studdert Kennedy believed that the answer to the existential problems of life and death faced by men in the trenches was the same answer that would solve the social and economic problems faced at home, a firm commitment to the Christian faith that would bring about God's purposes in England. He concluded his final address in his *Rough Talks by a Padre* with a rousing challenge to the soldiers, to fight in a way that would honor their war dead!

> They will have died in vain, our dead, unless we learn their twofold lesson, and take it well to heart. As England stands with swimming eyes, and looks upon the gardens of her gallant dead, help her to say with firm resolve: I will love the things for which my boys have died. And I will hate, with a bitter lasting hatred, the things that brought them to their death.[33]

In spite of Studdert Kennedy's hopes for the future and the sacrifices of England's soldier heroes, his understanding of England's past history and the enormity of its problems caused him doubt. "With the weariness of warfare upon us, and the weakness of great loss of blood to overcome, the future seems all black with clouds that are big with the rain of tears. It looks dark ahead."[34]

The chaplain heard these same concerns from the soldiers to whom he ministered daily. They, too, were concerned with the postwar world and how they would survive. They understood that they would need jobs and homes for their families. For them, the great issues of the day—war, peace, liberty, and honor—all boiled down to one issue: What would their lives look like after the war was over, and would they be able to earn a living wage? Studdert Kennedy's poem "Worry," reported the concerns of a soldier who had been blinded by a "whiz-bang." The promises he had heard from the politicians regarding postwar jobs were not comforting. He was concerned they wouldn't remember or be able to fulfill those promises.

"Worry"

Yes, I know they've been and promised,
But it's easy to forget.
When the shoutin's done and over
There's accounts to settle yet.
There'll be thousands same as me, sir,
Out to do what work they can,
Not disabled, but like me sir,
Not just everybody's man.
Will they find us jobs to work at
Where two 'ands can earn their pay,

For a wage enough to keep us
Free from debt, and pay our way?
That's the only thing as worries
When I sits me down to think,
Will I get my charnce of 'ome, sir,
And enough to eat and drink?[35]

While he was realistic about the challenges posed by the social and economic problems facing Britain, Studdert Kennedy was hopeful for the future. Indeed, hope was the only light that lifted his morale and enabled him to survive the long years of war and separation from his family. After the war, he recalled, "As I lay sick at the Front, I thought to myself we are going to bring something great and glorious out of the war . . . we are going to have a new order, a new world, a better day. And I believed it. I believed it more passionately and earnestly than I ever believed anything on earth. To me it was the only light which kept on shining through those years of blackness.[36]

Studdert Kennedy's hopes for the postwar world did not include acceptance of the conditions he had known before the war, instead he wanted radical social and economic change, a transformed England. In the poem, "Old England," he suggested sinking the "old England" with its poverty and social injustices to the bottom of the sea. Instead, he and his beloved soldiers were fighting for a new ideal, a new England. It would not descend magically from the heavens like a New Jerusalem but would have to be forged out of the blood and sweat of England's soldiers.

"Old England"

My old England were a curse.
It were sleepin', sweatin', starvin',
Wearing boot soles for a job,
It were sucking up to foremen
What'ud sell ye for a bob.
It were cringin', crawlin', whinin',
For the right to earn your bread,
It were schemin', pinchin', plannin',
It were wishin' ye were dead.
I'm not fightin' for old England,
Not for this child—am I 'ell—
For the sake o' that old England
I'd not face a single shell.
What I say is sink old England
to the Bottom of the sea
It's a new England as I fights for,

It's an England swep' aht clean,
An England where we'll see the things
Our eyes 'ave never seen.
Decent wages, justice, mercy,
And a chance for ev'ry man
For to make 'is 'ome a 'eaven
If 'e does the best 'e can.
It's that better cleaner England,
Made o' better, cleaner men,
It's that England as I fights for,
And I'm game to fight again.
It's the better land o' Blighty
That still shines afore our eyes,
That's the land a soldier fights for,
And for that a soldier dies.[37]

POSTWAR DISILLUSIONMENT

"Marching Song"

I can hear the steady tramping of a thousand thousand feet,
Making music in the city and the crowded village street,
I can see a million mothers with their hands outstretched to greet,
For the Army's marching home.

I can see a million visions that are dancing overhead
Of the glory that is dawning where the sky is burning red,
Of the Britain to be builded for the honour of the dead,
For the army's marching home.

I can see the broken women choking back their scalding tears,
Oh? The barren, empty greyness of their lonely, loveless years!
But their duty's to the living and they'll only give them cheers,
As the Army marches home.

I can see the crowd of children of the crest of yonder hill,
I can hear their little voices cheering, cheering loud and shrill,
'Tis that they may grow to beauty that our flag is floating still,
As the army marches home.

There's a crowd of wooden crosses in the wounded heart of France,
Where the cornfields used to glisten and the blood-red poppies dance,
Can't you hear the crosses calling us to give the Christ a chance,
Now the army's marching home.

O? We'll build a mighty temple for the lowly prince of peace,
And the splendor of its beauty shall compel all wars to cease,
There the weak shall find a comrade and the captive find release,
When the army marches home.

Of men's hearts it shall be builded and of spirits tried and true,
And its courts shall know no boundaries save the boundaries of the blue,
And it's there we shall remember those who died for me and you,
When the army has marched home.[38]

The armistice called for a cessation of hostilities on 11 November 1918. Members of the British Expeditionary Force who had served the longest were the first to be demobilized, with the remainder of British forces serving occupation duties in Europe and the Middle East.[39] Studdert Kennedy fell into this latter group and continued to serve the troops until the end of March 1919 when he returned to his family and his church in Worcester, and to his hopes for a better England.

Dashed Hopes and Disillusionment with Postwar Conditions

Unfortunately, the postwar England to which he returned was not a radically improved or changed England. The old social problems remained and were, if possible, even worse than before the war. Wartime economics had focused on war production and supporting the troops. Little had been spent on housing or home-front infrastructure. Initially, Great Britain experienced a postwar boom, with an explosion of pent-up demand for goods that had been unavailable during the war.[40] Shipbuilding saw a significant boom as firms set about replacing shipping that had been lost to submarine warfare. The majority of demobilized soldiers found work. But the clouds of economic trouble lay just over the horizon, with Britain's market dominance in textiles and coal challenged by the United States and Japan. Britain's European competitors were also in a strong economic position as most were not burdened by a huge war debt.[41] Britain's economic situation was further challenged by a unionized workforce that had won high wages and reduced working hours during the war, which increased the cost of the goods it hoped to export.[42] Demobilized soldiers added millions to the workforce. In May 1919, in spite of Britain's short-lived postwar economic boom, the Labour Ministry reported a million unemployed with more than 400,000 of them being demobilized servicemen. While unemployed and homeless servicemen demonstrated outside Parliament, the Labour minister, Sir Robert Horne, minimized the problems.[43]

> The marvel is not that 400,000 servicemen are unemployed, but that that number is not greatly exceeded. In some weeks demobilization took place at the rate of 170,000. Industry has been dislocated by the war and has to be readjusted to peace conditions. The usual markets for goods are not open. In these circumstances it is magnificent that 81 percent of the discharged men have been reabsorbed by industry . . . the present phase (is) a passing one.[44]

The phase did not pass, and unemployment problems increased while market dislocations, falling prices, reductions in wages, and recurring coal strikes plagued the country. By 1921 the postwar economic boom had ended, and, in October, Prime Minister Lloyd George called Britain's economic problems a depression, "the worst in over 100 years."[45] The year 1925 saw overall unemployment remaining near 11 percent with some sectors (iron, steel, and shipbuilding) experiencing more than 25 percent unemployment.[46] Hunger marches by the unemployed, many of them former soldiers, became a common occurrence. High unemployment, averaging above 10 percent, remained a sad reality through the remainder of the 1920s.[47] While the USA experienced the "Roaring Twenties," Great Britain experienced a very different economic reality. The newspapers of the time contain hundreds of references to Lloyd George's promise of an England "fit for heroes to live in." But the phrase was used more as an accusation and betrayal of their soldiers' trust then as a celebration of accomplishment.

After the war, Chaplain Studdert Kennedy returned to his role as a pastor at St. Paul's Worcester. His popular wartime publishing efforts and speaking skills, honed over more than three years in the war zone, provided him a platform from which to attack the social ills he encountered at home. The newspapers loved his headline-grabbing comments and ability to fill any venue with large crowds, eager to hear "Woodbine Willie, the war padre."

Studdert Kennedy was not happy with postwar England and the conditions he found. His wartime hopes for a revitalized England characterized by social justice were destroyed by the reality that confronted him and the demobilized soldiers who returned with him. It did not seem fair or just that those who had suffered in the war and shed their blood for their country should have to endure the trials of unemployment, homelessness, and hunger. In his 1921 book *Food for the Fed-Up*, he summarized his disappointment and disillusionment.

> We have been tried as silver is tried, we have passed through fire and water and had a surfeit of self-sacrifice, we have given our best and bravest, and shed our blood in rivers, and we trusted that God would bring us out into a wealthy place, into a new world. But it is no new world that we find ourselves in, but an old world grown older, a world of selfishness grown more selfish, of greed that has grown more greedy, and of folly that knows no limit to its foolishness. There has come upon us a great disillusionment. . . . Millions who gave up their all in

> a frenzy of self-sacrifice during the war are asking themselves bitterly what they gave it for. What's the good? And Who's to gain? We are fed up.[48]

Instead of great changes in social conditions at home, Studdert Kennedy perceived that very little, if anything, had changed. His wartime doubts regarding improved conditions proved prophetic, as the country seemed to have to returned to prewar normality. For Studdert Kennedy, "normal" meant a return to conditions that were damaging to the human soul.

> Life is just the same (as in 1914). There is the daily paper on my table, with its account of the daily strike. In its pages the poor blame the idle rich, and the rich blame the idle poor, and everybody blames Lloyd George. Everybody says that the country is going to ruin, and nobody believes it. Everybody says that the peace is a patched-up peace, and everybody believes it is as safe as the Bank of England, and that is of course a great deal safer than God. The great British Democracy is falling back into its old groove. The War is over. We are very tired, very irritable, and we want to get back to business as usual.[49]

In a May 1922 address at a men's rally, he sadly reflected on his hopes during the war and how they had been dashed by the peace. He informed his listeners of his passionately held hopes for the postwar world and concluded, "As far as I'm concerned, when I sit down by the fire and try to tot up what we have got. I find my dream has not come true. I have been trying to find the fruits of victory for two years and I have not struck any yet.[50]

Studdert Kennedy was especially vexed by the condition of the unemployed soldiers he met on the streets, usually homeless and begging for food. In his 1927 novel, *I Pronounce Them*, one of his characters, a former war chaplain, was likewise upset by the condition of the demobilized soldiers and connected their condition directly with the failure of politicians of the day. "It was disgusting that some of the decent working men who had served with him in France should be compelled to live as they did. He was heartily sick of politicians and politics."[51]

Studdert Kennedy often characterized the valiant soldiers who fought and died on the battlefields of France as images of the crucified Christ. In his poem, "Indifference," he once again equated those soldiers, now unemployed and homeless, with Christ. In postwar Britain they were sacrificed on a different calvary.

> "Indifference"
>
> When Jesus came to Birmingham they simply passed him by,
> They never hurt a hair of him, they only let him die.
> For men had grown more tender and they would not give him pain,

They only just passed down the street, and left him in the rain

Still Jesus cried, "forgive them, for they know not what they do,"
And still it rained the winter rain that drenched him through and through,
The crowds went home and left the streets without a soul to see,
And Jesus crouched against a wall and cried for calvary.[52]

Studdert Kennedy continued his publishing efforts after his return from France. His books *Lies* (1919) and *Food for the Fed Up* (1921) and poetry, *Peace Rhymes of a Padre* (1920), reflected his emotional disposition and disenchantment with peacetime conditions resulting from the war. *Lies*, in particular, communicated his disappointment with the peace and postwar conditions and blamed that disappointment on the profusion of lies that filled the land.[53] In words that echoed those of many returning warriors who had been disappointed with postwar life, his introduction to the book alternated between horror and hope, between bitterness of betrayed trust and the promise of his faith.

> This postwar world is black with lies—biting and buzzing round everything. . . . There are so many poor unfortunate beggars that cannot see any God for this cloud of lies. We must get out of it and get to God or—well I do not know what I see coming, but it is going to be something awful. There's a bad smell about—a very bad smell; it is like the smell of the Dead—it is the smell of dead souls. I can smell hell. If only men could smell once more the lilies that grew by the Empty Tomb! . . . In the future there must be, not death, but Resurrection. Get to work and bury the dead—bury the dead and make room for the living. There are too many lies.[54]

The book is also full of reminiscences of the war and his role in it. In the first chapter where he addressed lies regarding the Christian Bible, he once again raised the problem of evil, a subject he exposited fully in his wartime books and poetry. Discussing war, he stated, "If God wills war, then I am morally mad, and I don't know good from evil."[55] He exhorted his readers to work for peace with the Suffering God of the Bible. "I tell you God almighty can't make peace without your help."[56]

Studdert Kennedy had hoped for a new unity between those who had fought in the war together, a solution to the class warfare that characterized British industrial and economic life. Instead, postwar Britain continued to be riven with struggles between capital and labor, illustrated by the many strikes that plagued the British economy. Most concerning, for Studdert Kennedy, was that both sides in the struggle often resorted to "faith in force" to accomplish their goals.[57] He was also vexed by what he termed "street corner lies" that guaranteed "with a superior smile" that poverty and hunger would persist, that piously proclaimed "the poor shall always be with you." He passionately condemned that lie, "There is more blasphemy in those words than in the most lurid Sergeant's speech that ever turned the air in Flanders blue. It is sheer atheism."[58] His work also addressed the lies in liberty, equality, lust, human nature, and democracy, the social lies contained in theology and believed by Christians, Social Darwinism, lies about war, and the lie that suggested that postwar Britain forget the war and obliterate its memory through drug-induced amnesia. He saved some of his most damning invective for the political leaders that asserted that war could bring anything positive, that war was good for the character of a nation (recall Lloyd George's 1918 Wolverhampton speech).

> If this world-wide war has done us any good, it is because in its flames a certain number of old and soul-killing lies have perished self-destroyed. In the blood, the mud and the stench of the battlefield they worked themselves out to their final absurdity, while guns roared laughter from behind. Often and often the 9–inch guns have seemed to me to yell out above the rattle of a barrage, "you fools, you fools!"[59]

Studdert Kennedy was firmly convinced that the only remedy for the lies he condemned in his book was truth, a truth that would energize individuals committed to duty and sacrificial service to bring about transformational change in British society. He ferociously condemned those who possessed God-given abilities but refused to use them in the service of humanity. Note how he compared these failures to the most despicable pests of the battlefield.

> If the man of superior abilities is not a public servant, he is a parasite and more unworthy of his manhood than an ignorant and drunken pauper. If he uses his ability to serve himself at the expense of his fellowman, to get on and get over them, his success is the measure of his failure. He is like those enormous bloated flies that buzz round the dead on a battlefield. Filthy things, clothed in gorgeous colors, their bright green wings flashing in the sun as they seek the choicest morsels of the swollen and disfigured dead.[60]

Studdert Kennedy's next book, his 1921 *Food for the Fed Up* was an exposition on the Apostles' Creed. It is evident from his introduction that he was still struggling with the war and its aftermath. "Millions who gave up their all in a frenzy of self-sacrifice during the war are asking themselves bitterly what they gave it for. What's the good? And Who's to gain? We are fed up."[61] In this work, he suggested that Britain's only hope for social change was a revival of classical Christian ethics to address the problems of the postwar world. His message was particularly focused on the economic challenges facing Britain and declared that capitalism, labor, socialism, and communism were insufficient to solve the problems of the day.

> The revolutionaries hate Him (Christ) and declare that His Gospel of Love is opium to the people, who need to be fed fat with hatred, that they may be strong to revolt. Business is Business, and Christ has nothing to do with it, says the commercialist. Conscious labour or planned organization of social labour is the name of the expected Messiah of the New Age. Our hope of salvation is not a religious ideal, but rests on the massive foundations stone of materialism," says Mr. Belfort Bax, the Socialist. Christ tells the businessman that he is an immoral scoundrel, and the Socialist that he is a silly fool, and points another way.[62]

Studdert Kennedy condemned the capitalism and commercialism of prewar Britain and blamed it for the carnage of the World War. He viewed the war as man's self-imposed judgment and condemnation for a century of greed and selfishness.

> Just such a day of judgement has this Western world been through these last years. For a century the life of Europe rolled on, with its vulgar commercialism, its sordid money-grabbing, blinded by its surface prosperity and its idiotic trust in force, building its battle-ships and torturing its women, bloated with pride and self-sufficiency, counting its wealth and pointing at its wonderful enterprise, its growth in knowledge, and its supreme command of the forces of nature; and then came the day of judgement. In the flashlight of a million guns, in the groans of dying men and the wailing of countless widows, in the agony and bloody sweat of a continent wracked with pain, we were made to see whither we had been going and what it meant. . . . I have seen Him standing there time and time again, pointing His loving but relentless finger to the dead man at my feet, and saying, "That is what it means. That is what 'business is business," that is what "free and unfettered competition," that is what refined prosperity really mean—that boy with the swollen, shapeless face, with the great hole in his head and the brain tumbling out, that is what they really mean.[63]

He had become avowedly anti-war by 1921 and blamed Britain's political leadership for their failures during the war, during the postwar period, and finally in their efforts to achieve a lasting peace. In a poem he published in his 1920 *Peace Rhymes of a Padre*, he communicated his condemnation of and disillusionment with the politicians who had produced the Versailles Treaty. In the poem, his words recalled the wartime sufferings of the British soldiers, who he characterized once again as the Christ.

> "Dead and Buried"
>
> . . .
>
> I was crucified in Cambrai,

And again outside Bapaume;
I was scourged for miles along the Albert Road,
I was driven, pierced and bleeding,
With a million maggots feeding,
On the body that I carried as my load.
. . .
Yet my heart was still unbroken,
And my hope was still unquenched,
Till I bore my cross to Paris through the crowd.
Soldiers pierced me on the Aisne,
But twas by the river Seine
That the statesmen brake my legs and made my shroud;
There they wrapped my mangled body
In fine linen of fair words,
With the perfume of a sweetly scented lie,
And they laid it in the tomb
Of the golden-mirrored room,
'Mid the many fountained Gardens of Versailles.[64]

In Studdert Kennedy's poem, he expressed the bitterness of his soldiers who had gallantly endured the horrendous conditions of the war only to face final betrayal by the statesmen at the peace negotiations. His distrust of the politicians and his experiences of the war turned him into a pacifist and he worked with the "no-more-war" movement with the passion of one who has seen war firsthand and could describe its human impact from personal experience.

Studdert Kennedy's New Hope for Britain's Future

Studdert Kennedy, in spite of his strong condemnation of Britain's problems, believed that Britain could find redemption and justice for its people, but he could not trust in any political movement or party. For true transformation to take place, he proclaimed that a universal change in attitude was required, a "sense that Great Britain can never be truly great until every British life is lived as fully and as freely as it has power to live.[65] True greatness could come only through a change in the country's social conditions, a realization that the slums, unemployment, and homelessness were a tragic wound that would sink British hopes for the future. Transformation would require men and women who were dedicated to public service, who would sacrifice themselves in their efforts to accomplish social and economic change and were energized by an appreciation for the essential value of every human being.

> Men with the vision are not indifferent to this world, but are keen to make it perfect with a keenness that no worldly man can ever know. They detest slums

> because they poison eternal spirits; they loathe all waste of human life because human life is of infinite and eternal worth. They are true democrats, who cannot help seeing all men as equal, because they see all men as eternal.[66]

Studdert Kennedy believed that he was called to serve the men and women of Britain and hoped to fulfill his vision to bring justice and hope to postwar England. He understood that Lloyd George had failed in his promise to create an "England a land fit for heroes to live in," that perhaps the Prime Minister's dream had been an unrealistic expectation motivated by wartime necessity.[67] He believed that the peace had been betrayed by the politicians and that their efforts guaranteed another war.[68] Studdert Kennedy knew he could not trust political leaders to bring about peace or social transformation, and transferred the vision that had energized him on the battlefields of France to the streets and factories of Britain. As he had seen the battlefield as a crucifix, he now saw the cities of Britain overshadowed by that same great cross, that same great vision. In his 1921 book, *Food for the Fed Up*, he communicated his vision clearly, England would be changed only through faith.

> That is who we see Him in the world and in the church—crucified—crucified in every street of our great cities, crucified in every hovel of our slums, crucified on our markets, crucified on our battlefields, but for ever rising again. Again and again men cry that he is dead and buried, antiquated, impossible, mythical; again and again He comes back, takes hold on human hearts, and sends them out to preach His truth, aflame with the old new Love.[69]

CONCLUSION

Chaplain Studdert Kennedy suffered moral injury as a result of the breach of trust by the authority figures in his life: the broken promises made by politicians, the dashed vision of the church, and the death of his own idealistic hopes for a revitalized England. He had vainly hoped for a transformed England emerging from the war, an England that would eliminate the poverty, class war, and slums that had been too common before the war. We see his disappointment in the pages of his books *Lies* and *Food for the Fed-Up*, where he complained of the lies that buzzed about his spirit as he considered the postwar world. Failed military and political promises, a misplaced trust in the effectiveness of force, and the false hope that the crucible of war could produce a better England contributed to those lost dreams. He personalized his disappointment with the war and its outcome in his poem, "Fruits of Victory." In the poem, he introduced the reader to a mother who has lost her son in the war and was forced to face her barren future. She had willingly sent him to war in hope that her son's dreams for a better future would be accomplished. But, in the final analysis, she wondered if the sacrifice was worth the cost. This grief-stricken mother is a metaphor for all the mothers of England, for England itself (and for Studdert Kennedy), who had sent their sons to war, and now searched in vain for the fruits of victory in the postwar world.

"Fruits of Victory"

I would not call him back, my soldier son,
Though arms and lips are aching for his kiss,
I gave him once for all, my only one,
But not for this.
This world with sorrow piled up on its sin,
With poverty to crown the curse of war,
With children growing peaked, and pale, and thin,
This running sore.
I gave him for his dream of splendid things,
I gave him that a world of men set free
Might seek their God resurgent on the wings
Of Liberty.
I gave him that his victory might bear
the fruit of growing peace all down the years
I gave him that mothers in despair
Might weep these tears.
O God, who rent my heart out by the roots,
I do not ask thee give it back to me,
I ask thee of thy Justice show me fruits
Of Victory.[70]

Studdert Kennedy had experienced the conditions of combat and war that contribute to combat stress and had suffered both spiritual and moral injury as a result of his own decisions and the broken promises of Britain's leaders. He lacked guidance to direct him toward recovery from his invisible wounds or war, but his ecclesiastical background and intuitive nature moved him in a direction that would enable him to survive his injuries and emerge as a wounded survivor. In chapter 7, I'll discuss the self-prescribed purification process that enabled him to transcend his disillusionment regarding the war's outcome and to embark upon a journey of postwar social service and post-traumatic growth.

NOTES

1. William Blake, "Jerusalem," published in 1807.
2. Jonathan Shay, *Achilles in Vietnam* (New York: Touchstone Books, 1994), 6.
3. Ibid.
4. Carl von Clausewitz, *On War*, Eds. and Translators, Michael Howard and Peter Paret (Princeton: Princeton University Press,1976), 80.
5. Shay, *Achilles in Vietnam*, 15.
6. Jonathan Shay, "Moral Injury," *Psychoanalytic Psychology* 31, no. 2 (2014) 186.
7. G. A. Studdert Kennedy, *Rough Talks by a Padre* (London: Hodder & Stoughton, 1918), 43–44.
8. Blake, Jerusalem, 1807.
9. "Premier and an Honorable Peace: Final Emancipation from Reign of Force," *Leicester Daily Post*, Nov. 10, 1915.
10. "Asquith Aims at Getting Every Potential Man," *Dundee Evening Courier*, Dec. 21, 1915.
11. Prime Minister Asquith had famously used the phrase "wait and see" multiple times in answer to his House of Commons opponents on 4 April 1910 and he became known as "Wait and See" Asquith. His war leadership was not highly regarded, and he was replaced by Lloyd George in 1916. G. A. Studdert Kennedy, *Rough Talks by a Padre*, 70, 95–96. See also "Political Notes," *Middlesex Gazette*, April 9, 1910.
12. Studdert Kennedy, *Rough Talks by a Padre*, 69–70.
13. "Mr. Lloyd George on British War Aims and Manpower." *Birmingham Gazette*, 21 Dec. 1917, 1.
14. "Lloyd George's Policy," *Birmingham Daily Gazette*, "Dec. 11, 1918, 1.
15. "Lloyd George's Wolverhampton Speech," *Devon and Exeter Daily Gazette*, Nov. 25, 1918, 1.
16. "Lloyd George's Wolverhampton Speech," *Devon and Exeter Daily Gazette*, November 25, 1918, 1., It is possible that the phrase was not original with Lloyd George. An unhappy soldier, complaining of his low-wage job, said he had heard army recruiters using the phrase to enlist soldiers in the BEF. "I heard a speaker at a recruiting meeting whilst home on leave, when it's all over you will have this and that and England will be a land fit for heroes to live in." I should like to meet some of those speakers now." "An Ex-Soldier's Complaint." *Sheffield Evening Telegraph*, October 11, 1919, 2.
17. Harold Broughton, a private who served in Gallipoli, Egypt, and on the Western Front, recalled all the talk about the England being a land fit for heroes to live in. Speaking in 1984, he still did not think the promise had been fulfilled. "There was a lot of talk, and a talk of a land fit for heroes to live in. But it was a long time coming, and in fact I don't think it's come yet." Harold Boughton IWM 8667 TS, iwm.org.uk, accessed March 6, 2021.
18. William Blake, "Jerusalem," published in 1807.
19. "Fight for Right: Mr. Andrew Fisher on Death Better than Dishonour: A New Heaven and a New Earth After the Struggle," *Western Gazette*, March 17, 1916, 8.

20. Ibid.

21. www.prospectmagazine.co.uk/arts-and-books/almost-everything-you-know-about-the-hymn-jerusalem-is-wrong, accessed March 2, 2021.

22. Studdert Kennedy followed this same program when he worked with the Industrial Christian Fellowship beginning in 1922.

23. "The National Mission of Repentance and Hope." www.lambethpalacelibrary.wordpress.com/2016/05/13/the-national-mission-of-repentance-and-hope-1916/, accessed January 15, 2021.

24. G. A. Studdert Kennedy. "Sinner and Saint," in *Rough Rhymes of a Padre* (London: Hodder & Stoughton, 1918), 27.

25. Studdert Kennedy, *Rough Talks by a Padre*, 172.

26. D. F. Carey, "G. A. Studdert Kennedy: War Padre" in *G. A. Studdert Kennedy by His Friends*, ed. J. K. Mozley (London: Hodder & Stoughton, 1929), 130.

27. Studdert Kennedy, *Rough Talks by a Padre*, 66–67.

28. Ibid., 165–167.

29. Ibid., 161.

30. Ibid., 138–139.

31. G. A. Studdert Kennedy, *Lies* (London: Hodder & Stoughton, 1919), 143. See also G. A. Studdert Kennedy, *Rough Rhymes of a Padre* (London: Hodder & Stoughton, 1918), 17.

32. Studdert Kennedy, *Rough Talks by a Padre*, 88.

33. Ibid., 134–135.

34. Ibid., 199.

35. G. A. Studdert Kennedy, *More Rough Rhymes of a Padre* (London: Hodder & Stoughton, 1919), 25–27.

36. "Fruits of Victory, Woodbine Willie's Analysis of our Times." *Northampton Mercury*, May 12, 1922, 13.

37. Studdert Kennedy, *More Rough Rhymes of a Padre*, 73–76.

38. G. A. Studdert Kennedy, *Peace Rhymes of a Padre* (London: Hodder & Stoughton, 1920), 11–13.

39. Stephen Richards Graubard, "Military Demobilization in Great Britain Following the First World War," *The Journal of Modern History*, Dec. 1947, 19:4, 297–311. There were two demobilization plans. The first resulted from long committee work during the war and sought to minimize postwar unemployment. Soldiers who had jobs awaiting them at home would be demobilized first. The unforeseen consequence of this plan was that soldiers who had been serving years would be last to be demobilized. The plan resulted in soldier strikes and demonstrations. The government quickly reformulated the plan and conducted demobilization based on the length of time in service.

40. Martin Daunton, *Wealth and Welfare: An Economic and Social History of Britain 1851–1951* (Oxford: Oxford University Press, 2007), 179, 286.

41. Barry Eichengreen, "The British Economy Between the Wars" https://eml.berkeley.edu/~eichengr/floudjohnsonchaptersep16–03.pdf accessed Dec. 15, 2020, 6, 16.

42. Ibid., 10. See also Nicholas Crafts, "Walking Wounded: The British Economy in the Aftermath of World War 1," https://voxeu.org/article/walking-wounded-british-economy-aftermath-world-war-i, accessed 19 Jan 2021, 2–3.

43. "Government Complacence on Unemployment," *Sheffield Independent*, May 29, 1919, 1.

44. Ibid.

45. "Premier Unfolds His Unemployment Proposals." *Sheffield Independent*, Oct. 20, 1921, 1; Today, the economic dislocations of 1921 and 1922 are termed a severe recession.

46. Crafts, "Walking Wounded: The British Economy in the Aftermath of World War 1," 2.

47. Eichengreen, "The British Economy Between the Wars," 20. See also Daunton, *Wealth and Welfare: An Economic and Social History of Britain 1851–1951*, 180.

48. G. A. Studdert Kennedy, *Food for the Fed-Up* (London: Hodder & Stoughton, 1921), 7.

49. G. A. Studdert Kennedy, *Lies* (London: Hodder & Stoughton, 1919), 236.

50. "Fruits of Victory, Woodbine Willie's Analysis of our Times." *Northampton Mercury*, May 12, 1922, 13.

51. G. A. Studdert Kennedy, *I Pronounce Them* (New York: George H. Doran Company, 1927), 15.

52. Studdert Kennedy, *Peace Rhymes of a Padre*, 37–38.

53. William Purcell, *Woodbine Willie*: *A Biography* (London: Hodder & Stoughton, 1962), 167. *Lies* was the least favored of Studdert Kennedy works by his friends and was not included in the 1947 publication of the excerpts of his works, *The Best of Studdert Kennedy*.

54. Studdert Kennedy, *Lies*, ix–x.

55. Ibid., 6.

56. Ibid., 7.

57. Ibid., 38–42.

58. Ibid., 43.

59. Ibid.,143.

60. Ibid., 77.

61. Kennedy, *Food for the Fed-Up*, 7.

62. Ibid., 116.

63. Ibid., 310–311.

64. Studdert Kennedy, *Peace Rhymes of a Padre*, 70–73.

65. Studdert Kennedy, *Lies*, 81.

66. Ibid., 265.

67. G. A. Studdert Kennedy, *Democracy and the Dog Collar* (London: Hodder & Stoughton: 1923) 50–51.

68. G. A. Studdert Kennedy, "A Pageant of Truth," *John Bull*, Aug. 1, 1925, 15.

69. Studdert Kennedy, *Food for the Fed Up*, 261.

70. G. A. Studdert Kennedy, *Songs of Faith and Doubt* (London: Hodder & Stoughton, 1922), 26–27.

Chapter Seven

Purification

Acknowledgment, Confession, and Penance, 1919–1921

"The Nation's War Lie."
Woodbine Willie's Act of Penance
11 Nov 1921

An "open confession to God" Which, he said, he felt was due from him as an act of penitence because he did not rise high enough and become brave enough during the war was made by the Rev. G.A. Studdert-Kennedy ("Woodbine Willie") at the Central Hall, Westminster, London last night.

In an impressive address, he said he appealed to the troops during the war and encouraged them to fight on the ground that they were fighting for freedom and honour. He knew now that it was nothing of the kind. There was no freedom and there was no end to war. We had lied as a nation and besmirched our honour. We had broken our promises and gone back on our word in half a score of cases. We seemed to be further from peace in many ways than ever before.

What he should have known and what they all should have known, was that there was no freedom to be won by the sword, no honour to be vindicated by it, and no peace to be got out of it. It could only lead to worse and worse disasters.

In an impassioned appeal to those who might have lost dear ones he asked for forgiveness for their enemies, for they knew not what they did. They were mad, he said, he himself was mad, they were all mad out there. . . . He appealed to all to concentrate their whole thoughts and minds on the frustration of force. [1]

ACKNOWLEDGMENT AND CONFESSION

November 11, 1921, marked the three-year anniversary of the armistice ending the hostilities of the Great War. The date was marked by nationwide remembrances and a mass gathering at the Cenotaph, the great stone war memorial in Central London. Attended by the king, Parliament, and thousands of veterans and civilians, the highlight of the day was the observance of two minutes of silence to honor the nation's war dead. Studdert Kennedy is reported to have participated in those observances and was also scheduled to speak that evening at London's Central Hall, a Methodist institution near Westminster Abby. The large crowd gathered that evening expected to be entertained with Studdert Kennedy's rhetoric and racy speaking style. Instead, his speech, as reported in the popular press, was different than any he had delivered before, although its content was hinted at in his 1919 work *Lies*. It was, as he characterized the speech, his "open confession" for his own guilt related to the war. The speech was reported widely in the popular press.

Rita Nakashima Brock and Gabriella Lettini, in their work *Soul Repair: Recovery from Moral Injury after War*, observe that a first step in recovery from moral injury is the acknowledgment by veterans of the harm they have perpetrated. They must avoid the denial of responsibility and avoidance of the emotional toll that their experience of war has inflicted upon them.[2] It is nearly universally acknowledged that combat requires its participants to "stuff their feelings" in order to operate effectively in that environment. Brock and Lettini as well as Jonathan Shay encourage combat survivors of moral injury to unblock those feelings, face their own responsibility, and acknowledge it.[3] They must avoid denial. Studdert Kennedy voiced this same concern as he considered the effects of the war on the soldiers to whom he ministered and as he considered his own soul. The following quote, though long, captures the emotional necessity requiring "combat forgetting" while also recognizing the necessity to remember.

> A soldier must forget facts if he is to fight; . . . I know something of the methods used to keep up fighting morale. They consisted very largely in helping men to forget, in distracting their thoughts, in amusing, deluding, and drugging them. Our horror was, lest we remember—lest we remember. They were necessary methods; these things had to be. I did my share of it, singing comic songs when I had just taken a hundred funerals, talking nonsense with a dead pal huddled beside me with a lump of shrapnel in his stomach and wild agony in his still wide-open eyes, going over the top on a rum ration and the hope of a blighty.[4] It had to be. I don't cry out against any of it, not even the rum ration; I've had it myself. We had to stop mad dogs that ran amuck. It was necessary, then, this drugging of ourselves. It was necessary then, but it is fatal now. We cannot live on drugs. . . . That was very largely the Gospel of military morale—it had to be—and will have to be so long as War continues. But it is not a gospel for life.[5]

Studdert Kennedy, in his 1921 Armistice Day "open confession" was publicly declaring that he had taken the step to acknowledge his own role in the war and his contribution to its evil. In doing so, he rejected denial and the drugging of his conscience. The next step was even more difficult: his public confession of war guilt.

Jonathan Shay, in his 2002 work *Odysseus in America*, discussed his work with Vietnam War veterans suffering from PTSD and reminded us that the return from war has historically been accompanied by rites of purification for the acts committed and blood shed during war. In his work, he recounted how the ancient Greeks, Romans, and the medieval Christian church required these rites of both individuals and entire armies to prepare them for reentry to peacetime society.[6] He also noted that modern militaries have forgotten that tradition, with warriors often returning directly from war to families and home with little time for adjustment. He suggested that including the religious act of penance as a form of purification in a soldier's post-combat transition provides spiritual as well as psychological benefits.

> My clinical team has encouraged many of the Veterans we work with to avail themselves of the sacrament of penance. When a Veteran does not already know a priest he trusts to hear his confession, we have suggested priests who understand enough about combat neither to deny that he has anything to feel guilty about nor to recoil in revulsion and send him away without the sacrament.[7]

More accurately called the Sacrament of Reconciliation, the religious act involves confession, assignment of penance, and absolution by a priest. As an Anglican priest, Studdert Kennedy was well versed in the practice of this essential element of his Christian faith. It is evident that the 1921 Remembrance Day speech served as his very public confession for his own guilt relating to the war: his public support for the war, his encouragement of the troops to give their all in the pursuit of victory, and possibly his own perception of having "bloody hands." It was also an important step in his recovery process from the moral injury he experienced in the war. It is clear, however, that the trajectory he followed in that recovery was unfocused and chaotic. The year and a half after his return from the war, from 1919 to 1921, was filled with nearly frenetic activity: publishing two books of prose, a book of poetry, fulfilling his pastoral duties at St. Paul's Worcester, caring for his family, and speaking to large audiences throughout the country. His post-confessional life, from 1921–1929, was likewise filled with endless travel and speaking engagements for the Industrial Christian Fellowship and the peace movement. Committed to duty and self-sacrifice, this activity may have fulfilled a need to perform a penance for his sins, a sacrificial public service that took him away from his family and exhausted him physically. One wonders if he ever granted himself absolution, or even if that is possible.

To understand Studdert Kennedy's Armistice Day act of confession, it important that we understand the state of mind and spirit that motivated his speech that night, the deep spiritual impulse that drove him to publicly confess his sins before what would become a national audience. The following pages recount some history that has been addressed in previous chapters, but a brief summary of his experiences will help us understand Studdert Kennedy's state of mind in November 1921.

A MAN CHANGED BY WAR

We've come to understand, through these pages and our own experiences, that war changes people and, by all accounts, Studdert Kennedy was a changed man after the war. The accounts of war contained in his prose and poetry[8] reveal a man who had been profoundly influenced by his experiences. His writings are filled with vignettes of war, his thoughts under fire, and the adjustments, both spiritual and psychological, that enabled him to survive the carnage of the First World War with his faith and sanity intact. Although he survived the war, he did not emerge from that cauldron unscathed. William Purcell described him as both a sadder and wiser man upon his return from France.

> The man who disembarked at Folkestone on March 21st, 1919, was a very different person from the eager, ingenuous priest who had gone out at Christmas of '15. Like the wedding-guest after his encounter with the Ancient Mariner, he was a sadder and wiser man. . . . Like so many of his generation, he returned to civilian life embittered, above all conscious of the many, the very many, who did not come back at all.[9]

Studdert Kennedy was never diagnosed with "shell shock," the First World War term for what we now recognize as post-traumatic stress disorder (PTSD), a diagnosis that did not exist in his time. Considering the nature of his war experiences in France it is evident that he did suffer from the effects of combat and possible combat stress injury, with resulting mental and spiritual implications for his life. As discussed earlier, his three experiences in the front lines with the troops exposed him to the rigors of bloody and dangerous conflict. His writings are filled with those experiences and it is clear they had a lasting impact on his memory. In the last book he published just six months before his death, he recalled his early-morning excursion behind a sergeant during the Battle of the Somme, in 1916. Writing in 1928 he commented, "I can remember this night much more clearly than any single night last year."[10] He continued,

> Before the dawn broke, the Sergeant was dead, and many other mother's sons with him. But the question remained clearly formulated as a question in my

> mind, and burned all the more deeply into it because of the horror of that night. That is the way with war. It shouts and bawls its questions at you. It throws them at you stark, raw, quivering, and all shot through with pain.[11]

Combat veterans universally report a similar response to combat and the vividness of combat memories. Contemporary research into the impact of combat stress and psychological trauma reveals that individuals suffer from a number of common complaints: heightened startle response, intrusive flashbacks and dreams, depression, sleeplessness, damage to core beliefs, feelings of shame or guilt, and a continuing sense of grief.[12] Linda McClenahan, commenting on the experience of spiritual trauma in combat veterans, reports that veterans returning home from war often experience intense sadness about life, and guilt or shame related to the violation of personal moral codes (moral injury), and emotional numbing.[13] Studdert Kennedy exhibited many of these symptoms. William Purcell, Studdert Kennedy's biographer, commented that many of Studdert Kennedy's postwar friends and acquaintances considered him a war casualty. Because of his stature as a public speaker and author, he lived out his response to the war on a public stage.

> There were those who met him in these years who judged him to be definitely off-balance, as were so many who came back from the war to find what was left almost intolerable. If others were bitter, so was he; if others had been sorely tried, so had he. And the pain was made all the more acute by the uncomfortable capacity, common to those of deep sensitivity, to identify himself with the sufferings of others. True, the agony did not now come from encounter with the physical brutalities of war so much as from the spiritual mass-casualties, who staggered back into civilian life, as often as not to find themselves unwanted.[14]

Based on the evidence contained in his writings and the observations of his close friends, it is safe to conclude that that Studdert Kennedy should be counted among those moral and spiritual mass casualties of the First World War.

MORAL INJURY: GUILT AND GRIEF

As discussed in chapters 5 and 6, Studdert Kennedy experienced moral injury as a result of his own choices and commitments during the war and the violation of his trust by those in authority, resulting in an abiding sense of guilt and grief as well as distrust of civilian authority figures.[15] As a clergyman, Studdert Kennedy was generally opposed to war but was ambivalent regarding the First World War due to the obvious evil represented by the Germany's efforts in Europe. He chose to participate in the war as a noncombatant, supporting the spiritual needs of the British troops. He had signed on to support the war effort in 1915 and did so in the full and complete belief that Great Britain was fighting a just war against a foe that meant to do great harm to all of Europe, including England. Like other members of the clergy at the beginning of the war, he encouraged the members of his church to support the war fully, either by enlisting or through concerted prayer. After the war, he admitted that he did so only after much prayer and reflection.

> When I went into my study in August 1914 to decide what I as a Christian minister was to do about this business, I went in to one of those horrible hours of my life. I believed then as I believe now, only not so clearly or completely, that war was a disaster. I did not believe it quite so clearly and completely then because I, like many others, had a kind of hope and faith that war would have a purifying and uplifting effect upon the character of the nation as a whole, and that out of this valley of the shadow of death we should come a nobler and a purer people. I know now that this was a delusion, and that war is not merely waste of life, but is degrading and brutalizing to the spirit of man. But I decided to play my part in the war rather than protest against it, because I believed that, disastrous as it was, it was forced upon us, and that if we refused to accept the challenge a greater and more awful disaster would fall upon us—not merely upon us as a nation, but upon the world as a whole."[16]

By the conclusion of the war, however, Studdert Kennedy had clearly concluded that the war was wrong and that the armistice could not bring a lasting peace. This realization and his participation and support for Britain's war aims contributed to a sense that he had violated his own moral code, had suffered a moral injury.

"BLOODY HANDS"

Studdert Kennedy's writings indicate that he experienced guilt and remorse due to his contributions to the war effort that resulted in the deaths of so many of his beloved soldiers and close comrades. This sense of responsibility for the deaths of others is often referred to as having "bloody hands." As a noncombatant chaplain he was not responsible for sending any soldiers into combat. He had, however, encouraged the men of his own parish to enlist in the military and had preached to thousands of British Soldiers to boost their morale and to fight bravely for victory. He did so because he understood the war to be a divinely directed crusade to defeat evil. In one speech he delivered to the assembled troops in France, he commented,

> War may be a necessary evil at the present stage of our development, but all the allied nations are agreed that it is an evil, and that we must not sit down under its

> necessity, but must work, plan and scheme to eliminate it. To us it is an axiom of life that peace is a blessing, and war a curse. . . . We want a lasting Peace, and mean to get it. It is a War against War. . . . You may ask what we are fighting for, and I say: the Freedom of the Peoples, the Honour of the Nations and the Peace of the World.[17]

In 1916, after his experiences at the Battle of the Somme, recorded in the poem, "His Mate," Studdert Kennedy provided guidance to a new chaplain just venturing into the war and seeking guidance from a more seasoned veteran. That advice may have weighed on his conscience after the war, for the advice he provided, although accurate and effective, was also dangerous and contributed to the combat death of the chaplain, Theodore Hardy. Hardy was a gentleman over fifty years old who sought guidance regarding the best way to serve the Soldiers in the trenches. Studdert Kennedy advised him to accompany his soldiers into the most dangerous situations, even "where there was the most danger of death." He even suggested that "Most of us would be more use dead than alive!"[18] Studdert Kennedy's postwar recollection contained the comment that, "I was full of it." and reflected acknowledgment (possibly even regret) of his own hubris in that moment. Hardy followed Studdert Kennedy's guidance and was killed during combat just before the armistice, miraculously surviving nearly three years of war. Studdert Kennedy's advice, that Hardy go into the most dangerous areas with his soldiers, was certainly effective in terms of successful chaplain ministry, but it also contributed to his death. Studdert Kennedy did bear some responsibility for that death, and he may have felt some remorse and guilt for Hardy's death, a sense of having "bloody hands."

Studdert Kennedy's combat experiences at the Messines Ridge in June 1917 also affected him deeply. As he and the soldiers of his unit observed the early-morning explosion of nineteen subterranean mines that destroyed the German trenches and killed thousands of German soldiers, the chaplain suddenly realized the human toll that the explosions were causing, the killing and wounding of thousands of German troops who, even though they were the enemy, were still human beings. He reported that his conscience was seared as he observed the explosions and reflected on the human suffering they caused. In his 1927 novel, *I Pronounce Them*, his semi-autobiographical main character Father Jim recalled his emotional experience on that Messines battlefield.

> He was groping frantically after his faith. If that went he was lost, lost on a dirty stinking battlefield full of muttered curses and obscene smells. Memories of a hideous sin-blasted wilderness near Messines in which he had wandered for hours dodging death and waiting dawn came back to him. Life was like that without faith.[19]

But his memories of the Messines Ridge also bore a more personal sense of loss and responsibility. Roy Fergusson, his own military assistant, was killed during the battle, on the last Sunday of June, 1917.

In his book, *The Hardest Part*, Studdert Kennedy recounted Roy Fergusson's death. He had sent Roy on a mission that he hoped would guarantee his safety during a particularly dangerous artillery barrage, escorting the walking wounded back to a place of safety. Instead, while he carried out his chaplain's orders, Roy was killed by the shell fire engulfing the British lines. Studdert Kennedy took the death particularly hard and recorded his reflections on his friend's death and the hope of eternal life as he escorted the body to a place of burial. His reflection ranged widely over various issues, but he finally found comfort in the promise of the resurrection. He concluded the chapter with an emotional farewell,

> Goodbye, Roy, Old Chap. . . . Some day we shall meet. Some day she (his mother) and I will recognize you in a new and glorious body, quite different from this poor broken flesh, and yet in difference still the same, because there will be shining in it and through it the gallant, splendid spirit that is Roy; best of Soldiers, best of servants, best of pals.[20]

Although Studdert Kenney's intent had been to protect his friend, his orders had instead resulted in another combat death. Such events weigh heavy on the heart and conscience of military leaders, especially those with a sensitive and caring spirit like Studdert Kennedy.

The Messines Ridge played another important part in Studdert Kennedy's combat history. He was awarded the Military Cross (M.C.) for heroic actions under fire. The events leading to that award serve as an important window into his emotions and sense of guilt after the war. His award stated that he had moved both British and German wounded to safety and brought aid to them in spite of mortal personal danger. He had also braved intense artillery fire to dash to the rear and back to acquire morphine for a wounded soldier. Dismissive of his own bravery, he later reported that the facts of the situation were anything but heroic.

> A young soldier was wounded in the aid station, but there was no morphine to treat his pain.) "The pain—the pain—my Gawd—the pain. For Gawd's sake gimme something to stop the pain." There was no morphia. That was the horror. Someone must go for it. I went. I went because the hell outside was less awful than the hell in. I didn't go to do an heroic deed or perform a Christian service; I went because I couldn't bear that moaning any longer.[21]

Finally, the great weight of death wrought by the war and experienced by Studdert Kennedy certainly contributed to his need to confess before that Armistice Day audience in 1921. As he inescapably remembered the many soldiers who had died during the war, it is evident that his conscience reminded him of the fact that he had encouraged many of his own parish to enlist and had fired the enthusiasm of the combat troops to embrace an honorable death in order to defeat the German threat to British and European freedom. Studdert Kennedy felt a sense of responsibility for those deaths and he carried their memory with him. Jonathan Shay, in a stunning chapter titled "Among the Dead: Memory and Guilt," comments that combat soldiers universally carry the memories of the combat dead with them into their postwar lives. "I won't forget a thing" is the vow of a combat soldier to his dead comrades to keep faith with them, to keep their memory alive."[22] As Studdert Kennedy commented in *The Hardest Part*, "The dead weigh heavy . . . on the heart."[23] In effect, the chaplain became a spokesman for his dead comrades as he joined the anti-war movement and forcefully condemned the annual observances of Armistice Day that, he felt, glorified war. Studdert Kennedy faithfully kept this vow to his dead comrades. The pages of his books, poetry, and his public speeches all bear reminders of their deaths, often described in the gory detail that those desensitized by constant experience of wartime carnage can inflict upon the uninitiated. I believe that their voices continued to speak to him during his postwar years and weighed heavily on Studdert Kennedy's mind and spirit. His 1918 poem, "Waste," summed up his emotional response to the war. It may have also served as a personal evaluation (an incorrect evaluation, we might add) of his own contribution to that war, a waste!

Waste

Waste of Muscle, waste of Brain,
Waste of Patience, waste of pain,
Waste of manhood, waste of health,
Waste of beauty, waste of wealth,
Waste of Blood, and Waste of Tears
Waste of youth's most precious years,
Waste of ways the Saints have trod,
Waste of Glory, waste of God, —
War![24]

THE 1921 ARMISTICE DAY CONFESSIONAL SPEECH

After the Great War, Studdert Kennedy returned home to his wife and young family and found great popularity and influence as a public speaker, building on his wartime popularity with the troops. He was appointed as a chaplain to the king and received a new church appointment that would allow him to continue his public speaking ministry without extensive church responsibilities. But his postwar success was accompanied by deep disappointment and disillusionment with postwar Britain, a perspective he shared with other veterans (discussed in chapter 6). They had anticipated that the rivers of blood spilled on the farmlands of France and Belgium would purchase, if not a utopian world order, at least one that would provide jobs and a living wage for the soldiers who returned from the war. But postwar Britain suffered an economic crisis that resulted in widespread hardship for the working classes, now composed of many of the demobilized soldiers and working poor that Studdert Kennedy had served all his life. His public speaking and writing provided him a platform from which to voice his disappointment, to encourage reforms as well as to enable him to process his own psychological and spiritual wounds. His 1921 Armistice Day confession was an essential step in his unconscious effort to address his sense of disillusionment and responsibility for the war.

Studdert Kennedy's success between his return from the war and his Armistice Day speech in November 1921 guaranteed that his comments that day would receive a wide audience. His prior speeches had been widely covered by the Press as he prophetically addressed unemployment, the Trade Unions, the need for peace, and his condemnation of war. The Armistice Day speech reflected a crisis in his own conscience, one in which he recognized that he himself had promoted the lies he had condemned in his book by the same title and bore some responsibility for the war, some blood guilt. The speech also served as a personal catharsis as he publicly identified his own failures and confessed them in a venue that would ensure a national audience.

The speech, while serving to reveal Studdert Kennedy's spiritual struggles before a national audience, also served as a challenge to the nation and its leaders to repent of their own war guilt. In essence, he acted as an Old Testament prophet, calling upon England to pause and reflect upon its own sins in the war and to reconsider its ways for the future. His message reflected his conviction that Britain must reject its "faith in force" and discover a moral path to peace and prosperity. His speech was indeed noticed, but not with the positive result he intended. Some called it hurtful to veterans, others noted its harmful impact on war widows and orphans. His fellow veterans may have understood his intent, for many were suffering unemployment and the lingering aftereffects of war. Some wondered, "Why bring religion into it?"[25] Others looked on in pity and considered Studdert Kennedy's speech evidence of a weakness of character. One author took this approach in an article titled, "A Momentary Aberration."

> Much is likely to be heard of the extraordinary address delivered yesterday by the Reverend G.A. Studdert-Kennedy. In his Remembrance Day address yesterday, he made what may be called "a public act of contrition" for what he

> said during the war. . . . Anyone who knows Mr. Kennedy's writings, either in prose or verse, must be aware that he is a man of very powerful emotions. In such men, moods of elation alternate with moods of profound despondency. It is easy to imagine such a man, when the black hour is upon him, looking around upon the world as he sees it today and crying out in his haste. Especially is that true of a highly-strung nature after contact with the horrors of war, and after being badly mashed up in it physically. Probably no one will regret more than Mr. Studdert-Kennedy himself that he let such a despairing cry escape from the arena of his own spiritual conflict.[26]

There were, of course, other responses. Some saw Studdert Kennedy's confession as an attack on Christian support for the war and of the necessity for resort to arms in the face of tyranny and armed oppression. Reverend H. Woodward, also a former war chaplain, responded in a letter to the editor, "Some modern Englishmen seem to know better than God and Christ, and are anxious to try the experiment of allowing wickedness to have its full fling on earth."[27] G. G. Swann commented that Studdert Kennedy's words were not helpful, that maligning the motives for going to war would not "help to heal the wounds inflicted by it."[28]

Mindful of the reception his London speech had received, Studdert Kennedy attempted to explain his thinking in another speech he delivered on Nov. 27, two weeks later at Sheffield Cathedral. His speech was printed under the title, "Futile Victory: Padre's Regret for War Propaganda." In the speech, he explained that militarism was only encouraged by a military response, that the future would hold only more conflict if Britain continued the attempt to conduct its affairs with its "faith in force."[29] In the speech he again confessed that he had lied to the troops by encouraging them to fight for victory while promising that their efforts would bring peace.

> I led them to suppose that a crushing victory would inevitably bring them freedom, honour and peace, and in saying that I repeat that unconsciously and unintentionally I lied to them when I should and could have known better had I been simply faithful to Christ . . . that no positive good can be gained by force—freedom cannot be won by it—honour cannot be established by it—peace cannot be maintained by it.[30]

In doing so, we have an indication of the efforts to atone for and recover from the moral injury sustained by Chaplain Studdert Kennedy when he violated his own principles related to war. His confession on the national stage was his very public effort to find personal forgiveness and reconciliation.

These speeches marked a turning point for Studdert Kennedy, solidifying his opposition to the use of force that he maintained for the rest of his life. Contemporary research on combat stress injury and moral injury indicate that individuals must work through their war experiences and that finding forgiveness for war acts is an essential part of finding healing for the psychological and spiritual wounds of war. I commented earlier on Jonathan Shay's discussion regarding the need for purification after war as an essential part of the healing process. Rita Nakashima Brock and Gabriella Lettini assert that moral wounds that are left unaddressed "linger and fester."[31] Dr. William Nash emphasizes the essential aspect of forgiveness in the healing process, commenting that "overcoming guilt and shame depends on forgiveness."[32] Studdert Kennedy wrote on this subject in his 1923 book, *The Wicket Gate* and his comments provide an important insight that Jonathan Shay, in his *Achilles in Vietnam*, has also noted, that a "healing community" is essential in the process of reconciliation and recovery.[33]

> And if he (a brother) fell away, and was sucked back into the evil streets again, when his soul grew sick and he began to long for the clean air of the Christian Brotherhood, he would creep back some Saturday night when the Brethren were met in preparation for the Eucharist, and standing up before them all, would confess his fault and ask to come back into the family. And then the elder Brother, the "*presbyteros*," or priest, speaking for the family of God, would absolve him from his sin and take him back again to share in the common life. But it was the community that absolved, it was in the family that the power of healing and regeneration lay.[34]

For Studdert Kennedy, the soldiers and their family members to whom he had ministered throughout the war served as that healing and transformative community. To them he had preached the Mission of Repentance and Hope, to them he had encouraged selfless sacrifice in the pursuit of military victory, and among them he sought forgiveness and healing through his London speech. Members of liturgical church traditions understand that penance naturally follows confession. Acts of contrition are often required of penitents by priests, and a series of prayers or reflection may serve as an effective penance. But many penitents undertake more rigorous forms of penance, committing themselves to a continuing life of sacrificial or public service. These may also serve as a source of spiritual healing and recovery from moral injury.[35]

SACRIFICIAL SERVICE AS PENANCE

Studdert Kennedy had been raised with a strong commitment to the principle of duty and public service. Beginning in 1922, Studdert Kennedy became the Chief Missioner for the Industrial Christian Fellowship. The hectic schedule, the constant train travel from one speaking engagement to the next and the self-imposed exile from his family may have unconsciously served as a personal penance for the acts he confessed on that Armistice Day stage. The self-sacrifice and duty he recommended in the trenches was extreme. Although some have noted the relatively brief nature of his assignments there, those assignments involved searing experiences that accompanied him the rest of his life. Those experiences included serving as an "inexperienced undertaker" carrying and burying the dead, complaining of his aching shoulders, and wishing for the body of a more robust man.[36] He recounted being covered in the blood of his soldiers and of discovering and burying the body of a friend. He recounted his own mixed reaction, exaltation and horror, at the sheer magnitude of industrial-grade warfare and the thousands of lives sacrificed in an instant. He wrote of the mothers, wives, and children of those he ministered to and empathized with the tears they would shed upon receiving his letters, offering Christian comfort for their loss.

Upon his return home from the war, Studdert Kennedy continued the frenetic activity that had characterized his war service. He was unable or unwilling to rest, energized by his message and the needs he saw in postwar Britain. Like many returning from war, he may have been addicted to the adrenaline rush that accompanies combat and the exhilaration of surviving near death experiences. He rationalized his activity, both in the war and after, as the universal duty of all citizens of Great Britain and presented his own sacrificial service as an example to all. He communicated this philosophy of duty in his first postwar book, *Lies*, identifying "a driving sense of duty"[37] and self-sacrifice as the great responsibility of all members of a democratic state, "who are ever thinking of their rights and never of their responsibilities."[38] Characteristic of his postwar literature, he illustrated this peacetime principle with a battlefield recollection.

> But if this great Truth is to be worked into our lives as members of a democratic state it must be combined with another truth for which Christ stood—the truth that the secret of life is service. . . . If the man of superior abilities is not a public servant he is a parasite, and more unworthy of his manhood than an ignorant and drunken pauper . . . he is like those enormous bloated flies that buzz round the dead on a battlefield. Filthy things, clothed in gorgeous colours, their bright green wings flashing in the sun as they seek the choicest morsels of the swollen and disfigured dead.[39]

Studdert Kennedy practiced and exemplified this ideal of service and duty as a Christian responsibility. He felt that Christians, bishops, clergy, and laity were far too content to stand on the sidelines and let others take the lead in the affairs of the day. "We must have a red religion which burns and blazes and calls men—calls them to service, renunciation, and sacrifice."[40]

Beginning in 1922, Studdert Kennedy was given the opportunity to continue his life of sacrificial service with the Industrial Christian Fellowship, an organization whose purpose was to share the gospel of Christ alongside the working men and women of Britain. I will address this period of his live more fully in the next chapter. He agreed to serve as their public representative and to conduct speaking crusades throughout Britain. The organization also became involved in the labor disputes that were all too common during the 1920s. He found that he was perfectly cut out for this role, for the working classes included many of the very soldiers he had served in the war as well as the poor he had served in Worcester.[41]

Studdert Kennedy continued his life of self-sacrificial service and duty throughout the 1920s, dashing about the country by train, speaking at a men's group, church, or public venue where he could communicate the message of the Suffering Christ as it applied to the economic and social challenges of the day. He would then dash home to visit his family, where he now had three children, only to dash away again for another public engagement. Studdert Kennedy's great-nephew, Gerald Studdert-Kennedy, noted the impact this schedule had on him.

> The messenger's diary was controlled by Kirk, the ICF Director, who organized a gruelling schedule of engagements, which, it is worth noting, made increasingly heavy demands on the preacher's emotional and physical resources, and indirectly on his immediate family. Between 8 October and 17 December 1925, for instance, he made forty-six scheduled appearances, moving within ten days from Eastbourne to York, Accrington, Leeds, York again, London and Swansea.[42]

This hectic schedule continued until his death. In March 1927, he announced that his schedule was "completely full for the next eighteen months."[43] Studdert Kennedy was cautioned by friends regarding his hectic pace, but he ignored them, assuring them that he was up to the challenge. Subject to frequent bouts of asthma (made worse by being gassed during the war) and fatigued by his constant travel, Studdert Kennedy died in Liverpool on March 8, 1929, aged 45. At the time of his death, he was engaged in another speaking engagement. His friends attributed his death to Studdert Kennedy's driving sense of duty. In his 1927 novel, *I Pronounce Them*, his semi-autobiographical main character Father Jim engaged in overwork and a hectic work schedule to evade some significant emotional issues. "From that time on, he purposely piled on work for himself, refusing to think."[44] Perhaps Studdert Kennedy hectic schedule, like Father Jim's, was driven by a desire not to think about the war or to recall the images of the thousands of soldiers he had encouraged into no-man's-land as they also fulfilled their duty to God and country.

> When I last saw him, I told him he could not go on for long at the pace he was working, making lightning journeys north, south, east and west to deliver half a dozen sermons or speeches at each destination, with never a moment's thought for himself; but he laughed my fears away. . . . He died at the height of his power through reckless attention to duty and refusal to give in though he was gripped with illness and pain.[45]

Acknowledgment of one's role in war, confession of the sins one has committed, and the forgiveness of a caring and trusted community are essential elements in the recovery from the trauma inflicted by participation in war. Studdert Kennedy, although he did not enjoy the benefit of contemporary insights regarding recovery from Combat Stress and moral injury, intuitively followed just those steps. He also pursued an intense public service, possibly as a public penance to atone for his perceived contribution to the evils of the war. His steps served as both a spiritual and psychological atonement for his war transgressions and played an important role in his recovery from moral injury. Public service may also illustrate post-traumatic growth by survivors of trauma that benefit entire communities. Studdert Kennedy's efforts to transform postwar Britain through his opposition to war and efforts to abolish poverty are exemplary examples of post-traumatic growth by a war veteran. I'll detail his phenomenal efforts in the next chapter.

NOTES

1. "A Momentary Aberration," *Nottingham Journal*, Nov. 12, 1921, 3.
2. Rita Nakashima Brock and Gabriela Lettini, *Soul Repair: Recovery from Moral Injury after War* (Boston: Beacon Press, 2012), 114.
3. Ibid., Jonathan Shay, *Achilles in Vietnam: Combat Trauma and the Undoing of Character* (New York: Touchstone Books, 1994), 193.
4. A blighty was a wound that was serious enough to send the soldier home, but not so serious as to cause severe damage or death.
5. G. A. Studdert Kennedy, *Lies* (London: Hodder & Stoughton, 1919), 119–120.
6. Jonathan Shay, *Odysseus in America* (New York: Scribner, 2002), 152–153.
7. Ibid., 153–154.
8. *Rough Talks of a Padre* (1918), *The Hardest Part* (1918), *Rough Rhymes of a Padre* (1918), *More Rough Rhymes of a Padre* (1918), *Lies* (1919), *Peace Rhymes of a Padre* (1920).
9. William Purcell, *Woodbine Willie: A Biography* (London: Hodder & Stoughton, 1962), 151–152.
10. G. A. Studdert Kennedy, *The Warrior, the Woman, and the Christ* (London: Hodder & Stoughton, 1929), 18.
11. Ibid., 18.

12. William P. Nash and Dewleen G. Baker, "Competing and Complementary Models of Combat Stress Injury" in *Combat Stress Injury*, eds. Charles R. Figley and William P. Nash (New York: Routledge, 2007), 65–93.

13. McClenehan, Linda. "Post-traumatic Spiritual Disorder." Ministry and Liturgy.Com (vol. 40; no. 8) October 2013, 9–13.

14. Purcell, *Woodbine Willie*, 155–156.

15. Another form of moral injury occurs when a military member's chain of command or administrative actions place him or her in a position that results in the experience of traumatic injury. The moral injury can result in anger or distrust directed at the chain of command.

16. G. A. Studdert Kennedy, *Democracy and The Dog Collar* (London: Hodder & Stoughton, 1921), 47–49.

17. G. A. Studdert Kennedy, *Rough Talks of a Padre* (London: Hodder & Stoughton, 1918), 62–66.

18. Carey, "Studdert Kennedy: War Padre" in *G. A. Studdert Kennedy by His Friends*, 138–141.

19. G. A. Studdert Kennedy, *I Pronounce Them* (New York: George H. Doran Company, 1927), 228.

20. G. A. Studdert Kennedy, *The Hardest Part* (London: Hodder & Stoughton, 1918), 190.

21. G. A. Studdert Kennedy, *Lies* (London: Hodder & Stoughton, 1919), 226–227.

22. Jonathan Shay, *Odysseus in America: Combat Trauma and the Trials of Coming Home* (New York: Scribner, 2002), 80.

23. G. A. Studdert Kennedy, *The Hardest Part* (London: Hodder & Stoughton, 1918), 154.

24. G. A. Studdert Kennedy, *More Rough Rhymes of a Padre* (London: Hodder & Stoughton, 1918), 80.

25. Studdert Kennedy, *Lies*, 20.

26. "A Momentary Aberration," *Yorkshire Evening Post*, Nov. 12, 1921, 4.

27. "Letters to the Editor: Christianity and War," *Sheffield Daily Telegraph*, Dec. 14, 1921, 5.

28. "Letters to the Editor: Christianity and War," *Sheffield Daily Telegraph*, Dec. 17, 1921, 3

29. Studdert Kennedy, *Lies*, 38–39.

30. "Futile Victory, Padre's Regret for War Propaganda," *Sheffield Daily Telegraph*, Nov. 28, 1921, 6.

31. Brock and Lettini, *Soul Repair: Recovering from Moral Injury after War*, 75.

32. William P. Nash, "Combat Operational Stress Adaptations and Injuries," in *Combat Stress Injury*, eds. Charles R. Figley and William P. Nash (New York: Routledge, 2007), 54.

33. Shay, *Achilles in Vietnam: Combat Trauma and the Undoing of Character*, 188.

34. G. A. Studdert Kennedy, *The Wicket Gate* (London: Hodder & Stoughton, 1923), 183.

35. Shay, *Achilles in Vietnam*, 186–187. See also Robert Grant, *The Way of the Wound* (Oakland: Robert Grant, 1996), 88.

36. G. A. Studdert Kennedy, *The Hardest Part* (London: Hodder & Stoughton, 1918), 15. Interestingly, Father Jim, the semi-autobiographical main character in his 1927 novel *I Pronounce Them*, is described as "of middle height, broad and powerfully made" and had played football as a three-quarter back (16).

37. Studdert Kennedy, *Lies*, 64.

38. Ibid., 66.

39. Ibid., 77–78.

40. Ibid., 39.

41. Kirk, "Studdert Kennedy: I.C.F. Crusader" in *G. A. Studdert Kennedy by His Friends*, 172–173.

42. Gerald Studdert-Kennedy, *Dog Collar Democracy* (London: The Macmillan Press Ltd., 1982), 123.

43. "Mail: Mustard and Cress," *Hull Daily Mail*, March 31, 1917, 1.

44. G. A. Studdert Kennedy, *I Pronounce Them* (New York: George H. Doran Company, 1927), 281.

45. H. R. L. Sheppard, "Studdert Kennedy: A Friend" in *G. A. Studdert Kennedy by His Friends*, ed. J. K. Mozley (London: Hodder & Stoughton, 1929), 201.

Chapter Eight

Recovery and Post-Traumatic Growth

Studdert Kennedy's Campaign against War and Poverty, 1922–1929

Chaplain G. A. Studdert Kennedy emerged from his experiences of the Great War as a wounded survivor. While his gas wounded lungs recovered sufficiently to allow him to live an active life,[1] he carried invisible spiritual and psychological wounds. In these pages, I have interpreted his life in light of the contemporary understanding of Combat Stress, Moral and Spiritual Injury. It is often noted that individuals that experience the identical stresses of combat emerge from the experience with very different outcomes. Some deal with the experience and emerge relatively unscathed while others carry the experience with them throughout their lives, psychologically and spiritually wounded. A good deal of research has been conducted on how to provide our military men and women with the resources to achieve the first outcome, what is often called resilience. Studdert Kennedy's life serves as an excellent example of elements that contribute to resilience (discussed in chapter 2) as well as those that can defeat it. His postwar life also demonstrates the possibility of recovery and post-traumatic growth that can result from the traumas inherent in modern warfare.

A WOUNDED SURVIVOR

While Studdert Kennedy's spiritual resources and natural strength contributed to the resilience that enabled him to complete his tour of service with the BEF in France, it is clear that he did not emerge from the war unscathed. As one combat veteran commented to me recently as I described Studdert Kennedy's experiences, "every soldier has his limits."[2] Studdert Kennedy's three years and four months in the war zone tested the limits of his physical and spiritual strength. He had ministered in the midst of trench warfare and encountered his own share of "mud, blood, and smells!"[3] One is struck by the passion with which he conducted his ministry and the love he demonstrated for the soldiers he served. His comments to the deceased soldier Peter in April 1917 epitomized the care he felt for all those soldiers. "That's all I am, Peter, an informal and incompetent undertaker, with tears in my eyes and sorrow in my heart."[4] But that empathy, the magnitude of death and destruction, and the accumulated grief that he felt for his soldiers and their loved ones very nearly overwhelmed him. His assignments throughout the war theater brought him into personal contact with tens of thousands of soldiers and, I believe, aroused in him a sense of responsibility for the spiritual lives of the soldiers he met as well as their loved ones, a sense of responsibility too great for any one man to bear. The sheer magnitude of the human suffering he experienced caused him to question his faith and the goodness of God. He discovered that his faith was built on flawed foundations and a misunderstanding of God. In addressing his spiritual and cognitive dissonance he reframed that understanding, that God suffers alongside humans in their self-inflicted difficulties. Most important, he also came to understand the limits of his own responsibility for the suffering and grief of those he served, that his own resources were too meager to handle the pain, grief, and the questions of those he suffered alongside.

> And I hear a voice out of the darkness crying, "My God, My God, why? . . . The woman whose hope was murdered on the battlefields of France crying from the unconscious for the child she cannot have . . . a monotonous, interminable procession, some in anger, some sullen, some scornful, some brokenly submissive, but all in the dark and asking why? The question no mortal man can answer. *Yes, it needs a cross to meet it, and it needs a Christ to bear it and not break.*[5]

Studdert Kennedy understood that he could not bear everyone's pain and grief, that he had to share that burden. Ultimately, his faith saved him. He survived the war with his faith intact but changed. He returned home as one of the war's' walking wounded, "embittered, above all conscious of the many, the very many, who did not come back at all."[6] In chapter 7, I discussed important elements of Studdert Kennedy's recovery from his moral injury: the acknowledgment of his wrong choices, refusal to deny or forget those choices, and his efforts toward purification. Another important element in his healing journey, common in recovery and post-traumatic growth, was a commitment to public service.

POST TRAUMATIC GROWTH: ABOLISHING WAR AND POVERTY

Post-traumatic growth occurs when individuals who have experienced a traumatic event work through their trauma and build on that experience, or transform it, for self-benefit and the benefit of the larger community. Researchers report that trauma survivors "may reexamine many aspects of their lives and might recognize growth in domains such as personal strength, relationships with others, appreciation of life, spirituality and new possibilities."[7] Contemporary research recognizes that post-traumatic growth may occur but is not guaranteed for every survivor of trauma. The experience of post-traumatic growth does not completely eliminate the effects or symptoms of traumatic experiences, many of those remain for life. These walking wounded recognize themselves as trauma survivors. For those who experience post-traumatic growth, it has been observed to include the following characteristics,

> Survivors of trauma recognize and embrace new opportunities. They forge stronger relationships with loved ones as well as with victims who suffered in the same way. They cultivate inner strength through the knowledge that they have overcome tremendous hardship. They gain a deeper appreciation for life and their relationship to religion and spirituality changes and evolves.[8]

Public service often serves as a focus of these new opportunities for personal growth, observed in survivors of combat stress and moral injury as well as other traumatic experiences. A sexual assault survivor who establishes an emergency hotline for victims of sexual assault or a survivor of war trauma who becomes a counselor to similar victims exemplify this positive outcome. Studdert Kennedy's postwar service and ministry serve as an example of recovery from moral injuries as well as of post-traumatic growth, although I don't believe he ever fully recovered from his war experiences. We must remember that the contemporary benefits of psychological knowledge and understanding of combat stress, moral injury and PTSD were unavailable to the survivors of the First World War. Family stories of silent and stoic war veterans who never spoke of their war experiences are unfortunately ubiquitous.

As discussed earlier, Studdert Kennedy emerged from the war with serious regrets concerning his own role in promoting the war, both prior to and during the conflict where he preached support for Britain's war aims and encouraged his listeners to enlist and to fight valiantly in pursuit of victory. His publications between 1919 and 1921 communicated a serious disappointment in the postwar world and every facet of British society (discussed in chapter 6). An important element of his post-traumatic growth was his anti-war activism and distrust of Britain's political leadership in the use of military force in the pursuit of national aims. His 1921 Armistice Day speech in which he confessed his wrongdoing was a personal effort to seek forgiveness and to atone for his errors; to recover his mental, moral, and spiritual health. His national popularity gave him a speaking platform from which to actively oppose the nation's "faith in force" and to serve the larger community in which absolution and forgiveness could be found. Studdert Kennedy also believed in the transformative power of his faith, that God could transform lives through forgiveness and love. His postwar commitments and post-traumatic growth display that transformative power in action.[9]

Recovery from moral injury and post-traumatic growth is often found through selfless sacrifice and public service, as noted above.[10] Studdert Kennedy possessed a well-developed social conscience. He was devoted to the welfare of working men and women of Great Britain, opposed the warfare between the classes (capital and labor) and passionately hated the poverty that afflicted so many. His role as a "missioner" and champion of the Industrial Christian Fellowship (ICF), beginning in 1922, provided him the opportunity to pursue his own post-traumatic growth as he transferred the same passion that he felt for the soldiers in the trenches of France to the working men and women who toiled in the industries and mines of Britain. It is instructive of his mindset that he transferred the spiritual vision of the crucified Christ that he experienced on the Somme battlefield to the working-class slums of Britain.

> Inasmuch as ye have done it unto the least of these my little ones ye have don't it unto me." From that moment on I never saw a battlefield as anything but a Crucifix. From that moment on I have never seen the world as anything but a Crucifix. *I see the Cross set up in every slum, in every filthy overcrowded quarter, in every vulgar flaring street that speaks of luxury and waste of life. I see Him staring up at me from the pages of the newspaper that tells of a tortured lost, bewildered world.*[11]

Between 1922 and 1929, Studdert Kennedy effectively declared war on Britain's "faith in force" and on its economic inequalities: class warfare, slums, and poverty. In descriptive language that was often described as "racy" in the local papers, he passionately denounced the problems he perceived and which he committed himself to correct. The brotherhood of man, he said in his 1925 book, The *Word and the Work*, was "broken, wounded, torn, it bleeds on battlefields, is diseased in slums, it is covered with festering sores of vulgar luxury, it groans with hunger, and is rent by strife."[12] He blamed these issues on both the political leadership and on Britain's defective early-twentieth-century economic system and its woes. Condemning both, he stated, "a godless international policy has produced rats and rotting corpses in the Valley of the Somme, and . . . a godless commercial and industrial system produces gilded vice and filthy slums."[13]

The solution he proposed was fairly straightforward, even simplistic: abolish war and poverty! In a 1928 speech, reported in the *North Devon Journal*, he expressed the two goals that he had adopted as his public service and ministry. Military leaders and politicians, he said, "bragged and boasted behind their armaments because they quaked with fear. And there came to this generation the vision that war could be abolished from the face of the earth. (applause). That was an enormous problem; applauding the sentiment would not abolish the thing. *They had got to abolish poverty and war*."[14]

In the remaining pages of this chapter, I will outline Studdert Kennedy's efforts and thinking in regard to these two idealistic ambitions. I believe they fully illustrate his post-traumatic growth and demonstrate the transformative nature of Studdert Kennedy's response to the war's impact on his moral and spiritual perspectives, a direct result and response to his wartime trauma. I'll first address his anti-war thinking and efforts.[15]

STUDDERT KENNEDY'S EFFORTS TO ABOLISH WAR

Studdert Kennedy's opposition to the war and his commitment to eliminating it grew out of his experiences on the Western Front throughout his more than three years there. He hoped that the experience of war would bring about a positive change in Great Britain, that the sacrifices of the people from every class of Britain's social system as well as its great empire would be rewarded with a commitment to a new social order. But Studdert Kennedy's hopes were dashed by the reality of postwar Britain's return to prewar normality. With no positive change to outweigh the losses and carnage of the war years, the human impact of the war weighed all the more heavily on his spirit, and he came to the conclusion that war and its passions had no place in a Christian worldview, that it was ultimately a "waste of time."

> As I lay sick at the Front, I thought to myself we are going to bring something great and glorious out of the war. As far as I can bring it about, if we gain a complete victory, we are going to have a new order, a new world, a better day. And I believed it . . . and although the padre's is a soft job—and it is no good pretending that it is not—yet because he sees the boys he loves go down (die) the Padre's heart came nearer to breaking those days than the hearts of other men. . . . Hatred, bitterness and anger were a waste of time.[16]

As I consider these words, I note the unbearable weight that pressed upon Studdert Kennedy's heart as he remembered the men to whom he had distributed cigarettes, had written letters for, and who had listened to his sermons. Chaplains come to love the soldiers and sailors they serve, and their death, in peace or war, is a heavy burden. The "torrents of blood"[17] that weighed on Studdert Kennedy's spirit drove him to consider the necessity of war and its existential impact on human beings. Not only did war result in a multitude of human deaths, its fear, hatred, and animal behavior degraded the human spirit. While those who theorized about war or simply read about it as history might see it as a positive human endeavor, those who experienced it from the inside knew it for what it was, an absolute horror. "War was irrational, both morally and spiritually and was bad for everything. The world got nothing whatsoever out of war and never would.[18]

> He had been in a war and could not associate God with it at all. There was a force which from outside they would think was a clean thing. When they got inside it was all slimy with fear. The horrible thing about force was the degradation of the human element, the creeping, cringing, crawling, and loathing. War stank with fear. They bragged and boasted behind their armaments because they quaked with fear.[19]

Studdert Kennedy was always sensitive to the fact the horrors of war were not limited in its effects to just the battlefield. He had written to his soldiers' parents, sweethearts, wives, and children. He had a wife and sons at home and knew the pain of separation and the toll it took upon his family. Those on the home front missed their soldiers and were constantly fearful of the news that might arrive at any time. He spoke of these family members in his poetry: of a mother who lost her beloved son, of a wife who welcomed a wounded husband back home to watch him suffer the pain of his war wounds and memories, of a father whose world was destroyed on the battlefields of France, and of a sweetheart who heard of her lover's death from a chance encounter. Studdert Kennedy understood their fears, felt their grief, and wrote of it in his prose and poetry.

Studdert Kennedy described one of these war victims in a 1927 *John Bull* article titled, "The Woman Who Lost Christmas." This war widow had volunteered in his church and assisted preparing and distributing dolls to children during the Christmas season, but she finally gave it up, with the joy of the season too great to overcome the darkness of the grief that filled her heart.

> "I am too old to pretend any longer," she said, "and Christmas is all pretence. Dolls, dolls, it is all dolls, and I am too old to play with dolls. I would rather have the naked ugly truth about life than this beauty that is not true." But her

> wound was deep. She had lost her husband in the war after three weeks of married life, and she was the kind of woman who loves only once.

Studdert Kennedy, with tears in his eyes and sorrow in his heart for this good woman and the grief she bore to her grave, concluded that war was evil and that the promise of Christmas must be fulfilled in human experience. Christmas, he said, must be made true. "Love must become the law of life. War must be ended, and hatred killed. Cruelty to children and tyranny of greed must be abolished. . . . Christmas is the only thing that is good enough to be true.[20]

Anti-War Activism

Studdert Kennedy became a "no-more-war" activist and joined with like-minded organizers to argue for significant political and national legislation to outlaw war. He contributed his highly regarded oratory skills to the anti-war demonstrations and organizations that arose after the war. In July 1922, he joined the worldwide "No-More-War" rally. The London demonstration drew more than 15,000 participants in and as many as five million world-wide. Studdert Kennedy participated, speaking from a platform in Hyde Park.[21] The event was widely reported in the newspapers and Studdert Kennedy's address was a highlight. He spoke frankly about his own participation in the war and the decision that faced him in 1914 when the war broke out. He proposed that people should not have to agonize over that decision in the future. Eliminating war would preclude that necessity, "there must be no more war.'[22] He also supported a number of like-minded organizations.

Studdert Kennedy became a regular speaker at League of Nations Union (LNU) meetings. The organization, founded in 1918 to support the values of the League of Nations, became a leader in the British peace-movement and, at one time, boasted a quarter of a million members. In a 1923 LNU address, he warned that the memories of the war were already fading and that the dangers of another war would increase with time. Peace was a tenuous accomplishment.

> Already the tide was setting the other way, and people were beginning to forget, and in a generation, it would be intensely hard to explain to men the meaning of the valley of the Somme. . . . I don't think we are going to get rid of war until there have been martyrs for the cause of peace.[23]

He also participated in the 1924 Birmingham Conference on Politics, Economics, and Citizenship (COPEC). The conference addressed many issues facing the Christian church in 1920s England; the role of women in the church, children's education, the anti-war movement, and the right of individual servicemen to declare themselves as conscientious objectors to war. In a comment that elicited a good deal of notice in the press and condemnation by the public, he suggested that serving soldiers and sailors had the right to follow the dictates of conscience should they come to believe that a war was immoral, that they had the right even to mutiny. In the address, he once again reiterated the struggles of his own conscience when he considered his response to the war in 1914 and wished he had decided against participation. Referencing conscientious objection, he stated, "I want to claim with all my might, the right to mutiny. I hope that when a sailor or soldier feels that the cause he is asked to fight for is wrong, he will say so. And I hope the Church will support it. I know it's risky.[24]

Studdert Kennedy developed an ongoing concern that the annual observances of Armistice Day and the proliferation of war memorials in churches and town squares, instead of memorializing the brave sacrifices of Britain's heroes, were serving to glorify and promote war. In effect, he became a spokesman for the "glorious dead" who could no longer speak for themselves. "Year by year," says the Rev. G. A. Studdert Kennedy," I grow more terrified of Armistice Day. This fear is engendered because of its glorification of war. It must be more and more a day for the glorification of peace."[25] Instead of commemorating a great war victory, he suggested that "they could only be a blessing to this and every other country if all joined together in crying out with the voice of the million dead: "Never Again!"[26]

In a 1927 *John Bull* article titled, "The Accursed Thing!," he commented on his visit to the war memorial in Edinburgh, Scotland. While there he observed a war widow and her son visiting and observed their solemn reaction to the beauty of the memorial. He stated that he longed to take the son aside and tell him the truth about war, of its horrors. He feared that the memorial was communicating a beautiful lie, that war is glorious. He feared something even more terrible, that that child would himself be forced to fight a war that would be even more terrible than the one he had experienced in France from 1915 to 1919.

> Some months ago I went to see the Scottish National War Memorial in Edinburgh. I think it is one of the most beautiful things in the world. Scotland may well be proud of it. And yet I hate and detest it. I hate it all the more fiercely because it is beautiful. It is that most deadly and poisonous of all things, a deadly lie . . . there is not in it a single warning note. Anyone who has never seen war or known what it really means would come away believing that it was glorious and romantic. . . . For God's sake, let us be realists on Armistice Day. Do not be tempted by the hero worship in your son's eyes. Tell him the facts. This is the best tribute we can pay to the glorious dead. . . . They would tell the

> children if they could. Let us do it for them, and honour their memories on the altar of truth.[27]

Condemnation of the Bankers' Role in Propagating War

Studdert Kennedy used his "bully pulpit" on Armistice Day 1922 to remind England of those who bore financial responsibility for the Great War and of the conduct of war in general. His church, St. Edmund Martyr, on Lombard Street, was situated in the heart of London's financial center. In preparation for Armistice Day's two-minute silence, he delivered an address to a large audience that gathered during the lunch hour for an observance in the historic Royal Exchange. Participants received a prophetic reminder of their own responsibility for war and its propagation. Studdert Kennedy confronted the gathered bankers and insurance brokers with their own significant role in the propagation of war. The newspapers reported his speech and the stunning irony of its location.

> Woodbine Willie (Rev G.A. Studdert Kennedy, rector of St. Edmund Lombard Street) delivered a striking address at the Royal Exchange yesterday. The occasion was one of the most remarkable in the history of that historic building. More than a thousand city workers—many of them well-known figures in the banking and insurance world—attended during the lunch hour a special service "in preparation for the two-minutes silence on Armistice Day. . . . Wearing on his surplice the military cross, "Woodbine Willie" appealed to his hearers, as being men who had the power for peace or war, to concentrate the great system of the money market to the cause of peace. "Peace at any price is wrong," he declared, "but so is great wealth at any price. You can pay too dearly in human blood and lives for wealth." . . . He made no general charge, but appealed to them to cast out those men who helped to cause wars. . . . If civilization could not destroy war, war would destroy civilization.[28]

The message that war could not proceed without the financial support of banks and industry became a significant part of his message as he traveled throughout Britain for the ICF. He was fearful of another war and understood that once it started, it was impossible to stop. He encouraged his listeners to eliminate war by attacking its very roots. "You must stop war where war starts—in the counting houses and the financial bargainer's rooms. War starts in Lombard Street, wherever it ends."[29] But the blame for the war did not stop at the doors of the financiers. According to Studdert Kennedy, the bankers were part of a vast industrial civilization that redirected the warrior ethos of the ancient world into business. In his 1928 book *The Warrior, the Woman, and the Christ*, Studdert Kennedy created a historic narrative to describe this evolution from ancient culture to the industrial world. In his narrative, industry had abandoned its primary creative role and transformed into a destructive force, seeking wealth rather than a creative life-sustaining power. In this narrative, industry enslaved men, women, and children, incorporating them into a vast machine. The church, through its inaction, bore the blame along with industry.

> The women hypnotized and helpless were pressed with their little ones into mine and mill, and did nothing but work and breed prodigiously. . . . Every day the world became more and more like a battlefield. . . . The church as a whole was silent, and the shame of that silence clings to her yet.[30]

The evolution of this world was inevitable, away from human dignity and always toward war and destruction. Industry destroyed the human spirit even as it created the conditions for mass warfare, resulting in the First World War.

> The Industrial War became world-wide and, as the factory extended, the struggle for markets, spheres of influence, concessions, and opportunities for exploitation of natural resources became more and more intense. The warrior using his knowledge of applied mechanics armed himself with enormously powerful engines of destruction. . . . The very blood and bones of the peoples were built into engines of war. The sprawling filth of the slums extended as more ships put out to sea. It was ready to break, that great black cloud, in torrents of bloody rain. . . . Then suddenly the cloud burst and it rained blood upon the earth for four years.[31]

In Studdert Kennedy's narrative, industrial civilization was responsible for the mechanization of slaughter, for transferring the engineering genius of industry to the battlefield. "Industry and commerce had turned the world into a huge machine."[32] Industry had turned the battlefield into an abattoir, a kingdom of hell. He described this atrocity in his 1923 book *The Wicket Gate*, interestingly a commentary on the Lord's Prayer.

> The Battle of the Somme was a fitting climax to the whole tragedy of what might be called "murder by machinery"; it brought out the essential points and wrote them large in letters of blood and flame. To stand and watch the working of a 9.2 armour-piercing gun—to appreciate the beautiful exactness with which the monster moved, the unerring accuracy of his aim, the marvelous ingenuity of mechanical device which every part of it displayed—and then to consider the purpose for which the combination of God's gifts was being used, was to see the abyss of the modern tragedy, the nemesis of secularism, which uses the materials which God gave us for building the Kingdom of Heaven, to build the kingdom of Hell.[33]

Identifying the Church's Role in Propagating War

An important question that dogged Studdert Kennedy throughout his life was, "what role does the church have regarding war and its propagation?" He was aware of his own struggles in coming to terms with his support for the war. He was also aware of the condemnation by some sections of society for the church's role in supporting that war. In his book *Democracy and the Dog Collar*, he placed the argument against the church in the voice of a socialist labor opponent.

> This is one of my great grouses against you and your church. You have given and still give your blessing to the eyewash and cant of militarist nationalism. You bless colours, say prayers over guns, give the proudest place in your churches to war memorials, and talk and teach to children the petty, puerile, and flag-waving patriotism . . . (it) stinks, stinks with the stench of battlefields, the dry parched, sickening smell that calls up memories of an August day in the valley of the Somme.[34]

Studdert Kennedy believed that the church must acknowledge its past sins and renounce war. Otherwise it would lose its legitimacy and right to speak to working-class men and women. The church must repent of war even as he had repented and confessed at that 1921 Armistice Day speech.

> If the church of the twentieth century does not repent and proclaim open war against war; if she does not make good her right of entry into the factory, the office, and the counting-house; if she is content to remain a department of life, a State institution . . . and allows her members to be dishonest, and to comfort their consciences by pauperizing the poor with doles and easy charity.[35]

For Studdert Kennedy, opposition to war was a spiritual issue that the church could resolve only as it left its lofty churches and worked alongside the working men and women of Britain; in the streets, counting houses, industry, and mines. Only then could it speak effectively to the men and women who lived there. Only love could convince the church in this great endeavor, the love of Christ. Fear would oppose change and bring more war. "Fear it is that drives us out to war. Fear is the father of ferocity, and the forger of the sword. From the creative point of view, which is God's point of view, force is weakness, and only Love is power.[36] Ultimately, an end to war could only come if all of society worked together. "Trade Unions, churches and the League of Nations Union should band together to make the war attitude impossible."[37]

The Challenge of Memory in the Propagation of War

Studdert Kennedy was a realist even as he idealistically worked for the elimination of war and to establish worldwide peace. He understood human nature and the frailness of human memory. He knew that a new generation would soon arise that would not remember the horrors of the Great War. He also knew that many of the soldiers and survivors of that war would not, could not speak of their experiences, that the memories were too painful. The danger he foresaw was that each generation would have to experience its own version of the Battle of the Somme before it could understand the need for peace. He believed that day was inevitable and, when it arrived, he was fearful that even his own son would choose the path of war.

> So I believe it will be. Sometimes I see a day when I and my son will face one another with the choice between us—and maybe he will choose the other way from mine—and I shall have to watch him go, because I cannot make him see the Valley of the Somme, and he must make his own. It will be a bitter day.[38]

In a 1926 *John Bull* article, "The Answer's a Lemon," he communicated his final judgment and condemnation of war, a judgment that he would apply to the continuing class warfare between capital and labor that he believed characterized Great Britain of the 1920s.

> Great wars, great revolutions, and great strikes are all alike great nonsense, and that is all the greatness about them. They are tales told by fools, full of sound and fury, and signifying nothing, or worse than nothing. In point of cold fact, the Great War was one of the meanest and most sordid chapters in European history, and if history is ever honestly written it will appear as such. All the piteous panic-stricken weakness of human nature oozed out through those accursed years as pus and poison ooze from a stupidly neglected sore upon a sickly body.[39]

Like many who have suffered moral and spiritual injury as a result of their participation in war, Studdert Kennedy actively and passionately opposed war. His efforts in opposition to war are one element pointing to his recovery and post-traumatic growth from the effects of his injury. He also adopted another great challenge that was, if possible, even more formidable than the first. He committed his life to abolishing poverty in all its myriad forms in Britain.

WAGING WAR ON POVERTY, UNEMPLOYMENT AND CLASS WARFARE

"To the Princess at the Royal Wedding"

If flaunting feathers made fine birds,
And gilded braid were gold,
If coronets were honest crowns,
Not baubles bought and sold;
. . .
If we all glorious without,
Were glorious within,
Above the coward compromise,
That folly makes with sin'
Then through the thunder of these cheers,
No child would cry for bread,
Nor would the waste of living men,
Shame our poor wasted dead.
God's people were not pent like swine
In evil-smelling sties,
With clouds of filthy smoke to hide
The splendour of the skies.
Men would not walk the ways of death,
Nor labour in despair,
If all our hearts were golden as
The sunshine of your hair.[40]

Rev. G. A. Studdert Kennedy enjoyed a broad social experience due to his role as a clergyman in the Church of England. He came from humble Irish origins but, due to his wartime successes, enjoyed entrance at all levels of British society. As a military chaplain he was responsible to minister to the spiritual needs of all ranks within the military. As Church of England clergyman, Studdert Kennedy ministered to all ranks on England's stratified social ladder. As a king's chaplain, he preached regularly at Buckingham Palace and could speak of having conversed with the king on various topics of national concern. He reportedly spoke to a once and future prime minister[41] "like a Dutch Uncle" concerning economic problems and worked with numerous Church of England bishops in attempting to solve a vexing miners' strike.[42] He was also welcomed by the masses of English working men and women who flocked to his church services and packed his public meetings to hear his "racy" sermons.

In 1922, he became the chief missioner for the Industrial Christian Fellowship (ICF), headed by Rev. P. T. R. Kirk, also a Church of England clergyman and former military chaplain. The ICF was an organization that had as its goal to "carry a Christian message to the industrial masses,"[43] to bring Christianity into the workplace. An important aspect the ICF's efforts was to implement a social gospel to benefit the working class and bring about change through its good offices and, if possible, to influence social legislation. Its members included clergy, trade unionists, members of the government, and numerous volunteers. It was a significant voice during the turbulent economic times of the 1920s.

Studdert Kennedy's Hatred for Poverty

Studdert Kennedy officially became the ICF's "chief Missioner" in 1922 but had assisted in its efforts on a part-time basis since at least 1920. His commitment to the goals of the ICF and its social gospel was not newfound but grew out of his lifelong experience of poverty. His father had served in one of the poorest areas of England in his parish church at Leeds. Studdert Kennedy spoke of that experience as having been life changing. "I was brought up in one of the most damnable parishes in the North of England where people still live like pigs in hovels. There, when a child, I vowed that I would dedicate my life to stamp poverty out of the world."[44] During his years of ministry with the ICF, he was often accused of being a socialist, a charge that he denied.[45] But socialism as a potential solution for Britain's poverty certainly interested him. A 1913 "tongue-in-cheek" letter to the editor of the *Yorkshire Post* indicated his interest in the subject. In the letter he challenged a local correspondent to explain his assertion regarding the Socialist Party's imminent collapse, and to educate him in its impact.

> To the Editor of the Yorkshire Post: The Position of Socialism. Sir, I would be very much obliged if you would allow me, through your columns, to ask Mr. Millar if he would kindly publish a summary, however slight and inadequate it maybe of the "abundant evidence that the Socialist party in England is on the point of collapse." . . . I have not yet studied the subject sufficiently to proclaim myself a convinced Socialist, but I am in terrible danger of being caught by that incurable intellectual disorder. . . . If Mr. Millar is right, I am slowly but surely going mad. Surely as a man and a Christian, he cannot turn a deaf ear to this piteous appeal for help from a poor incipient lunatic—Yours, etc. G.A. Studdert Kennedy, St. Mary's Vicarage, Leeds.[46]

Later, probably at Rugby, Studdert Kennedy broadened his experience with the poor, children, and even tramps. In a newspaper interview in preparation for a 1926 ICF crusade in Coventry, he explained some of his early endeavors.

> "My first duties as a clergyman," he told a Midland Telegraph reporter this morning, "were to study children four to nine years of age and to work amongst

> the tramps. An infant school, two lodging houses, and a work-house were included in my first charge." One feels that the lessons he acquired of the moral impulses which accrued have followed him all the days of his life.[47]

During the war, he focused his empathy and care upon the needs of the soldiers fighting on the Front and of their families. He sought to bring the compassion of his Suffering God to the battlefield. Those who challenged his theological understanding suggested that his battlefield theology would change with the return of peace. He disagreed, stating that the ministrations of the Suffering God were as necessary in the slums as they were on the battlefield.

> I do not think so, unless Peace brings in the Millennium, and though I am an optimist I do not anticipate that. The vision of the suffering God revealed in Jesus Christ, and the necessary Truth of it, first began to dawn on me in the narrow streets and shadowed homes of an English slum. All that War has done is to batter the essential truth of it deeper in and cast a fiercer light upon the Cross. A battlefield is more striking, but scarcely more really crude and brutal than a slum.[48]

This concern for the poor and the social gospel remained with Studdert Kennedy throughout his life. Just a few months before his death in March 1929, Studdert Kennedy spoke at an ICF rally in Rugby. In the speech he challenged the hearers concerning poverty and their fear of it. He acknowledged that he feared it. He stated that he also hated it, though he had never been poor himself. Instead, he had walked with and ministered to the poor, and his experience convinced him of poverty's inhumanity and the need to eliminate it.

> Are you afraid of being poor? Opened the Rev. G.A. Studdert Kennedy? I am and have been all my life, although I have never been poor in the proper sense. I have never known what it was to wonder where my next meal was coming from and what would happen to my wife and my children, and yet I have always hated poverty. I have lived and walked among people who have been crowded together like pigs in hovels and in my early days I wandered in and out of those cottages. By doing so, I learned to loathe poverty, and it brought me to the service of Christ, for I believe that it is His will and commandment that the poverty which degrades the human soul should be swept off the face of the earth.[49]

Christian Responsibility to the Poor

In his role as an ardent opponent to poverty, Studdert Kennedy once again was faced with the question that a sergeant hurled at him in a battlefield trench as he went forward into "no-man's-land," "What was the church doing there?" He encountered it again as he and other clergy mobilized to confront Britain's social problems: poverty, unemployment and slum housing.

> We are often told that the Church has nothing to do with social questions; that there is no social Gospel; and that we should stick to our real busines of saving individual souls. There is truth in that warning, but in the way it is often put is just the half-truth which is the most dangerous sort of lie . . . but there is a degrading and destructive poverty which starves and stunts the human soul and makes death, not fulness of life. Against that the Church, if she be true to herself, and true to her Lord, must wage ceaseless and remitting war.[50]

He felt the organized church was responsible to mobilize its resources to defeat poverty and the social ills that accompanied it. But it was not just a corporate church responsibility, it was also an individual one. Every Christian bore a fundamental responsibility to defeat this great social ill. He felt it was a litmus test of an individual's Christianity; anyone who was not moved by the sight of hungry children, of unemployed workers loitering on the street, or of overworked miners striking for a decent wage to support their families should seriously consider the efficacy of their faith.

> He could not understand the present state of things having the approval of anyone who was not either soft in the head or hard in the heart, or both. He was sick to death of it, and the thing he was afraid of was not red revolution, but going on as they were, muddling along with millions of beastly, dirty, ramshackle cottages, and people housed like pigs, and starved children, and under-fed women. . . . Housing is not a class matter, and if you're not ashamed in your very bones of the houses people live in in this country you're not even a decent man, let alone a Christian.[51]

In the final analysis, for Studdert Kennedy, the social gospel was a "God thing!" He believed that a Christian social conscience and action were foundational to the church, that "The dream of a new and better social order is as much an essential part of the Christian life as is prayer, and communion with God."[52] Ultimately, the question boiled down to one important point for him, "I believe it is God's will that we should destroy poverty."[53]

This is the point at which the Studdert Kennedy and the ICF found common ground. The social goals that motivated Studdert Kennedy were shared by the ICF and its leadership. More important, the ICF was an organization that commanded a large force of volunteers and a visionary leader in the Rev. J.T.R. Kirk. The organization also enjoyed the backing of the Church of England and well-connected members both within government and the economic world. When Studdert Kennedy signed on with the ICF in 1922, he inherited a charter that enjoyed the blessing of the bishops of the Church of England. A 1922 report in the *Birmingham Gazette* explained this important document.

> The archbishops led the way in 1920 with the very full and impartial report of the committee which they appointed to investigate industrial and social questions. This report gave the authoritative attitude of the church on such questions as housing, wages, leisure, trade unions, unemployment, the rights and duties of property, women's work, and all the manifold problems of industrial life. . . . The Industrial Christian Fellowship set to work to translate this great creed into action.[54]

Unemployment

Unemployment served as a vexing problem that fueled many of the inequities that challenged Britain's economic system and were condemned by Studdert Kennedy. The percentage of British unemployed during the 1920s averaged 10 percent, with some industries experiencing much higher numbers. Unemployment insurance, "the dole," guaranteed some workers a minimum income while they sought work, but not all workers were covered, and it expired eventually. For Studdert Kennedy, it seemed especially unjust that many of the unemployed were the soldiers with whom he had served in France. In a 1924 interview with the *New York Times*, he blamed unemployment on

> overcrowded conditions in the British Isles, which he said has created serious unemployment problem from which the veterans of the great war suffer most. Many an Englishman who fought for three or four years in the war," he said, "is wandering the streets starving and out of work, wondering bitterly what all the great upheaval has been about.[55]

As Studdert Kennedy traveled the country to support the ICF's mission, he often spoke to the unemployed men gathered to hear his encouraging words. His heart was deeply touched by their difficulties and their hardness of life. Unfortunately, their problems were shared by even those who could find work, the working poor. In a speech titled, "Christianity and Industrial Life," an address that he delivered hundreds of times during his travels with the ICF, he commented,

> "I suppose you would not say I was wrong if I say we are in a devil of a mess." He continued, "If you went round to some of the unemployed meetings as I have done and if you had seen the state of the men's bodies and souls you would realize how awful their lot is. And if you went to the blast furnaces and the engineering shops in the great centers to see the work men are doing and how the world is run you would realize in some degree how hard their life is."[56]

As today, there were many uninformed opinions regarding the situation of the unemployed. Some believed that unemployment insurance would cause men to become slackers, receiving the "dole" while enjoying a vacation on the government's expense. Others said the unemployed were "work-shy," another term for lazy. It was widely believed that the unemployed were less capable or intelligent than those who had work. Studdert Kennedy railed against these misconceptions and stood up for the dignity of the unemployed as well as those who were fortunate to have continuous, if insufficient, work. Instead of character or intelligence deficiencies, he attributed the economic problems of the country to a broken social system.

> In opening, he drew a word picture of the misery of unemployment and told how he had led two thousand unemployed men to the Guardians for relief, and how he sang comic songs to cheer the hunger marchers from Leeds to London. He had seen some of the men in France, and he thought the present condition of things was an appalling disgrace to the country. He had heard it said in a comfortable room that these men were work-shy. To talk about the majority being work-shy was an abominable lie. They were men as good as any, mentally, morally and spiritually, and they were absolutely destitute but for the dole, and that was not sufficient to keep body and soul together. . . . There was something deeply wrong with our social system that we had not yet put right.[57]

Some of the most difficult economic and work conditions existed in England's coal-mining regions. Postwar Britain was plagued with nearly continuous coal strikes during the early 1920s, but the problems came to a head in late 1925 and resulted in the general strike of 1926. The ICF and Studdert Kennedy played a key role in attempting to resolve the vexing issues that led to the strike.

The General Strike and Coal Strike of 1926

An important example of the ICF's effort to move the church into the working world was its role in Britain's continuing coal strikes and labor's attempt to resolve the coal issue through the 1926 general strike. Rev. P. T. R. Kirk is reported to have played a key role in working with the bishops and union leaders to bring about a solution to the problem that has been described as "the closest thing to a British civil war in the last hundred years."[58] Studdert Kennedy played a role as adviser and intermediary and was present at ICF headquarters when the bishops met with representatives of the Miners' Federation in July 1926 to "confer on the possibility of securing a just settlement in the coal dispute."[59]

Studdert Kennedy conducted ICF crusades in the industrial areas and visited the mines. He observed the conditions of workers and their families firsthand and spoke with them concerning the conditions they endured. He had firsthand knowledge of conditions in the mines and understood that events were reaching a breaking point. In late 1925 he visited with Ramsay MacDonald,[60] head of the Labour Party and leader of the opposition, and implored him to take action. It is indicative of Studdert Kennedy's stature that he was accorded a meeting with the head of the Labour Party and future (and past) prime minister of England.

> Well I went to Mr. MacDonald in the House of Commons. I walked up and down his room and talked in a torrent.[61] I told him what I saw and feared ahead. I remember saying, "There is going to be a devil of a row, the devil of a row, and O God, Mr. MacDonald, we cannot afford a row. It does not matter two rotten old rust pins who wins the row, the people will pay for it, the women and children will pay for it. Can't we stop it before it's too late?" He agreed in the main with what I said. . . . But he was doubtful, very doubtful about stopping it.[62]

Studdert Kennedy's efforts proved unfruitful, and the general strike occurred, throwing the country into turmoil but, in the end, lasting only nine days. The coal miners' strike continued, however, until November 1926, with lockouts, some miners going back to work in violation of the strike, and general strife in the coal regions. The bishop's efforts to resolve the difficulties and bring peace to the warring parties encountered opposition in the press and from both political and religious leaders.[63] The bishops claimed a victory, however, stating that the presence of the church in these disputes proved the efficacy of the church as it sought to resolve social disputes through the application of its gospel responsibility.

> The Bishops, attempting to bring about resolution and reconciliation, proposed that the parties come to discuss for negotiations and proposed a solution based upon the government's own Coal Committee Report. The Bishop's solution was called the "Bishop's Memorandum" or the "Bishop's Terms." "The Bishops and the Free Church leaders he said, did not set out to harass the government. They fell back on the Coal Committee Report. They acted as mediators and negotiators and carried to the government the proposals of the miners. And they would do it again and again. They were ministers first of all of a gospel of reconciliation."[64]

Unfortunately the bishops' effort proved unsuccessful, and the miners' strike dragged on until the end of 1926. Many again asked the question that Studdert Kennedy had encountered so many times before, "What was the church doing there." In describing the bishops' and ICF's effort to the *New York*

Times during a brief visit at the end of 1926, he declared that the general strike itself had been a success, but the coal strike was a great source of grief for everyone involved. The bishops' intervention had resulted in one important accomplishment, that the working people of Britain understood that the church cared for the needs and concerns of everyday people.

> The General Strike in England was a triumph, there wasn't the slightest sign of revolution, but the coal strike has been a miserable, protracted piece of folly with bad leadership on both sides and a bad spirit. It has petered out now and settled nothing. Dr. Kennedy said he was one of the band of clergy, called the "Bishop's Terms," which tried to bring about peace in the miner's strike, but which was not able to accomplish much because of "untimely publicity thrown on their efforts," He was confident however, that their efforts made the working people realize that the church really cared for a just solution of the problem.[65]

Studdert Kennedy was not kind toward the politicians who had brought about the end of the coal strike with a disastrous defeat for the miners; a decrease in wages and extended working hours. Referring to events leading up to the 1926 strikes, he derided the government and owner's efforts in clear terms. "We needed vigorous national action in 1925, and all we got was a sloppy subsidy, granted by a sloppy government, to be used in a sloppy way."[66] In December 1926, he declared that the miners had not received a fair deal, that all who warmed their hands and homes on a coal fire (and everyone did) should be ashamed! He declared,

> "The miners had not had a fair deal. I don't want," he said, "to warm my hands and see a picture of want in the fire, and if you warm your hand in the fire and cannot see a picture of want in the mining villages you are too hard in the heart and too soft in the head. There is no blacker page in the history of man than the history of coal," proceeded Mr. Kennedy. "Christ has been crucified in it again and again. I don't care to what party you belong, or to what class you belong, when you take out your bit of coal you ought to look at it and be ashamed."[67]

In a 1927 *John Bull* article, he once again took up the case of the miners and the treatment they had received at the hands of the government and owners. His empathy for the struggling miners and their families was evident in the article, and he agonized that others did not feel the same passion and concern that he did. While the resolution of the strike did result in the distribution of coal to the country and a resumption of commercial life, it was no victory.

> A week or so ago I returned from a visit to the valleys of South Wales. . . . It is an utterly damnable state of affairs. . . . How can I make you see it? To be up to your ears in debt, and to work beyond your strength for a wage which even

> in a full week is not sufficient to keep up that strength; to be haunted by the fear that your health will fail, and to know that our wife is haunted too, and is secretly going short to feed you; to see no hope, no matter how hard you work, of ever getting out of debt; to have lost all your savings through the lapse of some wretched industrial insurance policy; to be living in a disreputable insanitary cottage in a dingy street between two barren hills, and looking forward to living there all your life; to wake in the middle of the night in a muck sweat of fear that you are going to be ill—that is a common-place of life inside a miner's mind. . . . The miners at present are beaten and broken men. What I want to insist upon is that this victory over the miners is not a national victory, but a national defeat and disaster.[68]

The disaster for the miners and the conditions of working people in general led to dissatisfaction on the part of many workers. This dissatisfaction provided an opening for revolutionary elements who sought drastic solutions. The ICF and Studdert Kennedy stood as a bulwark against their efforts.

Studdert Kennedy and the ICF: Anti-Communist Bulwark

The ICF and Studdert Kennedy played another essential role in 1920s Britain. Postwar Britain was flooded with various political and economic movements: communism, socialism, labor unions, liberals, Tories, and so on. The most dangerous of these was militant and revolutionary communism. During the 1920s, the full extent of the Communist Revolution in Russia was not yet understood, but reports were leaking from Russia of vast humanitarian abuses, of the destruction of the church and of the murder of priests and bishops. The ICF sought to oppose the efforts of communist agitators in Britain, surreptitiously at first and more obviously later, and to channel the dissatisfaction of Britain's workers into less dangerous directions. A 1922 newspaper article described the work of the ICF as guiding the current economic currents into "safe Christian channels."[69] A 1928 article was much clearer in describing the ICF's anti-communist role and efforts. The author stated that the ICF was not a political organization, but a Christian organization that sought to oppose the efforts of communist agitators by means of ICF missioners who worked alongside the workers and shared their work and home life.

> Much of the work lies in opposing the evil influence of Communist and anti-Christian propaganda which is being spread among the sorely dissatisfied workers throughout the length and breadth of the land. Outside the factories, by the dock gates. In public houses, at street corners where masses of unemployed men gather, the Communist speakers take their stand. Now, side by side with them, there appears the Fellowship messenger, urging men to a spirit of goodwill and sane patience, instead of allowing the bitter, revolutionary, and un-Christian

> doctrines of Communism and atheism to possess them. These men are not clergymen. They are men who have been through the mill of factory and workshop themselves. They are for the most part men who are trade unionists. They do not talk conventional religious platitudes, though they bring Christ's message. They deal in practical questions of economics, expounding the Christian Fellowship view on vital matters that are the greatest factors of present-day life in the work centers of the country. . . . And as a rule they get a better hearing and a more popular reception than do the mouthpieces of Communism that they are fighting.[70]

Studdert Kennedy shared in the ICF's opposition to communism. In his writings and speeches he denounced Karl Marx as the leader of a false religion and the enemy of Christianity.[71] He asserted that Christianity and communism were like fire and water, they could not mix.[72] In his 1921 book *Democracy and the Dog Collar*, he presented a discussion between two individuals he described as Mr. O.C. (organized church) and Mr. O.L. (organized labor). Speaking of Marx, he described him as the prophet of a doomed movement who was better off buried and forgotten. Speaking for the organized church, he said of Marx,

> It is extraordinary how impossible it is to get rid of the ghost of Karl Marx. *Das Kapital* is really the Bible of the working classes; they swear by it and don't read it, and could not understand it if they did. I am fed up with the whole performance. I believe that old gentleman ought to be buried. He was not really a prophet, he was only a disease.[73]

Studdert Kennedy understood, however, that communism possessed an appeal for working-class men and women who had been mistreated by the British social and economic system. "As a view of life it has strong attractions, especially for those whose conditions are intolerable. Its kingdom of comfort for all, its appeal to suspicious class hatred and force, give it a powerful hold over discontented men."[74] He disagreed with and opposed the Marxists' view of economic determinism, that men were destined by their economic situation to an inevitable fight to the death between the proletariat and the bourgeois, between workers and capital. He argued that Englishmen possessed one vital character trait that would defeat the Marxist effort, their independence. Englishmen possessed moral freedom to choose for themselves and that, when guided by God-given insight, would favor a democracy that would defeat communism and poverty and provide dignity for all.[75]

In only one element did Studdert Kennedy suggest that the church should mimic the communists. The church needed to get out of its beautiful cathedrals and into the streets and workplaces to oppose the communists where they were most effective, alongside the working men and women of Britain.[76]

Instead of propaganda, which he believed was based on lies, he suggested that the ICF and the church should counter communist propaganda with truth. Victory over the communist threat required an offensive mindset; passivity would be rewarded only by defeat. He stated that "these were days of propaganda, and the church must follow the example of the Communists, Socialists and politicians generally, and go out and speak from boxes at street corners, not to propagate, but to tell the truth."[77]

Ultimately, Studdert Kennedy was certain that communism would be defeated in England. He believed this because he had faith in God and in the workingmen of England with whom he had shared the years of grinding warfare in France. He believed in the ultimate goodness of the English worker and their love and commitment to family. Because they had accomplished victory in France, he also believed they would accomplish victory over communism and the deficiencies in the British social and economic system. While Studdert Kennedy was vehemently opposed to communism and socialism, he fully supported the goals of the labor movement.

> In its militant industrial and political aspects it (Communism) was the natural result of grinding poverty and a sense of intolerable injustice, but as a moral movement it was born at home. And there still lies its great moral and spiritual strength. It is not the political agitator or the paid socialistic spouter, but the love of his wife and kids that fires the soul of the best of the Labour men. It is that love which has made and will continue to make the movement irresistible until the wrongs it seeks to right are righted, and the injustices it seeks to remove are removed.[78]

Studdert Kennedy understood England and its people. He traveled throughout the industrial sectors of the country and knew that the message of the communists, while it commanded a hearing and promised great revolution, would not work in England. He believed that at its core England was not communist, and never would be. In his heart, he believed that the core of England was Christian.

> "The heart of England is still as Christian as can be," he said. In this connection he told how, while speaking to miners and working people in all parts of England during the coal strike, he found that Communism was only surface. He referred to Cook, the Communist leader of the miners in the great strike, as being "made a sort of king." "Communism, he continued, "that wretched thing they got from Russia, is the curse of trade unionism and of the whole working-class movement. I do not believe the amount of declared communism among the working people is important at all. It acts as a sort of ferment creating unreal fears on one side and unreal hopes on the other side. It is a sort of fanatical faith."[79]

Studdert Kennedy's Opposition to Class Warfare

The one danger posed by communism that Studdert Kennedy feared was class warfare. This was, of course, a central tenet of communism that Studdert Kennedy believed would fail, but class conflict was an ongoing reality in Britain's stratified social system and a daily reality in the industrial world to which the ICF sought to minister. The ongoing warfare pitted the unions and workers (labor) against the industrial owners (capital).

Throughout the 1920s, ongoing labour disputes pitted the industrial owners (capital) and the working classes (labor) against each other. Wildcat strikes and lockouts were a regular occurrence. Of particular concern were the coal miners, who, because of shifting market factors and a general fall in coal prices, saw their wages cut and working hours extended. When the miners walked out, the ripple effects on other sectors of the economy were extensive, with coal-dependent industries having to reduce or suspend operations altogether.

Studdert Kennedy spent a good deal of effort opposing this class warfare, often using somewhat questionable rhetoric[80] to oppose the Marxist and militant socialist efforts to fan the flames of economic conflict. He was emphatic about the answer to the problem. Capitalists and labor alike had to work against the passions that threatened to break out in open warfare, that characterized the competing interests as enemies on an inevitable collision course. Some strikes had resulted in open conflict and bloodshed, and Studdert Kennedy opposed this conflict as vehemently as he opposed warfare between nations. He believed that nothing good could come of war between nations, and he was even more certain nothing good could result from industrial and class conflict. He suggested that miners and owners reframe their thinking, that instead of enemies, they should recognize the essential interdependence of the miners' and owners' interests, that one could not exist without the other. Continued conflict would be devastating to all. He suggested that only one solution would bring peace and prosperity to both sides. "The only other way out of the difficulty was to make men feel that they were not workers first, nor employers first, but sons of God first."[81]

As we have seen in these pages, Studdert Kennedy was deeply troubled by the economic and social problems facing his country. He spent years working to bring about an end to poverty and championed the cause of the unemployed and underpaid workers who struggled to earn a living wage. He suggested that the only way to address these ongoing problems was to reframe the nature of work and endow it with a renewed commitment to human dignity.

STUDDERT KENNEDY'S SOLUTIONS

Studdert Kennedy suggested solutions that he believed would address the problems that he identified within the British economic and social system. He believed that those solutions began with an awakened conscience of those in society who had the means and ability to move government to find solutions that would work. He believed that a revived Christian faith and conscience accompanied by duty and sacrificial service would move Britain in a positive direction. An important element of his effort was to awaken the human conscience of the nation to empathize with those who faced hunger, unemployment, and homelessness. He painted word-pictures of the destitute and poverty stricken that he hoped would touch the hearts of the masses, even as he had been touched. But an awakened conscience was not enough; he also communicated a message for those who possessed wealth and position, that they bore a responsibility to solve the problems of the poor.

The message that he hoped to communicate to those in positions of power, whether political or industrial, was that those positions of power and wealth were accompanied with a responsibility to use their position in service to the greater community. In his 1919 book *Lies*, he compared the individual of wealth or power who refused to serve the public to the colorful and bloated flies that fed off the bodies of the dead on the battlefield. He did not direct his criticism only at capitalists but included the leaders of the trade unions, for they too possessed a great deal of power due to their position and the resources of the unions. He believed and taught that all those in power must wield their power in a responsible way to overcome," . . . the evils of poverty, overcrowding and sordid conditions of life."[82]

Studdert Kennedy aimed his criticisms and recommendations at owners and financiers as well as at the workers. For the workers, he encouraged that they provide an honest day's work for their pay and that they not abuse the "dole." But he reserved his harshest criticism for the wealthy industrialists and reminded them of the biblical truth "To whom much has been given shall much be required."[83] He based his criticism on the fact that the workers had little to look forward to but poor housing and meager pay and nothing to fall back on should they lose their jobs. The wealthy possessed vast resources and the benefits that accrued from those resources: adequate housing, healthcare, education, and leisure.

> Dealing with industrial problems, the speaker said that large profits were blamed by employers because they took big risks, but the greatest risk of all was that of unemployment. The worker had nothing to fall back on, and he should have payment for his risk.[84]

Studdert Kennedy rejected the calls of the communists that the wealthy's resources be redistributed to the masses, there was simply not enough to go around, but he reminded the wealthy that their wealth was accompanied by ethical and moral responsibility, it was a stewardship. That stewardship required that capitalists and industrialists utilize their resources to help the greater community address the problems and issues it faced. He reminded them that their wealth originated with the work of the masses and that they had a moral responsibility to care for the needs of those whose labor sustained their opulent lifestyles.[85]

> But that man who has the 10,000 pounds knows it is legally his own, and he gets it into his head that it is morally his own, and that he can do what he likes with it, that is moral wickedness. Christ would have called it sin. That money came out of the sweat and blood of human beings. It is a trust from God, and you have to put it to the best use possible use for his people. The idea that it is morally our own arises from a system of thought which leaves God out of consideration.[86]

Studdert Kennedy also attacked the capitalist concept of the "amorality of business," what he called "business morality." He rejected the idea that the businessman could ignore morality, seek profit at any cost, and follow the "let the buyer beware" approach. He believed and taught that ethics and morality must underlie all social interactions, that lies were unwelcome in business and daily interaction even as they were unwelcome in church. Defrauding one another and lying in business (and politics) led to the collapse of morality in every sphere of public and private life. "We can lie in business, we can lie in politics, we can lie in commerce—get that far, and there soon won't be anywhere we can't lie."[87]

Finally, Studdert Kennedy sought to instill in British society a transformed view of the workers who served as the foundation and lifeblood of the economy. He wished to elevate their public stature from that of uneducated wage slave to a place of honor, similar to that held by the soldiers who had won the war. He sought to elevate the dignity of work!

> We cannot get democracy until we recognize that the man who digs our country's coal is as much in the service as the man who kills our country's foes, and the man who drives the British trains as much in the service as the man who trains the British guns. . . . We must recognize it and honor labour accordingly. Half the trouble is that we do not honor the workman as we honored the soldier.[88]

Studdert Kennedy also hoped to elevate the self-perception of the workers themselves, that they would come to understand that they performed honorable service. Their work, he pointed out, whether in a coal mine or a coffee shop was an essential public service. He believed that the dignity of work should be viewed as sacramental service, that the worker's physical efforts should be equated with the sacramental service of the priest at the altar.

> I want the miner to feel when he is down there in his pit that he is not merely working for his wage—working for Friday night—a wage slave—but that he is a Priest of God, a Priest of Love called by God to produce warmth and power for his brothers in the world. I want him to feel that he is as much a priest down there in the dark, filthy black and streaming with sweat, as I am a priest when I stand at the altar and plead for the wants of men. The coal black is as white as my white robes, and sweat is sacramental wine poured in service of God's world. He is the right honourable the Collier, one of the greatest and worthiest servants of the human race. I want him to feel that way about himself, and I want other people to feel that about him.[89]

Ultimately, Studdert Kennedy wanted workers to understand that God accompanied them as they entered the workplace, as they descended into the mines. As he comforted his beloved soldiers with the knowledge that God would accompany them into the battlefield and "No Man's Land" to face the bullets and artillery shells of the enemy, God would accompany Britain's workers into their workplaces. He had introduced Britain's soldiers to the Suffering God. He also introduced Britain's workers to the "Worker God!"

> "Then Will He Come"
>
> When in the darkest depths the miner striving,
> Feels in his arms the vigour of the Lord,
> Strikes for a kingdom and his King's arriving,
> Holding his pick more splendid than the sword;
> . . .
> Then will He come with meekness for His glory,
> God in a workman's jacket as before,
> Living again the eternal Gospel story,
> Sweeping the shavings from his workshop floor.[90]

Studdert Kennedy's solution to Britain's economic and social ills found their foundation in his Christian faith. As he traveled Great Britain preaching the message of the ICF, he attacked the social ills of the country, laid blame and criticism at the feet of those who deserved it, and always found opportunity to visit the unemployed, the imprisoned, and the hungry. He used his own means to help others, even denying those means to his own family at times. His message was always based on Christian truth and the need for the awakening of Christian character and action. He hoped and prayed for the time when England would become a "city on a hill" and Britain's people would work with Christ to establish the New Jerusalem. It was this hope, this vision that drove and motivated him to work for the well-being of England and its citizens, even as it had motivated him as he served the British soldiers in France and Belgium.

> The vision of eternal life makes men see life as one. . . . All the earth becomes a sacrament. Every hill-top speaks of heaven, and every flower flames with God. Men with the vision are not indifferent to this world, but are keen to make it perfect with a keenness that no worldly man could ever know. They detest slums because they poison eternal spirits; they loathe all waste of human life because all human life is of infinite and eternal worth. . . . The men of vision cannot think of privilege except as another name for responsibility; wealth to them means work for others, and position a chance of wider service. . . . When you think of men as sons of God, you do not mind much whether they are princes or porters, publicans or prime ministers. The only thing that matters is that they are men. These men neither envy the rich nor patronize the poor, and they do not waste their time on hatred. To them a snob is, not so much a sinner, as a fool who is not really living . . . missing half his friends because he cannot see a man behind a suit of clothes. . . . In the light of eternal truth I can see a new London, the New Birmingham, Liverpool, Manchester, and Leeds, coming down from heaven prepared as a bride adorned for her husband.[91]

CONCLUSION

Studdert Kennedy always viewed the soldiers he served in France as the epitome of Christ's sacrificial offering as they fought and died on the front lines of freedom. In his New Jerusalem, he likewise saw God's presence in the workers who manned the blast furnaces and the mines who daily offered their sweat and labor on the altar of Britain's commerce. As he sought to defeat war and poverty, he hoped for a time when all would work together to create an idyllic Britain. In the context of Studdert Kennedy's post-traumatic growth and recovery from moral injury, I would judge that his wartime experiences and memories accompanied him throughout the ten years that he survived the war, and that those experiences drove and motivated him to publicly serve those who he felt needed his service the most. He successfully surmounted the physical, moral, and spiritual challenges of his wartime experiences, although he remained deeply changed by them.

In his own life, Studdert Kennedy sought to live what he described as a transforming life. He sought to transform Britain from what he had described as selfish and cruel to one that would recognize and celebrate the dignity of all human life and work. The epitome of that type of service was summed up in his view of Christ.

> The great man is the transforming man and Jesus is the transforming man par excellence. It is in that quality that I discover the key to crucial question we are trying to answer, "What kind of human life did Jesus live on earth? He lived a transforming life. He was in perfection the artist man, the creative warrior.[92]

Studdert Kennedy would probably not welcome the application of this description to himself. He was always self-effacing and too aware of his own failures and imperfections to develop a swelled head. He epitomized the transformative life as a frail and damaged human being who "put it all out there" for the people he served. He was beset by moral and spiritual challenges brought about by the war and by his dissatisfaction and disappointment with Britain's social and economic conditions and its failures to care for the most vulnerable. For them he dedicated his life in service and duty, often at great personal cost. Fueled by his war experiences and postwar disappointment, he built a life of service and sacrifice for the welfare of others. In my mind, this the very definition of post-traumatic growth and transformation.

Studdert Kennedy never abandoned the love he felt for the soldiers he had served in France. He transferred that love to Britain's unemployed and working men and women, often the very soldiers he had served in the war and to whom he committed his life and work during his postwar years. His efforts focused national and political attention on poverty and working-class conditions. He provided hope and encouragement for those masses as he preached Christ-inspired social change in thousands of halls, parks, and churches. His sacrificial efforts came at a price, however, both to his health and to his family. His asthma-damaged health gradually deteriorated due to the rigorous speaking and traveling schedule he pursued. His family was denied the presence of the husband and father that they had every right to expect after the grueling years of separation during the war. One wonders if the sacrificial schedule he undertook was driven by guilt he assumed for his role in the war as well as the fact that he survived while so many others did not. While I believe his efforts on behalf of the Industrial Christian Fellowship are evidence of post-traumatic growth, I understand that they are also evidence that he carried the wounds of mental, moral, and spiritual injury with him the rest of his life.

Contemporary warriors who face the rigors of combat benefit from the experiences of those who fought in the wars of the twentieth century. Lessons learned from their experiences and trauma have resulted in greater understanding of the psychological and spiritual challenges faced by war's survivors. They have also resulted in the development of resources to aid them in their recovery, for recovery is possible. Those resources include new treatments available to psychologists, medical personnel, and chaplains as they seek to assist today's war veterans. Our knowledge of combat stress, moral injury, spiritual injury, and PTSD is constantly improving and will benefit today's and future warriors and their caregivers who share the rigors and the lasting impact of the battlefield. These insights and continuing education serve as a resource to help us build the resilience that will enable us to survive and recover from life's inevitable traumas. The presence of a caring and healing community is an essential resource, and we must never be embarrassed to seek help there.

My personal takeaway from my reflection on Studdert Kennedy's life and my own experience of trauma is the conclusion that a strong personal faith is often severely challenged when faced with combat stress, moral injury, or PTSD. These experiences often reveal the imperfections and fallacies of dearly held beliefs inherited from family or adopted without serious reflection. Traumatic experiences may throw those beliefs into question or even reveal them as myths. We may discover that they do not address the questions that death and its associated griefs throw at us, that they do not sustain us in the face of trauma and war. We may suffer spiritual desolation. But continued reflection on these issues can serve as a source of resilience in the midst of trauma, as it can guide us to a new, more accurate understanding of faith and life stripped of the myths and misunderstandings that misled us in the first place. We can emerge from the painful process, like Studdert Kennedy, with a lasting hope tempered by a personal acquaintance with life's suffering. Perhaps this is wisdom.

> Peace does not mean the end of all our striving;
> Joy does not mean the drying of our tears;
> Peace is the power that comes to souls arriving
> Up to the light where God Himself appears.[93]

NOTES

1. Michael Brierly, "Geoffrey Studdert Kennedy: A Brief Life" in Michael W. Brierly and Georgina A. Byrne, *Life after Tragedy: Essays on Faith and the First World Evoked by Geoffrey Studdert Kennedy* (Eugene, Oregon: Cascade Books, 2017), 30.
2. 1st Baptist Salinas Men's Zoom Meeting, March 5, 2021. During the meeting I described Studdert Kennedy's war service. One gentleman, a former Army Medic and veteran of Desert Storm, made the comment that "Everyone who experiences war has his limits."
3. G. A. Studdert Kennedy, *Lies* (London: Hodder & Stoughton, 1919), 143. See also G. A. Studdert Kennedy, *Rough Rhymes of a Padre* (London: Hodder & Stoughton, 1918), 17.
4. G. A. Studdert Kennedy, *The Hardest Part* (London: Hodder & Stoughton, 1918), 60–161.

5. G. A. Studdert Kennedy. *The Word and the Work* (London: Longmans, Green and Co., 1925), 55–56.
6. William Purcell, *Woodbine Willie: A Biography* (London: Hodder & Stoughton, 1962), 152.
7. Vincent R. Stanrino, W. Patrick Sullivan, Clyde T. Angel and Loaunne W. Davis, "Moral Injury, Coherence, and Spiritual Repair." *Mental Health, Religion and Culture* 22, no.1 (2019), 102.
8. "Understanding Post-Traumatic Growth," *Psychology Today*. www.psychologytoday.com/us/basics/post-traumatic-growth accessed March 1, 2021 at 0839. See also Rita Nakashima Brock and Gabriella Lettini, *Soul Repair* (Boston: Beacon Press, 2012), 91, and Jonathan Shay, *Odysseus in America: Combat Trauma and the Trials of Coming Home* (New York: Scribner, 2002), 152, 175.
9. G. A. Studdert Kennedy, *The Warrior, the Woman, and the Christ* (London: Hodder & Stoughton, 1928), 152.
10. Shay, *Odysseus in America*, 152, 175. See also Rita Nakashima Brock and Gabriella Lettini, *Soul Repair* (Boston: Beacon Press, 2012), 91.
11. Studdert Kennedy, *The Word and the Work*, 57–58.
12. Ibid., 69.
13. G. A. Studdert Kennedy, *The Wicket Gate* (London: Hodder & Stoughton, 1923), 69.
14. "Age of Problems: Christianity in Industry," *North Devon Journal*, July 19,1928, p. 7. See also, "A Preacher's Power: Rev. G.A. Studdert Kennedy's Visit to Coventry," *Midland Daily Telegraph*, March 5, 1926.
15. Rita Nakashima Brock and Gabriella Lettini, *Soul Repair: Recovering from Moral Injury after War* (Boston: Beacon Press, 2012), 42. Brock and Lettini observe that many survivors of moral injury develop an aversion to war and participate in anti-war efforts.
16. "Fruits of Victory, Woodbine Willie's Analysis of our Times." *Northampton Mercury*, May 12, 1922, 13.
17. "Woodbine Willie at Tunbridge Wells," *The Courier*, June 1, 1923, 11
18. Ibid.
19. "Age of Problems: Christianity in Industry," *North Devon Journal*, July 19, 1928, 7.
20. G. A. Studdert Kennedy, "The Woman Who Lost Christmas," *John Bull*, Dec. 24, 1927, 15.
21. "No More War; Today's Call from the Nations; Hyde Park Rally." *Westminster Gazette*, Sat. 29 July 1922, 8.
22. "No More War Rallies, Hyde Park" *The Scotsman*, July 31, 1922. 9
23. "Alternative to War: The League of Nations." *Sunderland Daily Echo*, Monday May 14, 1923, 5.
24. "Ruling Out War: Rev. S. Kennedy on Individual Conscience," *Birmingham Gazette*, Thursday April 10, 1924., 6.
25. "Fear of Armistice Day," *Mansfield Reporter and Sutton Times*, Fri. Nov. 11, 1927.

26. "Army Padre on the Right Way to World Peace," *The Leader*, Friday June 23, 1922, 7.

27. G. A. Studdert Kennedy, "The Accursed Thing," *John Bull*, Nov. 12, 1927, 24.

28. "1000 at City Service, Woodbine Willie and the Power of Money." *Westminster Gazette*, Nov. 11, 1922.

29. "Where War Starts." *Yorkshire Evening Post*, Thurs. Sept 21, 1922.

30. Studdert Kennedy, *The Warrior, the Woman, and the Christ*, 308.

31. Ibid., 308–312.

32. "Socialistic Theories Exploded," *Shipley Times and Express*, Friday Oct. 6, 1922, 5.

33. Studdert Kennedy, *The Wicket Gate*, 245–246.

34. G. A. Studdert Kennedy, *Democracy and the Dog Collar* (London: Hodder & Stoughton, 1921), 206–207.

35. Studdert Kennedy, *The Wicket Gate*, 245–246.

36. Ibid., 86.

37. "World-Wide Demand for No More War." *Daily Herald*, Monday July 30, 1923. 2.

38. Studdert Kennedy, *The Wicket Gate*, 88–89

39. G. A. Studdert Kennedy, "The Answer's A Lemon," *John Bull*, May 29, 1926, 17.

40. G. A. Studdert Kennedy, *Songs of Faith and Doubt* (London: Hodder & Stoughton, 1922), 52–53.

41. Ramsay MacDonald.

42. G. A. Studdert Kennedy, "Let the Prince Speak Out," *John Bull*, Feb. 23, 1929, 9.

43. Gerald Studdert Kennedy, *Dog Collar Democracy* (London: Macmillan Press, 1982), 3.

44. "Like Pigs in Hovels," *Yorkshire Evening Post*, March 8, 1928, 9.

45. A 1922 editorial in the socialist paper *Forward* noted that a recent speech was proof of his conversion to socialism, after quoting extensively from his speech on unemployment, the author concluded, "Not bad for a King's Chaplain!" "The Socialism of a King's Chaplain," *Forward*, July 22, 1922, 5.

46. "The Position of Socialism," *Yorkshire Post*, July 17, 1913.

47. "A Preacher's Power: Rev. G.A. Studdert Kennedy's Visit to Coventry," *Midland Daily Telegraph*, Friday March 5, 1926.

48. Studdert Kennedy, *The Hardest Part*, 195–196.

49. "Woodbine Willie; Powerful Address on the Serious Results of Poverty." *The Advertiser*, Oct. 26, 1928, 14.

50. Studdert Kennedy, *The Word and the Work*, 6–7.

51. "Woodbine Willie at Abertillery: Christ's Social Message." *New South Wales Gazette*, Feb 5, 1926.

52. Studdert Kennedy, *The Word and the Work*, 65.

53. "Woodbine Willie at Hastings: Eloquent Message of Christian Fellowship." *Hastings and St. Leonards Observer*, Jan. 21, 1928.

54. "The ICF, The Church and Social Service," *Birmingham Gazette*, March 3, 1922

55. "King's Chaplain Talks to Princeton Classes," *New York Times*, Jan. 14, 1924, 19.

56. "Christianity and Industrial Life," *Hastbourne Chronicle*, April 29, 1922, 6.

57. "Woodbine Willie, Famous Parson's racy Address," *Portsmouth Evening News*, January 26, 1922.

58. Thomas O. Loughlin and Stuart Bell, "Is Studdert Kennedy Relevant to the Twenty-First Century." https://youtu/be/5FjAXPUjBVw. accessed February 1, Accessed February 1, 2021.

59. "T.U.C. Invitation to Miners, Church Intervention," *Birmingham Gazette*, July 15, 1926, 1.

60. Ramsey MacDonald was leader of the Labour Party from 1922–1931, and leader of the opposition in Parliament from 1924–1929. He also served as prime minister twice, first in 1924 and again from 1929–1935. He was leader of the Opposition and Labour Party when Studdert Kennedy met with him.

61. The setting sounds very similar to Studdert Kennedy's meeting with Chaplain Hardy during the war.

62. Studdert Kennedy, "Let the Prince Speak Out," *John Bull*, Feb. 23, 1929, 9.

63. "Confusion Worse Confounded," *South Yorkshire Times and Mexborough and Swinton Times*, Aug. 13, 1926.

64. "Triumph Claimed for Primate," *Nottingham Journal*, Feb. 22, 1927.

65. Britain Puts Hope in Fighting Spirit: King's Chaplain, on Visit Here, Says Nation Has Great Task, but Will Solve Problems," *New York Times*, Dec. 23, 1926. For additional information relating to the bishops' role in the events of 1926 see: Bishop's Coal Peace Plan Unacceptable," *Dundee Courier*, Aug. 5, 1926; "Mr. Cook's Two Voices," *Penrith Observer*, Aug. 3, 1926, 8; "Let the Prince Speak Out," *John Bull*, Feb. 23, 1929, 9; "Not a Fair Deal," *Birmingham Gazette*, Dec. 13, 1926. 3; "Come Off It Coward," *John Bull*, Oct. 15, 1927, 17; "Industrial Christian Fellowship: Rev. G.A. Studdert Kennedy on Socialism," *Gloucester Journal*, Saturday, Sept. 24, 1927; "Starving Out the Miners," *Daily Herald*, June 3, 1926; "The Peer and the Pup," *John Bull*, July 26, 1926, 17.

66. Studdert Kennedy, "Let the Prince Speak Out," *John Bull*, Feb. 23, 1929, 9.

67. "Not a Fair Deal," *Birmingham Gazette*, Dec. 13, 1926. 3.

68. "Come Off It Coward," *John Bull*, Oct. 15, 1927, 17.

69. "The ICF, The Church and Social Service," *Birmingham Gazette*, Wed. March 3, 1922.

70. "Woodbine Willie at Hastings: The Problem of Capital and Labour," *Hastings and St. Leonards Observer*, Jan. 21, 1928.

71. "The Problem of the Churches," *Perthshire Advertiser*, Jan. 19, 1929.

72. "Class War is Anti-Christian," *Peterborough Standard*, April 1, 1927.

73. Studdert Kennedy, *Democracy and the Dog Collar*, 59–60.

74. "Religion and Social Problems," *Western Morning and Mercury*, Nov. 25, 1924.

75. Studdert Kennedy, *Democracy and the Dog Collar*, 92.

76. "Modern Voices of Revolt," *Newcastle Journal*, Jan. 27, 1927.

77. "Defense of Bishops' Intervention: Dr. Temple Explains," Staffordshire Sentinel, Oct. 7, 1926.

78. Studdert Kennedy, *The Warrior, the Woman, and the Christ*, 306–307.

79. Britain Puts Hope in Fighting Spirit: King's Chaplain, on Visit Here, Says Nation Has Great Task, but Will Solve Problems," *New York Times*, Dec. 23, 1926.

80. "Woodbine Willie at Kirkby, Are All Men Equal, Is the World an Unjust Place?" *Mansfield Reporter and Sutton Times*, Mar. 31, 1922, 5.

> The conflict of the strong and the weak in society is the quite inevitable result of the wide differences between the inherited capacities of one individual and another. This is the root cause of what is popularly called the Class War. . . . Class has not merely an accidental economic but an inevitable biological basis.

81. "Woodbine Willie at Kirkby, Are All Men Equal, Is the World an Unjust Place? *Mansfield Reporter and Sutton Times*, Mar. 31, 1922, 5.

82. G. A. Studdert Kennedy, "Why Class Hatred?" *John Bull*, Feb. 7, 1925, 13.

83. Luke 12:48, The Holy Bible.

84. "Woodbine Willie at Tunbridge Wells," *The Courier*, June 1, 1923, 11.

85. He also suggested that the wealthy should teach their children the responsibility of wealth and not to flaunt their privilege. "Woodbine Willie on Playing the Game." *Western Daily Press*, May 11, 1925.

86. "Woodbine Willie at Hastings: Eloquent Message of Christian Fellowship." *Hastings and St. Leonards Observer*, Jan. 21, 1928.

87. Studdert Kennedy, *The Wicket Gate*, 226.

88. Studdert Kennedy, *Lies*, 83.

89. Studdert Kennedy, *Democracy and the Dog Collar*, 99.

90. Studdert Kennedy, *Songs of Faith and Doubt*, 7–8.

91. Studdert Kennedy, *Lies*, 265–267.

92. Studdert Kennedy, *The Warrior, the Woman, and the Christ*, 152.

93. Kirk, "Studdert Kennedy: I.C.F. Crusader" in *G. A. Studdert Kennedy by His Friends,* 171.

Chapter Nine

A Survey of G. A. Studdert Kennedy's Works, 1917–1929

I am providing a survey of Studdert Kennedy's publications to support my discussion of the impact of war and moral injury on the thinking of its victims. While Studdert Kennedy's focus during the postwar years shifted to the economic issues afflicting the working classes, his many postwar works are filled with references to the war, evidence of its continuing impact on his thinking and emotions. Between 1917 and 1929, Studdert Kennedy published eight books of prose, four books of poetry, one novel, and numerous articles in various publications. This is an amazing publishing record, especially since he was fully engaged with the war, his family, and the ICF during those years. I have not found an explanation for his motivation to publish, but his opposition to propaganda, which he defined as lies, and commitment to the truth was an important element of his pastoral ministry, chaplaincy, and mission with the Industrial Christian Fellowship. One goal is evident in his publishing, to communicate Christian truth and encouragement for the Christian community. But he also sought to influence the wider British public to a revival of Christian faith and a revitalized social order based upon Christian truth and ethics, to "build Jerusalem in England's pleasant land."[1]

Studdert Kennedy's subject matter ranged from his experiences in the war, to the exposition of truth (the Apostles' Creed and the Lord's Prayer), marriage and divorce (his one novel, *I Pronounce Them*), and to Christian leadership and the establishment of a Christian social order (*The Warrior, the Woman, and the Christ*). In reading these works, I was struck by the breadth of his knowledge and interaction with the scholars, poets, and thinkers of his time: Darwin, Marx, Wells, Bergson, Milton, Browning, and a host of others. In 1968 Gerald Studdert-Kennedy, his great-nephew, however, described his great-uncle as "no intellectual" but as someone who instead possessed an ability of "reproducing and simplifying arguments that appealed to him from more learned sources"[2] in the service of his rhetoric. My own conclusion is that Gerald Studdert-Kennedy was a bit too harsh on his great-uncle.

What is clear from his writings is the impact of the war on Studdert Kennedy's thinking and writing. Every book, whether prose or poetry, contains images of the war and discussion of his concept of the Suffering God who offers solace to those who suffer from its impact. The battle of the Somme shows up in a number of his works, and becomes a metaphor for the carnage, loss, and evil that is war. His story about tripping over the dead German soldier at the Messines Ridge shows up a number of times, accompanied by his vision of the cross suspended over the battlefield. Studdert Kennedy seemed to interpret all of history in the light of his experiences during the war and sought to bring an end to war itself as well as the poverty and social problems that it produced. Finally, in his last book, the 1929 *The Warrior, the Woman, and the Christ*, he constructed a grand narrative of history that attributed the ills of society to the warrior impulse that imbues business and that led to the great outpouring of blood during the First World War. He suggested that creative conflict between the man and the woman, transferred to the wider world, could create a transformed society guided by Christian ethics and social justice.

Studdert Kennedy's works are certainly dated and contain comments regarding gender, eugenics, and equality that many would find objectionable. But they also contain the passionate words of a man who sought to transform his world through the only way he knew, through his faith. His works also offer an insight into the impact of war on an individual and the impossibility of escaping its memories. It is clear, at least in Studdert Kennedy's experience, that the memories and emotions elicited by war continued to influence his thinking years after his survival of the conflict. For many, there is no end to war once it has been endured. In the following pages, I will provide a brief overview and synopsis of Studdert Kennedy's published works with a special emphasis on his war memories and influences.

ROUGH TALKS BY A PADRE (1916)

Rough Talks by a Padre is Studdert Kennedy's first published book and grew out of a series of sermons he preached at the great British military base at Rouen, France where he was first assigned chaplain duties. D. F. Carey, in his contribution to Studdert Kennedy's posthumous biography, *G. A. Studdert Kennedy by His Friends*, explained that the sermons grew out of a need to address the moral conditions of the troops and to provide an opportunity to utilize Studdert Kennedy's obvious rhetorical skills. The sermons were preached to "great crowds" on Sunday evenings during Lent of 1916. The highlight of the series was achieved on Good Friday, during which Carey reported that the gathered soldiers responded to Studdert Kennedy's final address with a great cheer. "There was the awe, the hush, the silence, and then the roar, and it meant real homage from men who were, hundreds of them, going to their death."[3]

Studdert Kennedy's foreword, written in 1916 at the headquarters of the Physical and Bayonet Training, BEF school (after his participation in the Battle of the Somme in June 1916), concluded with the hope that it would assist his readers in their search for truth as they sought to untangle the "mystery of life."[4] The titles of the chapters are not necessarily indicative of the content of his messages. "What the (blank) is the Church Doing Here, What Are We Fighting For, What Stands in the Way, Are We Going to Get It, Shall Our Dead Have Died in Vain, Reaction and What it Means and Must War Continue" all addressed the challenges and questions the soldiers of the BEF were facing as they confronted the might of the German army. The concluding chapter, "Why Aren't All the Best Chaps Christians?" is a rework of Studdert Kennedy's chapter contained in *The Church in the Furnace*, "The Religious Difficulties of the Private Soldier."

The first chapter was a reply to a question Studdert Kennedy had heard in the trenches, and which occupied him throughout his time in France and even during his postwar efforts on behalf of the poor working classes of Britain. "What the (expletive deleted) is the Church Doing." in war was a question asked of chaplains then and continues to be asked today. Studdert Kennedy noted that he had asked himself the same question as he served as an ineffective stretcher bearer and as an amateur undertaker lying on his "belly muttering the burial service over a broken body lying in a shell hole."[5] He questioned how the "spirit of the bayonet and the spirit of the Cross could be reconciled" in that hell of a war. He found his answer in the sacrificial and sportsmanlike efforts of his soldiers as they went into no-man's-land to retrieve a wounded German soldier Studdert Kennedy had discovered. He answered the question with these words, "It is trying to keep the hope of Heaven alive in the midst of a bloody hell. It is trying to fill the army and to keep it filled with the Spirit of the Cross, the spirit of strong love of Right which will triumph at all costs in the battle against wrong."[6] He hoped to preserve the essential spirit of the English people, the spirit of sportsmanship enlivened by Christian love.

The following chapters ranged over many issues: comparisons between the English and the Germans, with the English exhibiting the superior characteristics; exhortations to fight for Freedom, honor and peace; discussions relating to true freedom; the disease of sensuality and condemnation of prostitution,[7] the evil of the war and the mountains of dead,[8] the Suffering God and his story regarding the officer who asked him in the hospital, "What is God like?"[9] It was here that he first recorded his great vision of the cross overarching the world that would guide him throughout his ministry.

> Ever and always I can see set up above this world of ours a huge and towering cross with great arms held out east and west from the rising to the setting sun, and on that Cross my God still hangs and calls all true men to come out and share his sorrow and help save the world.[10]

Studdert Kennedy concluded that sermon with a challenge to the soldiers of the BEF, that they would vow, before God and their dead comrades, that, "I will love the things for which they died, and hate the things that brought them to their death."[11] Studdert Kennedy certainly knew how to stir the men's hearts and emotions. No wonder they responded with a great roar! He concluded the sermon, and chapter, with these stirring words.

> Once more I bid you see the army of brave sorrow as it marches down the years, and I bid you look to the rear and see the faces of your dead. Proud they are and tearless—glad to be in that train; in Africa and in the Hell Fire of the Somme, men who died the soldier's death on a thousand known and unknown battlefields of this world war. . . . Will ye indeed forever love the things for which we died?[12]

Studdert Kennedy completed the sermon with a call to serve Christ as they served their honored dead.

In the concluding chapters Studdert Kennedy addressed the politics and social problems back home in England. He attacked class warfare and poverty and shared his hopes for the future, that the men of all classes who shared the trenches of the Great War could work together after the war's completion. In "Must War Continue?" he addressed the history of war and asserted that war was an inevitable element of the human condition that could only be conquered by faith. In words that he would repeat from many pulpits after the war, he declared, "Our task when the war is over looks immense and terrible. Poverty at home and fear abroad. Problems everywhere."[13] If Britain could not solve its problems, Studdert Kennedy did not hold out a great deal of hope.

> This much is certain: we shall be poorer, much poorer, than we have been in years. All classes will be poorer. And this fact implies another. We can be sure of this too. Our social problems, which were very complicated and difficult before the war, will be ten times as complicated and ten times as difficult after it. These are two broad certainties on which we can count.[14]

He was certain England would lead the postwar world as it followed the ethics of Christ. The concluding chapter was titled, "Why Aren't All the Best Chaps Christians, and is a rewrite of his chapter from *The Church in the Furnace*, "The Religious Difficulties of the Private Soldier." I'll discuss the content of that work in the following section.

THE RELIGIOUS DIFFICULTIES OF THE PRIVATE SOLDIER (1917)

Studdert Kennedy's first foray into publishing was a chapter in a book of articles by military chaplains titled, *The Church in the Furnace*. He attempted to address the common questions about war and God that he had heard from his soldiers during his service in France. He immediately tackled the most difficult problem they faced. "The first great difficulty of the private soldier is war."[15] In doing so, he addressed theodicy, the problem of evil, and discussed the transcendence and immanence of God. He also introduced his understanding that God in Christ suffers alongside humanity. Studdert Kennedy suggested that God's power is limited by his creation of man's free will, that war is not God's will but the result man's free will, which God would not violate.

The article also included concepts that he would expand in later works. It is clear that he was on a trajectory that would fully expound his understanding of the Suffering God.

> God suffers in every man that suffers. God, the God we love and worship, is no far off God of Power, but the comrade God of love: He is on no heavenly throne, He is up in the trenches, under the guns: for every wound a man receives there is pain in the heart of God, and every cry of agony finds echo in God's soul.[16]

Studdert Kennedy displayed an ability to speak to the soldiers in language they could understand. He continued, "God is not a bad Staff Officer, but a gallant and fatherly Colonel who goes over the top with his men."[17] After establishing this foundation, Studdert Kennedy addressed questions regarding the multiplicity of religions, hypocrisy, and the seeming indifference of God to prayer. He addressed a situation that would often arise in later works, what he termed the "selfish" prayers for protection he heard being offered in the trenches. His advice was that the soldiers instead develop an "utter indifference to death and danger which is one's duty to cultivate."[18] In the following pages he also addressed the truth of the Bible and the "muddle" of the church and the ineffective parsons they had found in the civilian world. He condemned their "affected fashion" and the "dry rot" they projected from the pulpit.[19] Studdert Kennedy asserted that these clergy stood in the way of the church's effectiveness with the common soldier, that Christ could break through to them. Unfortunately, he suggested that the church itself was a great obstacle in this process, like barbed wire that the men had to negotiate in order to reach the truth, for the church had produced a "mist of many lies that dims the vision now."[20] The subject of lies and truth is one that would dominate his thinking and preaching after the war.

Studdert Kennedy's concluding paragraphs would certainly have captured his soldiers' attention. He wrote that he had been writing his essay for the book while engaged in battle at the Messines-Wytschaete Ridge and that his thinking had been paralyzed by the events there. But his thoughts always returned to the soldiers he served. "One picture remains with me: a wooded ridge wrapped in a thick black cloud of battle smoke through which I peered anxiously, knowing that the men I had learned to love were fighting for their very lives.[21]

The chapter in the *Church in the Furnace* was so effective that it was reworked by Studdert Kennedy into a pamphlet titled, "Why Aren't All the Best Chaps Christians" that was distributed widely to British troops in France. It was also included in his 1918 work *Rough Talks by a Padre.*

THE HARDEST PART (WRITTEN IN 1917, PUBLISHED 1918)

The Hardest Part has been described as "the most famous, the most notorious" and the "true gem of his many works."[22] The book was written as a reflection of God informed by Studdert Kennedy's experiences while he served in the trenches with the 17th Brigade of the 24th Division of the British Expeditionary Force during June of 1917.[23] The book was put into its final form while he served at the "Army Infantry School, B.E.F." and contained many of the themes that he developed in his earlier works as well as themes to which he would return in his later efforts. Studdert Kennedy explained the purpose of his book in his introduction, that the question posed by a hospitalized officer he visited (who we first met in his "Religious Difficulties of the Private Soldier"), "What is God like," had become the foundation of his wartime reflections and was the theme of the book.

> All my experience has grouped itself round and hinged itself upon the answer to this question, asked me at the beginning, "What is God like?" because it appears to me to be the only question that ultimately and really matters and must be answered. The form of meditations which the answer takes is the result of an experience which much surprised me.[24]

Studdert Kennedy focused the entire book on his theme, the nature of God, as revealed through his experiences in combat at the Messines Ridge. Each chapter title contains "God" and presents a different aspect of the Divine. Chapter titles include: God's nature, God in nature, God in History, God in the Bible, God and Democracy, God and Prayer, God and the Sacrament, God and the Church, and God and the Life Eternal. Many of the chapters were dated to a specific day during the battle, some even with a specific time.

Studdert Kennedy rejected the traditional view of God, of a mighty potentate sitting on a throne. Instead he presented and developed his concept of the Suffering God, revealed in the crucified Christ. For Studdert Kennedy, this was the only understanding of God which made sense in the trenches of the Great War. It was the only understanding of God which would enable him to minister with compassion to the wounded soldiers and their dead comrades that he encountered and served alongside during those years of the war.

In Studdert Kennedy's battlefield meditations, he introduced us to the "dead Bosche"[25] that he tripped over on the battlefield though whom he eventually came to see the crucified Christ overarching the battlefield; the limitations of God due to his creation of human free will;[26] the revelation of the Suffering God in creation; and the long-suffering soldiers who exemplified the crucified Christ.[27] In their sacrifice he came to appreciate the Glory of God.

> All men are learning to worship patient, suffering love, and the muddy hero of the trenches is showing us Who is the real King. . . . I know nothing in my real religion of the Almighty God of Power. I only see God in Christ, and these men have shown me—*Him.* I have seen in them His glory.[28]

Death was an all too common experience on the First World War battlefield, and Studdert Kennedy included it as a common theme in *The Hardest Part*. He reflected on the faith of a soldier praying fervently during an artillery barrage only to be killed as his chaplain offered him a Woodbine cigarette; described the deceased Peter, shot through the forehead at his trench, who reminded Studdert Kennedy of the Apostle Peter and caused him to muse on the effectiveness of the church during the time of war; and to a young corporal who had received communion three days before the chaplain was confronted by his broken body and led him into a reflection on the importance of this central sacrament of the church.

> In the days of peace the Broken Body and the Blood outpoured seemed to have so little to do with ordinary things in life. But here, broken bodies and pools of blood are the most ordinary things in life. So ghastly ordinary, always bodies, broken battered bodies, and always blood. Is it wrong to see in them His Body

> and His Blood—God's Body, God's Blood? . . . God suffers in man's suffering, and man, if he be man, suffers with God.[29]

As Studdert Kennedy reflected on life eternal and the awful reality of the battlefield he acknowledged that effective soldiers considered themselves dead already, that to survive the war would be a surprise. He acknowledged as well that "Every man who dies in a bayonet charge dies mad,"[30] a theme he applied to himself when he made his great confession on Armistice Day, 1921. He confessed that England, as a nation, depended upon false stimulants and drugs to "hide from the hideous facts of war,"[31] a theme to which he would return in his postwar book *Lies*.

Studdert Kennedy's *The Hardest Part* demonstrated this chaplain's passionate love and commitment to the soldiers with whom he served in the war. He understood their language, their temptations, and the "conspiracy of silence"[32] that would characterize their postwar years, with most refusing to talk about the hellish experiences they had endured. But the book also reveals his passionate desire to understand and know the Suffering God who suffered alongside those soldiers and comforted their souls as they fought and died for England.

I agree with Stuart Bell and Thomas O'Loughlin that Studdert Kennedy's *The Hardest Part* is indeed a gem. It should be counted among the classics of war literature and theology. Few works of theology approach the vibrance or immediacy of Studdert Kennedy's musings, nor do they come close to the understanding and compassion for the human condition that Studdert Kennedy displays. Contemporary events such as 9/11 and the Covid-19 pandemic confront us once again with the reality of human suffering. Perhaps the theology of the Suffering God can comfort us as we face life and death, as we face eternity.

ROUGH RHYMES OF A PADRE (1918)

Studdert Kennedy began writing poetic verse to accompany his speeches, and to artistically encapsulate his ideas in a version that would appeal to those who would not otherwise have given him a hearing. His friend and military biographer D. F. Carey reported that Studdert Kennedy produced his first war poetry at the suggestion of another chaplain, Rev. F. B. MacNutt when they were both engaged with the National Mission of Repentance and Hope, described earlier in the book. "I thought that if he could put the stuff of the addresses, he was giving the soldier into soldier-dialect verse, in the style of Kipling, it would go down marvelously in the Army."[33] Studdert Kennedy "gave it a go" and produced "The National Mission: A Sermon in a Billet," quoted earlier in the book. Studdert Kennedy produced four volumes of poetry which were also combined in a number of anthologies. While his poems are not counted among the great First World War Poets like Wilfred Owen, John McCrae, and Siegfried Sassoon, possibly due to the religious nature of his work, they are still read and quoted by contemporary writers and preachers. From my research, the one that appears most often is, "His Mate," also quoted earlier in this book. Gerald Studdert-Kennedy, who was somewhat critical of his great-uncle's poetic abilities, commented on this lack of critical reception in his *Dog-Collar Democracy*.

> Studdert Kennedy's verse has not found its way into anthologies of writing from the war. But unlike other highly popular versifiers of the period who have long since sunk without trace. . . . His verse is still read and recited in sermons and, with some regularity, on religious broadcasts.[34]

The subject matter of the poems was, as mentioned earlier, designed to support the content of his addresses to the troops, and later to his congregations and the vast crowds who attended his ICF crusades. To use a description he loathed, they were even propagandistic. To illustrate this point, Studdert Kennedy introduced his questions about God in his poem, "The Sorrow of God: A Sermon in a Billet." The poem itself was rather long, taking up eight pages in the book, but it flows easily. In the poem, he first asked the question that had challenged him from the beginning.

> But it ain' the same out 'ere you know.
> It's as different as chalk fro' cheese,
> For 'arf on it's blood and t'other 'arf's mud,
> And I'm damned if I really sees,
> Ow the God, who 'as made such a cruel world,
> Can 'ave Love in 'Is 'eart for men,
> And be deaf to the cries of the men as dies
> And never comes 'ome again.[35]

As the soldier reflected on the comrade who had died and all the death surrounding him there, he concluded that God's role in the war, if he had any love at all for humanity, was the most difficult of all. In words that provided the title for his wartime theology, *The Hardest Part*, Studdert Kennedy penned these inspired words.

> The sorrows of God mun be 'ard to bear
> If 'E realy has love in his 'eart,
> And the 'ardest part I' the world to play
> Mun surely be God's part.[36]

Studdert Kennedy answered the solder's question with emotion-laden words.

So the Father God goes sorrowing still
For 'Is world what 'as gone to sea,
But 'E runs up a light on Calvary's 'ight
That beckons to you and me.
The beacon light of the sorrow of God
'As been shinin' down through the years,
A flashin' its light through the darkest night
Of our 'uman blood tears.[37]

The thirty poems in the book covered the full gamut of war issues that the soldiers were facing. Death ("Today Thou Shalt Be with Me," "Death," "Wait," "His Mate), wartime prayers ("Prayer before and Attack," "Thy Will be Done"), the necessity of cigarettes to the soldier ("The Secret"), the reasons behind their participation in the war ("What are We Fighting For," "In an Irish Brogue"), a mother's response to the loss of a son ("A Mother Understands"), and thoughts and yearning for home ("Paradise"). One poem stands out as an example of the moral injury that is the subject of this book. Studdert Kennedy reflected on the thoughts of a soldier as he considered his actions in the war. The poem is titled, "What's the Good?"

Well, I've done my bit of scrappin',
And I've done it quite a lot;
Nicked 'em neatly wiv my bayonet,
So I needn't waste a shot.
'Twas my duty, and I done it,
But I 'opes the doctor's quick,
For I wish I 'and't done it,
Gawd! It turns me shamed and sick.
There's a young 'un like our Richard,
And I bashed 'is 'ead in two
And there's that ole gray 'aired gezer
Which I stuck 'is belly through.
Gawd, you women, wives and mothers,
It's such a waste of all your pain,
If you knowed what I'd been doin',
Could yer kiss me still my Jane?[38]

The soldier regretted his actions but realized that it was necessary to defeat Germany and to bring peace to the world again. But the memories would stay with him, and he wished he could get them out of his mind.

'Struth I wish 'e'd stop 'is lookin',
And shut up 'is bloomin' eyes.
'Cause I keeps on seein' Richard
When I whacks 'im and 'e cries.[39]

In the end, the soldier condemned the war as a "bloody rotten waste"[40] and acknowledged that he would never tell his wife of these experiences for, "It would turn your 'air all gray."[41] But the memories would remain, as all survivors or war and moral injury attest, "We'll just 'ave a bloody mem'ry to disturb us when we rest."[42]

It is clear that Studdert Kennedy's poems were created to serve his rhetoric, but the poems also stand alone, often very powerfully so. My favorite poem, and which brings tears to my eyes every time I read it is his "Well."[43] It is another long poem (eight pages) and is the first poem in *Rough Rhymes of a Padre*. I'll quote just a few verses here.

And then at last 'E said one word, . . .
'E just said one word—"Well?"
And I said in a funny voice,
"Please can I go to 'Ell?"
And 'E stood there and looked at me
And 'E kind o' seemed to grow,
Till 'E shone like the sun above my 'ead,
And then 'E answered, "No,
You can't, that 'Ell is for the blind,
And not for those that see,
You know that you 'ave earned it, lad,
So you must follow me.
Follow Me on the paths o' pain,
Seeking what you 'ave seen,
Until at last you can build the 'Is"
Wi' the brick o' the "might 'ave been.'
That's what 'E said, as I'm alive,
And that there dream were true.
But what 'E meant—I don't quite know,
Though I knows what I 'as to do.
I's got to follow what I's seen,
Till this old carcass dies;
For I daren't face in the land o' grace
The sorrow of those eyes.
There ain't no throne, and there ain't no books,
It's 'Im you've got to see,
It's 'Im, just 'Im, that is the judge
Of blokes like you and me.

And, boys, I'd sooner frizzle up,
I' the flames of burnin' 'Ell,
Than stand and look into 'Is face,
And 'ear 'Is voice say—"Well?"[44]

MORE ROUGH RHYMES OF A PADRE (1919)

Studdert Kennedy returned from France in early 1919 and continued his popular publishing endeavors begun with his book of war poetry, *Rough Rhymes of a Padre* (1918). His *More Rough Rhymes of a Padre* (1919) and *Peace Rhymes of a Padre* (1920) met the growing demand for his poetic work. He also published a book of prose in 1919, titled *Lies*. These works reflected his deep empathy and pathos resulting from his participation in the war and his own attempt to come to terms with his emotions and hope for the future. A brief review of his literary efforts during these three years provides a window into his efforts to reconcile his support for and participation in the war with the growing realization that the Great War in particular, and generally all wars, solves nothing.

The poetry of *More Rough Rhymes of a Padre*, like his earlier *Rough Rhymes of a Padre*, were focused on the battlefields of France and Belgium. Studdert Kennedy filled it with the pathos of war, death, hope for the future, and thoughts of home. It demonstrated that the Padre empathized closely with the mind and spirit of the soldiers he served throughout France. In "I Know Not Where They Have Laid Him" Studdert Kennedy reflected on a mother's desire to know the location of her son's burial and the pain she experienced at his loss, a pain that no man could know. In "No Retaliation," he reported on the battlefield impact of a labor strike in the munitions factories back home, resulting in more soldiers' deaths due to the British inability to respond to German attacks.[45] In "Comrades Mine" he mused on the death of "Six heroes of Ligny Thilloy, August, 1918." He commented that they had "taught me how to die, how a soldier ought to die, duty done without a sigh, Comrades, mine."[46]

An important poem that revealed the condition of the author's spirit during the last year of the war was his "Come Unto Me" subtitled as a shell-hole meditation. In the poem, Studdert Kennedy reflected Jesus's words found in the Bible, "Come unto me all ye who are heavy laden and I will give you rest." Studdert Kennedy responded to the Lord, "It is not rest I crave, Not rest but strength to save the wounded and console their pain."[47] He further reported his own spiritual condition and the condition of his comrades, that they were lost in "no-man's-land" blindly following trails in the mud that lead them in circles, with no escape.

Come unto me,
It sounds like mockery,
A voice that calls a wounded man
Across a weary space
For we would come to Thee,
We long to see thy face,
But we are wounded sore
And evermore
Our weakness binds us,
Darkness blinds us,
We stretch our hands out vainly toward the shore,
Where thou art waiting for thine own.
We groan, and try, and fail again.[48]

The voice calling them to rest did so in futility for they felt they were condemned by the war and their blindness to wander forever in battlefields. Instead, the chaplain implored the calling voice, the voice of his Lord, to come to them. The answering voice responded, "I come."

In "Old England," Studdert Kennedy discussed the home front and why he and his soldiers were fighting. They weren't interested in the old England, but in a hopeful future England that would be characterized by universal justice and a living wage for all. He spoke for his soldiers, commenting that they weren't fighting for the poverty and conditions they had left, but for a brighter future. As he described the Old England, it was clear that there was nothing attractive about it.

What I says is sink old England,
To the bottom of the sea.
It's new England as I fights for,
It's an England swep' aht clean,
An England where we'll see the things,
Our eyes 'ave never seen.
Decent wages, justice, mercy,
And a chance for ev'ry man. [49]

The poet reflected a universal war weariness and cries for an end of the war in "A Song of the Desert," situated "On the Hindenburg Line, 1918." Studdert Kennedy's poem reflected on all the "songs of battlefield" he had penned and commented that his "soul sighs for release, it wanders in war's wilderness and cries for peace—for peace."[50] This was his great desire after nearly four years of war, and the desire of the soldiers he ministered to throughout France. Although his book of war poetry contained some rays of hope for the future, he concluded the book with a poem that reflected the spiritual condition of the war-weary troops and possibly his own. It certainly reflected the hopelessness and the futility of war. In "Missing, Believed Killed," the chaplain took the hope of the scripture and transformed it into a hopeless dirge,

> O grave, where is they victory?
> O death, where is thy sting?
> Thy victory is ev'rywhere,
> Thy sting's in ev'rything.[51]

PEACE RHYMES OF A PADRE

Studdert Kennedy's next book of poetry, *Peace Rhymes of a Padre*, published in 1920, reflected on the return of the BEF from France to the shores of England. Once again, the poet demonstrated a deep understanding of the men and women he served. Jonathan Shay, in his book *Odysseus in America*, has commented on the great difficulty that soldiers face in returning from war,[52] and Studdert Kennedy's poetry is deeply reflective of those challenges. His poetry was filled with hopes for the future tempered by the grim realities of the present tinged with the constant remembrance of the steep costs of the war. Titles like "Demobilized" and "Marching Song" reported the end of war and the demobilization of the troops. "The Spirit" reflected on conditions at home in the midst of economic turmoil and unemployment. It was dedicated, "To all ex-service men left out in the cold."[53] In the poem, a demobilized soldier reflected that he and his mates fought for more than the celebrations that marked the war's end, they fought for a true and lasting peace. This peace was not evident in the political wrangling that followed the war. Studdert Kennedy insisted that they must remember what was truly important, the attainment of peace!

> I remember—I remember,
> I'm not going to forget,
> Till we've done the job we started,
> Till the flag of peace is set.[54]

Religious themes continued to dominate Studdert Kennedy's work, with the sacrifice of Christ a constant reminder of the sacrifices of his beloved soldiers. Reflecting on the way in which the postwar Britain sought to move on after the war, the author related how a busy Birmingham simply ignored the Christ. Studdert Kennedy painted a picture of a lonely veteran, formerly standing watch in a flooded frontline trench, now sitting in the rain, homeless.

When Jesus came to Birmingham, they simply passed him by,

> They never hurt a hair of him, they only let him die.
> For men had grown more tender and they would not give him pain,
> They only just passed down the street and left him in the rain.[55]

In "The Pensioner," the poet focused on a veteran's wife whose husband had been severely wounded in the war and was effectively a "war widow." In the poem, she reflected that she received a meager war pension that in no way took the place of a healthy husband, or of the child that he had promised her, but was never born, and never would be.

> But my pension won't buy kisses,
> An'e'll never kiss again,
> 'E aint got no kissin' in 'im,
> Ain't got nothin' now—but pain.
> Nor as I would ever change 'im
> For the strongest man alive.
> While the breath is in my body
> Still I'll mother 'im—and strive
> That I keeps my face still smiling,
> Though my 'eart is fit to break,
> As I lives a married widow,
> So I'll lives on for 'is sake.[56]

In "Dead and Buried" Studdert Kennedy followed what would become a favorite theme as he condemned the politicians and the Versailles Treaty, which he felt would only buy more bloodshed. In "High and Lifted Up" he again presented his concept of the Suffering God in the crucified Christ of love and rejected the vision of God as a grand king. He stated that that vision of God was only an anthropomorphism, "All that showy pomp of splendor, all that sheen of angel wings, was simply borrowed from the baubles that surround our earthly kings."[57] The book of poems concluded with three poems: "It Is Not Finished" and "It is Finished" that sandwich a poem dedicated to his son, Patrick, for whom he wished, "the poet's open eyes."[58] In the concluding poem, he called upon his readers to follow him and the "wounded God" as they engaged the battle to bring about a "new day under a new sun."

> There's an army thronging round Him as
> He takes the road tonight,
> Can't you see your sons and brothers lined
> Before him left and right?

Can't you hear their voices calling you to
Join the host and fight
For the God who marches on.[59]

LIES (1920)

Lies, Studdert Kennedy's book of prose published in 1919, is probably one of his most authentic and passionate works. It received a ready reception in post-war Britain, with publishers commenting that it was a work that would challenge its readers to significant thought. It enjoyed many reprints throughout the 1920s and 1930s. It reflected Studdert Kennedy's postwar disappointment with the peace and the postwar world. His biographers and friends, however, found it less than appealing, completely omitting it from the 1947 collected works, *The Best of Studdert Kennedy*. Writing in 1962 William Purcell, Studdert Kennedy's biographer, commented that Studdert Kennedy's literary efforts were not always successful and proposes *Lies* as his evidence.

> Nor did he always succeed himself. *Lies*, which came out a year or so before *Food for the Fed-up*, lacks its cogency, smacks more of the street corner stand, and therefore has less in it of abiding value. . . . The latter (*Lies*) as a book has died.[60]

While *Lies* may lack the lasting impact for theology and pastoral care of Studdert Kennedy's *The Hardest Part*, it does provide us with a window into his soul as he confronted his disappointment with the postwar world and disillusionment with the outcome of the war. It is clear from the content of *Lies* that Studdert Kennedy had not yet recovered from the war. Published only six months after he returned from France, the wounds of war were still fresh upon its pages. In the introduction he commented, "there's a bad smell about, a very bad smell; it is like the smell of the Dead—it is the smell of dead souls. I can smell hell."[61] In chapter 1, writing on the Bible as the book of broken dreams, he recalled the nightmare war years,

> By all the concentrated horror of these four ghastly years, by the broken hearts of widows and their lonely, loveless lives, by the agony of England, and by her bloody sweat God call us all to honest, fearless thought.[62]

His purpose, as he explained it, was to apply Christian principles to the challenges of the postwar world and to individually address and destroy the lies that stood in the way of that process.[63] Again recalling his days in the trenches, he commented that he meant to address each lie in the same way that he was required to destroy the "chats" (lice) that afflicted him there, one by one.[64] In the following pages, he did so, singling out Darwin and Bismarck and their twin philosophies that led to the Great War. In chapter 3, he condemned the class warfare that resulted from England's industrial revolution and called for a return to cooperation. He especially ridiculed England's "faith in force" and recalled the great lesson of the war that "an appeal to force is fundamentally wrong, it is worse than a crime, it is a blunder."[65] In "Lies and Liberty" he appealed to workers to abandon their dependence on handouts and to commit to "not only the ability to work but the enthusiastic desire to work hard"[66] with a sense of duty to create a better life for all.

In "Lies and Equality" he attacked the kind of state that produced the "hell-fire" of the Great War, a Germany that ignored the value of the individual. He stated,

> We have been fighting the barbaric and anti-democratic idea of a state which refuses to recognize the value of the individual life, and looks upon men as made for states, and not states as made for men. We have been fighting for the root truth of Democracy that all men are of equal value in God's sight, and that no men are to be counted as cannon fodder to feed the idol of political power based on force.[67]

He suggested that the way to address that problem was through service, that selfless service was one of the key lessons of the Great War, a lesson that was in danger of being lost.

> A soldier in a bowler hat said to me, "This 'ere war is just fizzling out." The demobilized man has lost something. There is something he is feeling round for, like a man who has lost his cigarette case and hasn't a fag in the world. What is it? It is his sense of service. He left it in the pocket of his khaki clothes. That is the danger. We cannot get Democracy until we recognize that the man who digs our country's coal is as much in the service as the man who kills our country's foes, as the man who drives the British trains as much in the service as the man who trains the British guns.[68]

In the "Lies of Lust," Studdert Kennedy called for the end of the abuse of women and called for the recognition of the essential unity of male and female. He suggested that women possess and could contribute essential qualities that Britain needed to enter a new age. Sounding far more modern than the church of his time, he commented that lust "dwarfs the growth of the woman soul, and the woman mind for with the world of the future is crying and without which our dreams can never come true."[69]

In the remainder of the work, Studdert Kennedy suggested that the answer to the problems of postwar Great Britain was to be found in personal faith. He returned repeatedly to his theology of the Suffering God who "rules because He serves, who is supreme because He suffers, who is strong because He is weak,"[70] and who called humans to serve with Him in bringing about a better world. The lies of forgetfulness: materialism, drink, lust, furious action and even traditional religion were rejected. He posited that the world wanted to forget the recent past, to indulge in narcotics to dull the pain of the remembering of the war. He suggested that forgetting was futile, that it would only bring about a repeat of the past. He continued,

> Shall we forget? Shall we drug ourselves and fall asleep and allow it all to fester underneath the skin of life until it bursts again into an open bleeding sore. . . . God forbid. It shall not be. I've done with drugs. I want to live. God—Great God of Life—teach me to remember; teach us to remember—we must not forget![71]

He concluded that the answer to the problems he had illuminated was sacrificial service in which each individual would assume responsibility for his/her own burden. He suggested that a passionate spirit was the answer, that the people of Britain must follow Christ with a "red religion which burns and blazes and calls men—calls them to service, renunciation and sacrifice."[72] He concluded *Lies* with a vision of his hope for Britain, seeing a "New London, the New Birmingham, Liverpool, Manchester, and Leeds coming down from heaven prepared as a bride." The only alternative he saw to this vision was "darkness and sorrow."[73]

FOOD FOR THE FED-UP (1921)

Published in 1921, Studdert Kennedy's *Food for the Fed-Up* was an exposition of the Apostles' Creed and an attempt to breathe life into what he termed its outmoded form. His biographer, William Purcell, described it as "the best of Geoffry's books of this period, (it) was a tremendous piece of sustained apologetic."[74] He suggested that contemporary people were enamored with the idea of progress and had abandoned the ancient gods and beliefs as outmoded. He believed that the Apostles' Creed, one of those ancient beliefs, was actually an effective living creed that, if properly understood, could provide guidance for life and the transformation of British society. Studdert Kennedy introduced his theme with a wartime reflection, that First World War soldiers often spoke of being "fed up" with events, leaders, or the war in general. The impact of being "fed up" could have disastrous consequences for an army, "An army of men who are fed up can have no hope of victory, because they have no will to win."[75] Studdert Kennedy applied this wartime conundrum as a diagnosis of Britain's postwar condition, that the country was "fed up."

> We have been tried as silver is tried, we have passed through fire and water and had a surfeit of self-sacrifice, we have given our best and bravest and shed our blood in rivers, and we trusted that God would bring us out into a wealthy place, into a new world. But it is no new world that we find ourselves in, but an old world grown older. . . . There has come upon us a great disillusionment. . . . Millions who gave up their all in a frenzy of self-sacrifice during the war are asking themselves bitterly what they gave it for. What's the good? And Who's to gain. *We are fed up.*[76]

Studdert Kennedy continued that the only cure for the "fed up" state was solid food for the soul, the solid food found in the Apostles' Creed.

In the pages of his exposition, Studdert Kennedy found ample opportunity to expound on the problem of evil, his theology of the Suffering God and associated themes. Of God's responsibility for war, disease, and pestilence, Studdert Kennedy answered that this God "must be an evil-minded blackguard, with a nasty disposition like a boy pulling the wings off of flies."[77] He condemned the idea that God sends suffering into the world to test men, and stated that men have used this idea to sanction the infliction of harm on others. Instead, human suffering was the result of evil in the world, through human will.[78] He also presented his understanding of God as the Suffering God. In this postwar work, however, he added an important element, that the Suffering God was in fact triumphant as a result of the resurrection of Christ.[79]

Studdert Kennedy's central vision of the cross overarching the battlefield was again referenced in this work, but in its pages he confronted a new enemy, poverty, which he characterized as "a reproach to the gospel and a wound in the heart of Christ."[80] Studdert Kennedy transferred his vision of the battlefield Crucifix to the slums and market places of England.

> That is how we see Christ crucified and risen again in ourselves, and that is how we see Him in the world and in the church—crucified—crucified in every street of our great cities, crucified in every hovel of our slums, crucified on our markets, crucified on our battle-fields, but for ever rising again. Again and again men cry that he is dead and buried, antiquated, impossible, mythical; again and again He comes back, takes hold on human hearts, and sends them out to preach His truth, aflame with the old new Love.[81]

Studdert Kennedy may have transferred his battlefield visions to the cities and people of England, but he did not leave the memories and sights of the battlefield behind. Images of war fill the pages of *Food for the Fed Up*, which is not surprising since it was published only two years after his return from France. The "valley of the Somme"[82] once again characterized all the evil of the war while images of a "broken Flanders village" with a crucifix that was "looked up to by broken, battered bleeding men" offered some hope.[83] Images of "a hundred children burned to death" and "a battalion of fine men cut to pieces"[84] were used to illustrate points that have little to do with warfare. He continued to voice his opposition to war, a theme which he had introduced in his 1919 work, *Lies*. He blamed the failure of politicians for the wars that have consumed humanity[85] and bemoaned the fact that peacetime promoters of the various ideologies promoted achievement of their objectives through class warfare and their "faith in force."[86] The author's judgment on his nation's faith in force revealed by its resort to national rearmament was that it only revealed the nation's spiritual failure, "Our military power is an exact index of our spiritual and moral impotence."[87]

Studdert Kennedy's solution for the "fed up" and disillusioned condition of postwar Britain, of its "spiritual and moral impotence" was faith and commitment to the power of creative Love. "There is no other Power but His, which is the Power of Love. God is Love, and all power belongs to Love. There is more real power in that simple truth than in all the massed armies and navies of all the nations of the world."[88] Rather than business as usual and the "Godless prosperity" that produced the "boy with the swollen, shapeless face, with a great hole in his head and the brain tumbling out,"[89] Studdert Kennedy concluded the book with a plea for a return to Christian ethics and culture.

> Can we not see that Godless diplomacy, Godless commerce, and Godless pleasure are worse than crimes; they are stupid, sinful blunders. We must have light. There is no other light, there is no other standard, than that which shines in His Face. We must see it, and we must guide our ships towards it, or we must perish on the rocks; and as I write the rocks are near, and I can hear the breakers beating on a cruel shore.[90]

DEMOCRACY AND THE DOG COLLAR (1921)

Democracy and the Dog Collar marked Studdert Kennedy's transition from a focus on daily pastoral concerns and duties to a national stage and subject matter. He joined the Industrial Christian Fellowship in 1922, but he had been speaking at the organization's meetings for at least a year before his association with the group was finalized. The ICF's mission was to bring Christ and the church into the workplace, which meant that much of its message addressed the economic issues of the day. Studdert Kennedy's *Democracy and the Dog Collar* fit this message perfectly. In its pages he provided a defense for that effort. In effect, he answered the question that he faced so often, "What is the church doing here?"

Studdert Kennedy presented his economic questions and solutions through a dialogue between Mr. O.C. (organized church) and Mr. O.L. (organized labor). In this exchange, he used Mr. O.L. to voice many of the complaints regarding the church and to ask why the church sought to enter Britain's workplaces. He used Mr. O.C. to answer those questions and to suggest that Britain's labor problems could be solved by Christian principles and ethics. In its pages, he condemned communism, scientific socialism and Marx, describing him as a failed prophet that was "better left buried."[91] Studdert Kennedy was balanced in his condemnation of the economic ideologies of the day, and condemned Manchester Capitalism with the same vigor [92] he had directed at communism.[93] Through Mr. O.C.'s argument, Studdert Kennedy presented an impassioned plea to stop class warfare and the resort to force to achieve labor's objectives and instead proposed that all the classes of society work together to defeat poverty, even as they had cooperated to defeat Germany during the war.

> The best friends of Labour today are the men of goodwill in every class of society, who are convinced that it is wrong to seat and oppress the working people and that somehow or other the problem of poverty has got to be solved.[94]

It was in the pages of this work that Studdert Kennedy presented a theology of work that predated Pope John Paul II's 1981 encyclical *Laborum Exercens* on the dignity of work by nearly sixty years. Studdert Kennedy hoped that the worker would begin to see himself or herself as a "Priest of God, a Priest of Love called by God to produce warmth and power for his brothers in the world." But it was not only the worker whose perspective he hoped to change, he hoped that all of British society would adopt this same view.

Studdert Kennedy found ample opportunity to include images and questions regarding the war in *Democracy and the Dog Collar*. In its pages, he answered the charge that the church was simply a servant of international capitalism and had supported the war with patriotic sermons that led to the mass slaughter of Britain's workers. He used this opportunity to express his own misgivings about the war and the struggle he had experienced in deciding to support it. In the end, he felt he had no choice due to the circumstances, but he now rejected "the lie that the kingdom of heaven could be won by force."[95] Studdert Kennedy, as Mr. O.L., also condemned militant nationalism for its sins during the war.

> It stinks, stinks with the stench of battle-fields, the dry, parched, sickening smell that calls up memories of an August day in the valley of the Somme. Can patriotism ever be redeemed, and can the nations of the Empire ever be anything but a menace to the welfare of the workers of the world?[96]

In answer, Studdert Kennedy defended the peaceful love of one's country, even as he loved England's beautiful countryside, but agreed that militant nationalism was an evil that should be destroyed, replaced by the Christian love of the neighbor. Mr. O.L. responded that it was fine for the church to take a pacifist line after the war, just when the workers needed the church's support as they considered the need to forcefully to change the system that had oppressed the workers for so long. "During this last bust up your pulpits rang with patriotic sermons and talk of the Great Sacrifice, but now that it is over and the workers have come back to a land that it needs heroes to live in, you suddenly turn pacifist."[97]

Studdert Kennedy, as Mr. O.C., responded passionately, condemning all resort to force. Certainly the years of war in the trenches of Europe had taught them the ineffectiveness of force to bring about anything positive.

> The very first thing that any true friend of Labour has got to make quite clear to the workers today is that there is just as little to be got out of industrial war in the long run as there is out of international war, and that little is considerably less than nothing. If we have learned anything from the past five years of hell, it surely ought to be that war never gets anything or anywhere. It is in every case a disaster which it is the bounden duty of every sane thinking person to hold out against till the very last ditch. It is and it never can be anything but a pure and unmitigated disaster.[98]

Studdert Kennedy also raised the issue of the Sovereign God and the problem of evil, transferred from the battlefield to the coal mine. Mr. O.L. condemned the God who had "made the slums of Birmingham, he had no use of God whatsoever. He got sick of teaching kiddies who lived in pigsty's to do God's will and be content. . . . (God had) arranged that there should be poor pits and rich pits, and that therefore there must be poor miners and rich miners. That's religion isn't it—God's will be done?" Studdert Kennedy, as Mr. O.C. responded characteristically, "No, that's not religion. It is the oldest enemy of true religion."[99] Instead, Studdert Kennedy concluded that both communism and capitalism were failed ideologies, that the Christian ethic taught in the Sermon on the Mount guided by the "travail pain of God" (the Suffering God) was the only guide to bring social transformation to England.[100]

SONGS OF FAITH AND DOUBT (1922)

Studdert Kennedy published this book of poetry in 1922, coinciding with his new assignment with the Industrial Christian Fellowship. He often used his poetry to support his rhetorical activities, and many of the twenty-five poems in the volume reflected his new association with the ICF and the working people of Britain. Poems relating to economic issues, especially poverty, filled its pages. But the themes that had occupied his thinking in prior years also showed up: the failed utility of war ("Fruits of Victory"), his disdain for the traditional view of the sovereign God ("The Soul of Doubt" and "*Fiat Voluntas Tua*"), and his own sense of failure in light of the goals and challenges he faced (Roses in December). In "The Bolshevist's Speech" and "The Beggar's Soliloquy" he presented the communists' argument for revolutionary change and then argued that a culture transformed by Christian ethics would banish poverty and war.[101] Two poems that most effectively communicated Studdert Kennedy's themes in this volume were "Then Will He Come" and "To the Princess at the Royal Wedding."

In "Then Will He Come," the very first poem in the book, Studdert Kennedy proclaimed his God as the workman's God. His focus was now transferred from the trenches of France to Britain's furnaces, humming engines, and the sweating coal miner, "Holding his pick more splendid than the sword." (Note that the images of war were not far from the poet's mind). As Studdert Kennedy had seen Christ in Britain's soldiers as they sacrificed themselves on the battlefields of France, so he saw God working alongside Britain's labor force.

> The will He come with meekness for His glory,
> God in a workman's jacket as before,
> Living again the eternal gospel story,
> Sweeping the shavings from His workshop floor.[102]

Studdert Kennedy addressed Britain's glaring divide between wealth and poverty in his very effective poem addressed, "To the Princess at the Royal Wedding." As a chaplain to the king, Studdert Kennedy had the opportunity to experience the opulence of royalty firsthand, but had also lived among the poor. In this poem he compared the beauty of the princess, arrayed in her wedding finery, feathers, braided gold, and coronets, with the daily experience of the working poor who were "pent like swine in evil-smelling sties." He attributed the great divide to the failure of Britain's conscience, "If we, all glorious without were glorious within." The evidence of Britain's failed humanity, the poverty of its children and unemployed men, was an embarrassment to the heroes who died in the war and had hoped for a better postwar England.

> Then through the thunder of these cheers,
> No child would cry for bread,
> Nor would the waste of living men,
> Shame our poor wasted dead.[103]

Studdert Kennedy concluded the poem with a veiled plea for the transformation of Britain's conscience, that to eliminate poverty and despair, it would take a national change of heart. "If all our hearts were golden as the sunshine of your hair."[104]

Studdert Kennedy's *Songs of Faith and Doubt* did not achieve the same popular success as his war poetry. Most of the poems in the volume did find their way into his 1927 anthology, *The Unutterable Beauty*. Interestingly, his "To the Princess at the Royal Wedding" did not. Perhaps it had been a bit too effective, hitting too close to home for his Royal acquaintances.

THE WICKET GATE (1923)

Studdert Kennedy published *The Wicket Gate* in late 1923 as he served with the Industrial Christian Fellowship. In his opening pages, he related having traveled around Britain and hearing masses of people ask, "What shall I do?" as they realized the evils of poverty and unemployment that had descended upon England out of the earthquake of the war.[105] Recalling Bunyan's Pilgrim's Progress that his mother had read to him as a child, he suggested England's masses were like Christian viewing the road from the Wicket-gate, and had no idea how to get from the city of destruction to the heavenly city.[106] Most tellingly, Studdert Kennedy suggested that these masses didn't really know what they needed, which he identified as "plain bread," peace with God and Truth.[107] Instead of seeking these elements in revolution, he suggested that both could only be found in God, as understood through the words of the Lord's Prayer.

In his exposition of the Lord's Prayer, Studdert Kennedy presented a defense of the Christian faith as it related to the problems of postwar Britain. In its words he found hope for the future, dignity for the worker, and a relief from poverty. All this would be accomplished as individuals gave themselves in word and deed to a vital faith that would transform the world. It is interesting to note that Studdert Kennedy communicated complete support for the labor movement, which he characterized as a thoroughly spiritual effort, as opposed to communist and socialist efforts, whose goal was revolution.[108]

Studdert Kennedy included in these pages all the themes that have been identified in earlier works: his opposition to war,[109] the futility of force and its foundation in fear,[110] the "rotting corpses in the Valley of the Somme,"[111] his opposition to the traditional understanding of the Sovereign God[112] and his condemnation of what he called "business ethics," which were actually a complete lack of ethics.[113]

Studdert Kennedy concluded *The Wicket Gate* with yet another image of the Valley of the Somme, presented as the sum of all evils, a rampant secular materialism that had abandoned any vestige of humanity. He challenged the church to take its place in the world and to work to overcome the impact of the secular industrial and commercial world with true faith, a personal and vital relationship with God and God's truth.

> The Battle of the Somme was a fitting climax to the whole tragedy of what might be called "murder by machinery"; it brought out the essential points, and wrote them large in letters of blood and flame. To stand and watch the working of a 9.2 armour-piercing gun—to appreciate the beautiful exactness with which the monster moved, the unerring accuracy of his aim, the marvelous ingenuity of mechanical device which every part of it displayed—and then to consider the purpose for which the combination of God's gifts was being used, was to see the abyss of the modern tragedy, the nemesis of secularism, which uses the materials which God gave us for building the Kingdom of Heaven, to build the kingdom of Hell.[114]

Studdert Kennedy's final challenge to Britain's church sounded very much like the program of the ICF, a challenge to take the church out of its massive buildings and to move into the homes and workplaces of the common people.

> If the church of the twentieth century does not repent, and proclaim open war against war; if she does not make good her right of entry into the factory, the office, and the counting-house; if she is content to remain a department of life, a State institution . . . and allows her members to be dishonest, and to comfort their consciences by pauperizing the poor with doles and easy charity . . . she will discover that neither doctrinal orthodoxy nor ecclesiastical correctness can save her from the doom which God pronounces on all rotten institutions . . . that God's election is an election to service and not to privilege.[115]

THE WORD AND THE WORK (1925)

Studdert Kennedy's 1925 *The Word and the Work* is based on a series of Lenten reflections he presented during Lent (March to Easter) of the same year. These reflections took as their focus a number of verses from the first chapter of the Gospel of John. In these seven chapters, Studdert Kennedy challenged the church to reflect upon its presence in the world, to ask if it was effectively representing the living Word (Christ) who had been communicated to the world as the eternal rational reality. Studdert Kennedy took his argument a step further, challenging individual Christians to evaluate their faith. If their faith in Christ did not motivate them to personally address the wrongs of the world—poverty, disease, and war—then it was a fraud. "If you feel no longing to right wrongs, to war against injustice and cruelty, to defy tyrannies, to abolish ugliness and dirt, look out! You are standing on a rotten piece of ground."[116] Studdert Kennedy's desire to abolish poverty was front and center in this series of reflections. He countered those who suggested that the church should stay out of social problems with the assertion that it was the duty of the church to "wage ceaseless and unremitting war against" the "degrading and destructive poverty that starves and stunts the human soul."[117]

Studdert Kennedy's presentation was based on important verses in the first chapter of the Gospel of John. He argued that the message of the Gospel, communicated through the eucharistic bread and the corporate community of God, should motivate believers to transform the world. He taught, "The dream of a new and better social order is as much an essential part of the Christian life as prayer, and communion with God."[118] Of course, the new social order could only come about if the old order was understood completely. He viewed that order as, "broken, wounded, torn, it bleeds on battlefields, is diseased in slums, it is covered with festering sores of vulgar luxury, it groans with hunger, and is rent by strife."[119] Even worse, it turned workers into a "prostitution of the human personality. . . . The miners' cottages in many of our colliery villages tell us, just as plainly as though it were printed in great flaming letters on a hording, there are souls for sale."[120] His final judgment was that the current order was a vast world machine that sentenced human beings to sweat and blood, the tears and terror of mankind." [121] Studdert Kennedy understood that most individual believers wanted their church to be a refuge from the world, not a force to defeat its evils. He challenged them to wake up to their responsibilities, otherwise they would face destruction.

> But if your altar is a refuge, if you put your fingers in your ears to shut that awful voice outside; if you have built a private sanctuary for the comfort of your little soul, then look out! It is going to fall on you; the winds of God are coming to blow it all away, and you may cry after it with many tears . . . the wrath of God's Love will burn and burn and burn until there not even left the ashes of regret.[122]

While Studdert Kennedy challenged contemporary Christians to address the world's poverty and social problems, he also encouraged them with a vision that included participation in a vital community and a hope for a transformed social system based upon the Sermon on the Mount.

In common with his other works, *The Word and the Work* was also peppered with war illustrations:[123] the despair of war widows and parents,[124] his condemnation of war,[125] his condemnation of the view of God as an Eastern Monarch,[126] and the story of his tripping over the dead German soldier, and the vision of the Crucified Christ over the battlefield, and the slums of Britain. It is evident that his understanding of that vision had developed over time, and it achieved its fullest expansion in this treatment.

> On June 7th, 1917, I was running to our lines half mad with fright, though running in the right direction, thank God, through what had been once a wooded copse. It was being heavily shelled. As I ran I stumbled and fell over something. I stopped to see what it was. It was an undersized, underfed German boy, with a wound in his stomach and a hole in his head. I remember muttering, "You poor little devil, what had you got to do with it? Not much great blonde Prussian about you." Then there came light. It may have been pure imagination, but that does not mean that it was not also reality, for what is called imagination is often the road to reality. It seemed to me that the boy disappeared and in his place, there lay the Christ upon His Cross, and cried, *"Inasmuch as ye have done it unto the least of these my little ones ye have done it unto me."* From that moment on I never saw a battlefield as anything but a Crucifix. From that moment on I have never seen the world as anything but a Crucifix. I see the Cross set up in every slum, in every filthy overcrowded quarter, in every vulgar flaring street that speaks of luxury and waste of life. I see Him staring up at me from the pages of the newspaper that tells of a tortured, lost, bewildered world. "Ever and always I can see set up above this world of ours, a huge and towering cross with great arms stretched out East and West, from the rising to the setting sun, and on that Cross my God still hangs and calls on all brave men and women to come *out* and share His sorrow and help to save the World.[127]

I'll conclude my treatment of Studdert Kennedy's Lenten reflection with a beautiful element that is unique among the canon of his works, his view of the world as a poem, and God as the great Poet. "There is a real poem written by God Himself, and there are a million million versions of it, in a million million minds. . . . No one can read the poem unless he is in spiritual communion with the poet, who is God."[128] According to Studdert Kennedy's commentary, each individual saw the world through the poetic element that she was formed by, and this served as the basis of individual views of the world. The goal of the spiritual life was to "discern the true meaning of life, reading God's poem in full sympathy with the poet."[129] Through this discernment and understanding, Studdert Kennedy believed a transformational community would arise that could bring about the New Jerusalem in the world.

I PRONOUNCE THEM: A STORY OF MAN AND WIFE (1927)

In Studdert Kennedy's only novel, the author told a story that he stated he had wanted to preach but had been unable. The fiction recounted the lives of a number of married couples whose marriages had ended as a result of unfaithfulness, drunkenness, physical abuse, and desertion. The great question the author addressed was the condition of the "innocent partner," the husband or wife left behind by the departing spouse. Could they remarry, or should they remain forever single and celibate, still linked to the departed spouse through the indissoluble bond of Holy Matrimony. He also posed the question, "If they did remarry, or choose to live in sin, what legal, social and ecclesiastical ramifications would they face?"

Two of his characters, Charlie and Masie, had known each other since childhood, but Masie had married a drunk and abusive man. After the breakup, Charlie came back into the picture to rescue his childhood sweetheart. "Little Robin" was the young adult daughter of the Rector of St. Philips church and had fallen for a war veteran, a former airman "Peter the Splendid," who, it turned out, wasn't really splendid at all. After their marriage, he became an abusive drunk and deserted her for a woman he had met in Paris. Uncle Jim, the Reverend Jim Counihan (the semi-autobiographical alter ego of Studdert Kennedy), had been deserted by his wife Phyllis, a self-absorbed woman who had never loved anyone but herself. Charlie and Masie, Little Robin and Jim all had a decision to make. As they each considered establishing a new relationship for the future, were they willing to suffer public gossip and excommunication from the church for love? Charlie and Masie decided to take just that step, building a beautiful life together. Robin and Jim considered the step, were madly in love, but retreated from the brink at the last moment in order to allow Father Jim to continue his self-sacrificial ministry to the poor of Britain.

Studdert Kennedy set his novel in postwar England, and its pages are filled with ex-soldiers who had killed in the war (Peter and Charlie),[130] a young woman who had lost a beloved beau (Robin),[131] and thousands who were struggling with unemployment and labor troubles.[132] Studdert Kennedy's favorite passions and themes provide the setting. Father Jim served in the slums and encountered the poverty stricken who lived two families to a flat, filled with sick and dying children.[133] One character, while reflecting on the evils of war, noted that, "the women always suffer."[134] Another character condemned class warfare while also discussing the characteristics of the classes that made them so different.[135] Most important, Studdert Kennedy had Robin and Jim discuss the nature of God, rejecting the traditional viewpoint while recognizing that God was crucified in Christ.[136] Ultimately, the Curate Jim lived out this self-sacrificial love as he committed his life to serving the poor.[137]

The main character in the drama, Father Jim, was a semi-autobiographical figure representing Studdert Kennedy. Like the author, Jim was Irish, spoke with an Irish brogue, was a chaplain in the war, was absentminded, was overworked, and had made a name for himself as a preacher and was traveling around the country.[138] He "worked to forget" his love for Robin,[139] leading one to wonder if the real Studdert Kennedy had worked to forget the memories of the war that plagued him. Most poignantly, Father Jim related having cried only twice, once in the story and the other "while they stood together to watch the remnant of the 137th Brigade march down the road from Fonquevilliers to Souastre after the show on July 1st, 1916."[140] This was Studdert Kennedy's unit with which he served in June 1916 during the battle of the Somme. Jim, like Studdert Kennedy, recalled the spiritual desolation and challenge to his faith that he experienced at the Messines ridge in 1917.

> He was groping frantically for his faith. If that went he was lost, lost on a dirty stinking battlefield full of muttered curses and obscene smells. Memories of a hideous sin-blasted wilderness near Messines in which he had wandered for hours dodging death and waiting dawn came back to him. Life was like that without faith.[141]

Finally, Studdert Kennedy asked the question about the church and whether it should be reformed. In one section he discussed how the church had taken too spiritual an approach in dealing with poverty, ignoring and accepting the poor's horrendous living conditions while encouraging their spiritual patience with their earthly lot. The most important challenge he posed for the church was the question of whether it would be realistic about the marital and sexual challenges posed by the modern world for Christians. Would the church continue to impose outmoded moralistic rules on men and women while the culture changed and provided new freedoms and opportunities for both?[142]

Studdert Kennedy used his novel *I Pronounce Them* as a vehicle to communicate what he considered essential truths to a public that might not give him a hearing otherwise. Most would not darken the doors of a church or attend an ICF rally. But they might purchase a novel to read, and by so doing would encounter truths that Studdert believed were essential if his generation was going to build a New Jerusalem.[143]

THE WARRIOR, THE WOMAN, AND THE CHRIST (1928)

Studdert Kennedy's 1928 work, published only five months before his death in March 1929, was most closely related to Studdert Kennedy's war works, as in its pages he sought to answer the question that had nagged at his conscience throughout the war and after. He had posed the question in his 1917 publication, "The Religious Difficulties of the Private Soldier. *"The first great difficulty of the private soldier is war."*[144] That great difficulty had not been put to rest by the armistice, but had nagged at his mind, dominating his waking and sleeping thoughts. "That was the way with war, it shouts and bawls its questions at you. It throws them at you stark, raw, quivering, and all shot through with pain."[145] *The Warrior, the Woman, and the Christ* was Studdert Kennedy's attempt to rationalize the reality of war and to propose its elimination. His work also challenged the two great ideologies that posed the greatest challenge to Christianity during his time: Darwinism and Marxism. He felt that these two belief systems taught that destructive conflict was the inevitable fate of the human race and would result in the destruction of civilization if left unchecked.[146]

Studdert Kennedy's *The Warrior, The Woman, and the Christ* also proposed a counternarrative that would support a Christian interpretation of history to oppose that proposed by Darwin's theories and the Marxist historical narrative contained in Marx's *Das Kapital*. While the genesis of the book, according to Studdert Kennedy, arose from a question posed to him by a sergeant in the trenches, its theme was actually announced in his 1925 book of Lenten addresses, *The Word and the Work*. There he proposed that Darwin's concept of natural selection, the "survival of the fittest" resulted in a world envisioned as a "brutal battlefield." Instead, Christianity revealed that, "The ultimate nature of the world was being revealed to man in Christ as being, not a battlefield, but a home, and its final law as being, not the law of the jungle, but the law of the family."[147]

Studdert Kennedy asserted that the question that gave rise to his line of thought had originated from a comment made during the 1916 Battle of the Somme by a sergeant (who would be dead before the night was over) as they sought protection in the trenches from exploding German shells, "This ain't exactly a b_____y mother's meeting, is it sir?" The chaplain had responded, "Plenty of blood Sergeant, but no sort of place for mothers." The question that arose from the conversation, that prompted his thinking for this book, was, "Why does the soldier always associate the woman with the priest?"[148]

In developing his answer to the sergeant's question, Studdert Kennedy wondered if faith had always been associated with the feminine. He realized that the differences between the sexes was the most elemental conflict in the world, that understanding those differences was a key to bringing peace to the world. He suggested that conflict is an essential condition in the world, and that there were two types of conflict, destructive and creative. Destructive conflict was ubiquitous, evident in Darwin's survival of the fittest and Marx's conflict between the economic classes. Creative conflict was a constructive alternative, and served as the human ideal for every relationship, especially that between man and woman.

> Because the relationship between a man and a woman can be the deepest, most intimate and searching relationship into which two persons can possibly enter, conflict is inevitable, and the danger of its degeneration into destructive conflict is correspondingly great. The perfection of this relationship carries with it the Kingdom of Love. As we succeed here, we succeed everywhere, failure here is the most disastrous of all.[149]

The goal of the Christian church was to facilitate this creative conflict in the home and to exhibit its perfection in Christian community. According to Studdert Kennedy, men were, by nature, warriors. When led by the laws of the world their effect was destructive. But Christ was the perfect example of manly character and leadership, leading through love rather than domination or hatred. "Jesus was and is the transforming man par excellence. . . . He lived a transforming life. He was in perfection the artist man, the creative warrior."[150]

In Studdert Kennedy's argument, women were, by nature, creative. "Agriculture, house building, boat making, pottery, basket weaving, leather work, all the primitive arts and crafts were started and for ages were carried on by women."[151] The central role of women was the mystical work of creation, of bringing life into the world. Due to their different roles, and the presence of sin in the world, these different roles led to domination of the woman by the man. This destructive conflict had evolved in history and resulted in constant wars, in domination of one group over another, of the evolution of warriors into competing capitalists that resulted in the mechanization of civilization, the subjugation of women, and ever greater conflicts. The most recent result, for Studdert Kennedy, was the Great War.

> The very blood and bones of the peoples were built into the engines of war. The sprawling filth of the slums extended as more ships put to out to sea. It was ready to break, that great black cloud, into torrents of bloody rain. . . . Then suddenly the cloud burst and it rained blood upon the earth for four years.[152]

Studdert Kennedy suggested that the Christian faith could transform the relationship between the sexes and establish harmony between the man and the woman in the home, which would serve as the basis of a transformed society and a transformed world. Through their inspired creative relationship, peace and harmony would result.

> This led us to the enunciation of the great principle of creative conflict as underlying all social and individual development. A creative conflict is one in which there is no possibility of victory or defeat for either side, without grievous loss to both, nor any possibility of any premature peace short of perfection. Both sides must live in vital and mutually vitalizing conflict working out an increasing but never finally completed unity. . . . It is imperative now that the creative purpose of inevitable conflict should increasingly become a consciously creative purpose, and that work should take the place of war as the main business of life, and the artist supersede the warrior man. This growing consciousness of a creative purpose and the substitution of work for war is the quintessence of the process of civilization in its highest sense and is nothing more or less than the birth and growth of charity or creative love, which is the other name of God.[153]

Studdert Kennedy concluded *The Warrior, The Woman, and the Christ* with a passionate plea to the women and men of the world. To the men, he said, "The warrior must not be tamed. He must not become meek and mild and lose his fire and attack. He will need it all if the world is to be built up as a home. He will need to work and to think as he has never thought before."[154] He gave the greater challenge to women, who he felt bore the greatest ability to defeat war.

> But O, for Christ's sake, remember that you must carry a home in your heart. You must make the world a home. You must inspire the warrior man to build it. You must make him turn from war to work. You must say to him—I will not bear babies to be made cannon fodder of. But above all, you must be mothers. Whatever career you adopt and follow, whatever work you do, you must be Mothers. Even though your lot may be the hardest of all. . . . God made you to bear the future in your heart and you must not shirk it.[155]

Studdert Kennedy's last book, though written ten years after the war, was nevertheless full of his reminiscences of the war and of its impact upon him. As noted earlier, the genesis of the book originated with a question posed by a sergeant during his time at the Battle of the Somme, in June 1916. He reported that that event was a more vivid memory "than any night last year."[156] He also reported that the questions with which he grappled during the war were still there, for they had been thrown at him, "stark, raw, quivering and all shot through with pain."[157] The spiritual challenges he faced during the war still haunted him, as he recalled, "laying in no-man's land at night and watched a dark moving object approach not knowing if it was friend or foe." As he had posed his question to the dark object, he also posed it to the universe. "who goes there."[158] His descriptions of the war were as vivid in this late work as any in of his other works, full of blood and death. "Then suddenly the cloud burst and it rained blood upon the earth for four years. The children went out to die. Millions of them went out to die."[159] His condemnation of the war continued to be just as vehement. "If we go out to war it is from weakness, not strength. If we arm, it is because we are afraid. If we slay our enemies, it is because we are too stupid, cowardly, and too slothful to face the strain of making them our friends."[160] Finally, as he had introduced the book with the sergeant's question in the trench, he concluded with a reference to the same sergeant's question and stated that he understood why the sergeant had posed his "joke." As always, for his answer he returned to the Alpha and the Omega, the beginning and the end, The Christ.[161]

JOHN BULL ARTICLES (1925–1929)

Studder Kennedy began a four-year relationship with the weekly journal *John Bull* beginning in 1925. These articles, for the most part, paralleled his public speaking efforts in support of the Industrial Christian Fellowship and Britain's poverty-stricken working poor and unemployed. They also contained his opposition to war and reminiscences that communicated its continuing impact on its veterans, the war widows, and their children. He used his annual Armistice Day article to condemn the possible glorification of war through its annual observance and hoped to instead use the day as a memorial to communicate the evils of war. As a group, these articles provide a good insight into his postwar thinking as he operated on a national stage.

"Why Class Hatred?" (February 7, 1925)

This article addressed a subject that was one of Studdert Kennedy's perennial favorites. It was a key message that he delivered while traveling for the ICF and he had included the subject in his wartime messages as well. The focus of his article was the competition between capital and labor, which came up in a discussion with a gentleman outside a political meeting. "If these labour fellows keep on making trouble, I'm going to invest all my capital abroad where I've got a bit of security."[162] Studdert Kennedy gained an insight through the discussion, that the root of the struggle between capital and labor was really the struggle for power. He suggested the that the wise use and application of power by men and women dedicated to unselfish service was the greatest need for a democracy.

"Modern Dens of Thieves" (April 11, 1925)

In this Easter message, Studdert Kennedy recalled the gospel message that God's house should be a house of prayer. Instead, he suggested that it had become, like all of England, a den of thieves. His point was that the insatiable human desires for money, sex, and power had completely overtaken the world and every human, including husbands and wives, continuously put out their hands imploringly, "What can you give me?" During the war, they had experienced "these terrific outbursts of bloodshed when we turned God's world into a shambles, (they) are all part and parcel of the same infinite beastliness. Man's lust for power is as insatiable as his lust for love."[163] In the final consideration, Studdert Kennedy suggested that only God could fulfill the great emptiness in the human heart that manifested itself as lust.

"A Pageant of Truth" (August 1, 1925)

This article was one of Studdert Kennedy's Remembrance Day works in which he suggested that the nation should remember the horrendous nature of the war rather than to sentimentalize it. The pageant he suggested would consist of all those who had profited from, contributed to, or suffered from the war, telling their truth. "Our dead are glorious, all brave men are glorious, but because glorious men are murdered that does not glorify murder."[164] He condemned war and the resort to war and regretted the outcome of the last one. "As I write it looks as though this sixth winter of unemployment and depression were going to be the bitterest of all. The clouds of industrial war are black and lowering at home. . . . We seem to have learned little."[165]

"The Devil's Press Agent" (November 14, 1925)

In this Armistice Day article, Studdert Kennedy condemned the perpetrators of "the poison gas" of propaganda. He charged that the great delusion of war was fostered by those seeking power who spread abroad the delusion that war was inevitable. They fanned the flames of fear of other nations and politicked for armaments as an insurance against war while encouraging the lie that battlefield deaths were honorable. "Armistice Day can be taken over by the subconscious gas factory and made into a projector of subtle poison for the people's minds." He suggested that the answer was to face the facts and to adopt a "fixed determination to serve the truth, and see that their sorrow (of deceased soldiers) shall not be in vain."[166]

"The Great Christmas Sham" (December 19, 1925)

In his Christmas message, Studdert Kennedy pictured the Baby Jesus walking the streets of England and pointing out the disease and poverty that filled the streets and slums of the country. Studdert Kennedy discovered that this judge made him uncomfortable. "I don't know what to do. This is terrible judgement. I could have stood up to the old judge seated on his throne and threatening his everlasting hell better than I can stand up to the baby of Bethlehem. . . . The baby makes me condemn myself, and that is beastly uncomfortable." Different elements of British society came under judgment: England's prisons, the industrial warfare, the Irish settlement, and the folly of war. England's insufficient charity also came under the child's steady gaze and was declared to be shameful. "If England would only secure a greater measure of justice for the downtrodden and oppressed, then it would be Christmas indeed."[167]

"Are You a Thief?" (February 20, 1926)

Studdert Kennedy again addressed poverty and the needs of the workers, particularly the coal miners, in this article. His rhetorical question, "are you a thief?" he understood would be answered in the negative by most people. When asked if a landlord was charging a poverty-stricken worker a fair rent, he thought the answer might prick a conscience or two. The nation was embroiled in economic turmoil, and it appeared everyone was pursuing their own selfish interests. He suggested that each person should reconsider. "If we are all going to think only of our own interests, or those of our own class or section, there is nothing for it but a fight." Instead, he appealed to the nation's higher nature. "Let us try, you and I, to be honest with ourselves . . . to do our bit to put things right, even if it does mean a bit of sacrifice."[168]

"The Answer's A Lemon" (May 29, 1926)

The "Great Strike" of 1926 served as the subject matter of this article, and Studdert Kennedy compared the industrial strife engulfing the nation with the Great War and the results of that conflict.

> Great wars, great revolutions, and great strikes are all alike great nonsense, and that is all the greatness about them. . . . In point of cold fact, the Great War was one of the meanest and most sordid chapters in European history, and if history is ever honestly written it will appear as such. All the piteous panic-stricken weakness of human nature oozed out through those accursed years as pus and poison ooze from a stupidly neglected sore upon a sickly body.[169]

Studdert Kennedy suggested that the Great Strike and the continuing coal difficulties were as pointless as the Great War had been. Instead of conflict and fighting speeches, he countered that everyone needed to come together with "intelligent co-operation" to discover solutions that would benefit all: workers, owners and the nation itself, which depended on the coal. "It is now or never. For God's sake, for the children's sake, let's get down to it."[170]

"The Poisoner of Manhood" (June 26, 1926)

The "dole" and unemployment were the subject of this article. Studdert Kennedy defended both and pointed to those who castigated the unemployed as lazy and characterized the dole (unemployment insurance) as encouraging sloth on the part of workers. He explained that few workers actually enjoyed receiving the dole, that instead they preferred the dignity of work. Unemployment, he explained, resulted in depression and low self-esteem on the part of the those seeking work. It also resulted in strife at home as husbands and wives got on each other's nerves. The dole, in the face of starvation, was preferable. "Anyone who worked in the bad old days before unemployment insurance began would be driven to desperation by the idea of abolishing it. . . . Old Bill's life is not a bed of roses now, but it was a bank of stinging nettles in the days gone by." He concluded that the British economy would improve and would resort to unemployment insurance only in extreme circumstances, and they would perfect unemployment insurance. In the meantime, "the trouble is in the devil and not the dole, and with patience we shall scotch the devil yet."[171]

"The Peer and the Pup" (July 26, 1926)

Propaganda, which Studdert Kennedy defined as lies, and the coal difficulties was the subject of his July 1926 article. He discussed the propagation of lies for both good purposes and bad, promoted by politicians and orators. He singled out a gentleman, by the name of Lord Hundsdon, for particular criticism. The gentleman, while "referring to the granting of poor relief to miners' families said, 'While the miners are our enemies we should not feed them. We did not feed the Germans, and I do not for the life of me see why we should feed the miners." Studdert Kennedy condemned the lie that the miners were an enemy in any sense of the word. He continued that those in power bore a serious responsibility to the truth, and that the truth was often dull. The greatest danger was that good people with pure intentions would tell lies in order to accomplish honorable purposes. They should always protect themselves from that danger. The cause of the coal miners was an important one. "They need no liars; they can stand upon the truth. Let us have it at all costs, however dull, complex, and bitter it appears to be. It is the only thing that will get us coal and feed the collier's child."[172]

"All After the Jam" (September 25, 1926)

Britain was still dealing with the coal issues in September 1926, and Studdert Kennedy suggested the reason behind the continuing struggles and lost productivity resulted from disagreements over the "jam, and not over bread and marg." He suggested that workers and owners alike wanted the finer things in life, but where was the limit? While everyone quibbled, the mines lay idle and the workers unpaid. Rather than struggling with each other, Studdert Kennedy suggested that "economic facts demanded that we should not cease production for five minutes, and we have ceased for five months."[173] Instead, all should set their sights on "higher jam," that provided by God, and come together to solve the coal crisis.

"King Wenceslas Exposed" (December 20, 1926)

In Studdert Kennedy's 1926 Christmas article, he introduced his readers to a communist friend who criticized Good King Wenceslas and his charity as a sham, useless and ill targeted. The king only helped one poor peasant, rather than all the poor in his kingdom. In condemning the good king, the communist also condemned all Christian charity as pointless. He accused the church, along with the wealthy capitalists, of "bleeding the workers dry," then salving their conscience with a bit of charity. Studdert Kennedy admitted that there was a bit of truth in the communist's charge, but that the communist did not understand the true nature of the king's effort, for he had trudged through the snow to provide his gift, suffering the cold to do so. Studdert Kennedy suggested that Britain's well-to-do should consider the poor and do their bit to defeat poverty. But they should do so out of a heart of love and not of compulsion. "True charity is honest love, and it is the only cure for Communism. . . . Start off with that peasant, maybe he digs coal for a living. Start with him, but for the Lord's sake, don't end there."[174]

"A Rank, Barefaced Fraud" (April 2, 1927)

In this article, Studdert Kennedy attacked employment insurance companies that were perpetrating fraud on the workers who had contracted with them to provide financial resources in the event of unemployment. In establishing unemployment insurance, the British government had "outsourced" the role to private companies. Employees paid a small portion of their pay to the company and the company contracted with them to provide funds in the event they lost their job. The problem, as identified by Studdert Kennedy, was that the companies were unfaithful in their responsibilities, failing to pay or delaying payment to those who had lost their jobs, with obvious results of unpaid bills and hunger. When the defrauded unemployed workers took the companies to court, the companies had the resources to delay the legal processes while the workers sank deeper into hardship. Studdert Kennedy called upon the government and the business world to correct this fraud being perpetrated against the workers. Speaking to the workers through the article, he said, "I am ashamed of myself for not discovering how things were before today. But I know now, and I beg you to take a tip from one who always wished you well. Don't let them have any more of your money."[175]

"A Jolly Good Gamble" (July 23, 1927)

Studdert Kennedy discussed the challenge of helping the "D" (the down) and the D.O. (down and out), usually those who had ended up in prison. He commented that many of the "down" were difficult to help as they needed "guts" as much as they needed a helping hand. But the ex-cons he had come across were severely damaged by life, and usually possessed a questionable character. They could deliver a slippery lie with ease. But he believed that even these individuals deserved a chance. One in ten would succeed and lift themselves from the mire if provided a helping hand. Of the nine failures, Studdert Kennedy acknowledged that it could be depressing, but that one success made it all worthwhile. What Britain needed in this case were sportsmen and women, those who could gamble on humanity. "It was a game and a great game, and it was started by the greatest sportsmen of all when he said, "Follow me and I will make you fishers of men."[176]

"Come Off It Coward" (October 15, 1927)

Studdert Kennedy returned to the ongoing problems of the coal miners in his October 1927 article. He had visited the mines and observed the condition of the miners and their families firsthand, and he found their condition deplorable. He attacked the idea that the government and nation, in gaining victory over the coal strikes of the previous two years, had in fact won a victory. In fact, he stated, the result was a great disaster. Only propaganda and lies perpetrated the idea of a victory. He challenged the nation to use all of its resources at the national level to seek a solution to the coal problem. Propaganda and lies would not suffice.

Studdert Kennedy empathized with the problems of the miners. "To be up to your ears in debt, and to work beyond your strength for a wage which even in a full week is not sufficient to keep up that strength . . . to see no hope, no matter how hard you work, of ever getting out of debt; The miners at present are beaten and broken men."[177] Studdert Kennedy challenged the nation to cooperate in the discovery of a positive statesmanlike policy to solve the coal problem. Their great challenge was to find people who would destroy propaganda and finally, "take the misery of the coal mines to heart."[178]

"The Accursed Thing" (November 12, 1927)

"The Accursed Thing" was Studdert Kennedy's 1927 Armistice Day contribution to *John Bull.* In it, the author reported having visited the Edinburgh National War Memorial. He found it beautiful and hated it because it was so beautiful. He feared it would promote and glorify war rather than remind the nation of war's brutality and death. During his visit, he observed a war widow and her son visiting the memorial and longed to take the child aside to inform him of the great lie that the edifice perpetrated; he longed to tell him the truth about war and its evils. He knew that no veteran would inform the child, they were too damaged to share their experiences. Many suffered from the continuing effects of shell shock, "in asylums now, plenty of them, biting their nails and scratching themselves, shivering at every sound, the men who went mad with fear." He believed the glorious dead, the heroes of the war, would tell that child the truth if they could. Otherwise the glorification of war would serve only "to humbug our defenseless children so that when the trumpets blow again, they will troop out like sheep to the slaughter. . . . For God's sake, let us be realists on Armistice Day. Do not be tempted by the hero worship in your son's eyes. Tell him the facts. This is the best tribute we can pay to the glorious dead. . . . Let us do it for them and honour their memories on the altar of truth."[179]

"The Woman Who Lost Christmas" (December 24, 1927)

Studdert Kennedy's Christmas 1927 article returned once again to the subject of war and its impact on the families of those killed in the war. In the article, he recounted the story of a woman who had been widowed after only three weeks of marriage to her soldier husband. She had served the church faithfully for years, but finally came to the point that she was overcome by despair. For years, she had assisted with the church's Christmas preparations, preparing dolls for the children. In her collapse, she declared, "I am too old to pretend any longer," she said, "and Christmas is all pretense. Dolls, dolls, it is all dolls, and I am too old to play with dolls. I would rather have the naked ugly truth about life than this beauty that is not true."

In his reflection, Studdert Kennedy held out the promise and beauty of Christmas. He had comforted her before her death, and hoped she knew the fulfillment of heaven. But he also hoped that all humanity could find the peace and beauty of Christmas. "It must be made true. Love must become the law of life. War must be ended, and hatred killed. Cruelty to children and tyranny of greed must be abolished . . . and a little child shall lead them. Christmas is the only thing that is good enough to be true."[180]

"Two Terrible Photographs" (April 7, 1928)

Studdert Kennedy's 1927 Easter article began with two photographs of communist Russia in which students were pictured being taught that God did not exist. Studdert Kennedy suggested that the God they detested and denied was in fact the traditional nature of God that he also denied, the Sovereign God who ruled by force and fear, who was used by medieval priests and leaders to keep the faithful in line. "But before we judge or condemn them let us look to home and lay what their terror teaches us to heart. So long as we seek peace in preparing for war and call in Christ to bless aeroplanes and bombs; so long as we continue to let people rot in slums while we preach to them contentment and the hope of heaven." then we are still worshipping the old gods and not the Christ of Easter. The true Christ of Easter, risen and vital, would transform England and its social ills. "We have done our best to kill him during these years of war and so-called peace. He has risen and gone before us into Galilee." In concluding, he suggested that these truths could defeat Russian communism and build a new world.[181]

"They're At It Again" (February 18, 1928)

In this article, Studdert Kennedy returned again to his anti-war passion. He had heard both a British military leader and an American admiral suggest that war was inevitable, and that preparations were even then being made for the next war. While arms negotiations eliminated outdated weapons systems, the nations perfected and fielded more modern technology that was ever more deadly. He ascribed much of the talk about the inevitability of war to military men who were the best of men, but who also bore a mental defect, an inability to conceive of peace.

"But there is no other necessity of fate behind it. Do not be bamboozled by any talk of economic necessity for war. War is inevitable unless and until men learn to think and see straight—but no longer." Studdert Kennedy knew that every nation bore the seed of militancy, a central danger spot for the future. "We are all born with a tendency to this form of lunacy, and are liable to catch it, but it perpetuated and handed down through the military and naval tradition which continues unchanged in a world of incredibly rapid change."[182]

"Plain Facts for Parents" (May 19, 1928)

This article represents a rather unfortunate direction for Studdert Kennedy as he rather too passionately argued that birth control ought to be imposed to limit the "diseased, degenerate, and physically and mentally deficient from having children." He observed that medical science had made great strides in enabling such children to survive, but the results were rather unfortunate. "We must face and deal with the problem of the unfit, or civilization will perish and time will write an epitaph upon her grave."[183]

"Let the Prince Speak Out" (February 23, 1929)

Studdert Kennedy observed that the coal mine problem had become intractable. He had heard that the Prince of Wales had commented that the problems in the mines were "damnable." He suggested that the prince should also visit the mines of Wales to apply his good efforts to these ongoing social ills. He related that he had visited Ramsay MacDonald in late 1925 and had implored him to do something about the coal mines and the problems there. He had talked to him "like a Dutch uncle." But the once and future prime minister, while agreeing with Studdert Kennedy, doubted that much could be done. "It was not revolution that I feared. It was poverty, dirty, gray, shameful poverty. It was poverty that I know the Prince has seen in Durham and declares to be damnable." He mostly feared that the children and their mothers would pay with their hunger and poverty. I pray that the Prince might not only pass the hat round but blow a trumpet blast so loud that it can be heard all over the Empire, and when he has got silence, I pray that he may be moved to say: 'This cannot go on. It is damnable.'"[184]

"Confound their Politics . . . Woodbine Willie's Last Message" (March 29, 1929)

In Studdert Kennedy's last message, submitted to *John Bull* before his death, he reflected upon the general election that was then being waged within the country. He challenged the voters to ask the politicians, whether they be socialists, liberals, or conservatives, whether their policies would actually work; were they efficient?

> What we want to know is what those who propose to take their places can do to persuade or compel those at present engaged in industry to combine and make it decently efficient. And so put to an end this shameful business of doctoring starvation with indifferently administered charity poultices. It is this practical test of efficiency that we must apply to all their pleas and proposals

Studdert Kennedy asserted that the British were tired of the failures of their leaders, and the continuing waste of human life in the slums and coal pits. Instead they wanted change guided by science that would bring about the dignity of Britain's workers. He knew that the politicians would "turn on their propaganda guns, but we are accustomed to them now." They were only lies, "signifying bankruptcy of thought and initiative." He finished with a last plea, "This is one of the richest countries in the world, and there are children wanting boots."[185]

CONCLUSION

I'd like to conclude this section with another Studdert Kennedy quote that captures his overall purpose in writing and answered the question that was posed to him in so many ways. It appears that, at every turn, he was asked, "What is the church doing here?" The question was often posed with expletives, especially during the war. But his peacetime activities also elicited the same question, often accompanied by expletives voiced by the politicians upon whose toes he had stepped. He always sought to care for the down and out, those in greatest danger of personal and spiritual damage. While his answer, provided in his wartime work, *The Hardest Part*, applied specifically to the war, in practice it also applied in spirit to postwar Britain.

> Here at last I find an answer to that questions, 'What the—is the Church doing here?' It is trying to keep the hope of heaven alive in the midst of bloody hell. It is trying to fill the army and to keep it filled with the Spirit of the Cross, the spirit of strong love of Right which will triumph at all costs in the battle against wrong. It is to help the fighting men against two temptations, the temptation to dull despair which endures because it has to endure, and not because it wills to conquer, and the temptation to become brutalized, and to live as do the brutes.[186]

NOTES

1. William Blake, *Jerusalem*, 1810.
2. Gerald Studdert-Kennedy, "Woodbine Willie: Religion and Politics After the Great War," *History Today*; Dec 1, 1986; 36, 12; 40.
3. D. F. Carey, "Studdert Kennedy: War Padre," in *G. A. Studdert Kennedy by His Friends*, ed. J. K. Mozley (London: Hodder & Stoughton, 1929), 124.
4. G. A. Studdert Kennedy, *Rough Talks by a Padre* (London: Hodder & Stoughton, 1918), 12.
5. Ibid., 23.
6. Ibid., 31.
7. Ibid., 107.
8. Ibid., 122.
9. Ibid., 129.
10. Ibid., 130.

11. Ibid., 141.
12. Ibid., 144.
13. Ibid., 199.
14. G. A. Studdert Kennedy, *Rough Talks by a Padre*, 161.
15. G. A. Studdert Kennedy, "The Religious Difficulties of the Private Soldier" in *The Church in the Furnace*, ed. Frederick Brodie MacNutt (London: Macmillan and Co., 1917), 379.
16. Ibid., 391.
17. Ibid.
18. Ibid., 397.
19. Ibid., 403.
20. Ibid., 404.
21. Ibid., 405.
22. Thomas O'Loughlin and Stuart Bell, "G.A. Studdert Kennedy: The Man," https://youtu.be/cnrZ3mgzVj4, accessed Feb 24, 2021.
23. Carey, "Studdert Kennedy: War Padre" in *G. A. Studdert Kennedy by His Friends*, 125.
24. G. A. Studdert Kennedy, *The Hardest Part* (London: Hodder & Stoughton, 1918), xiv–xvii.
25. Ibid., 10–11.
26. Ibid., 28.
27. Ibid., 71.
28. Ibid., 73–74.
29. Ibid., 136.
30. Ibid., 180.
31. Ibid., 181.
32. Ibid., 196.
33. D. F. Carey, "Studdert Kennedy: War Padre" in *G. A. Studdert Kennedy by His Friends*, ed. J. K. Mozley (London: Hodder & Stoughton, 1929), 132.
34. Gerald Studdert-Kennedy, *Dog-Collar Democracy* (London: Macmillan, 1982), 109.
35. G. A. Studdert Kennedy, *Rough Rhymes of a Padre* (Hodder & Stoughton, 1918), 18.
36. Ibid., 19.
37. Ibid., 23.
38. Ibid., 75.
39. Ibid., 77.
40. Ibid., 77.
41. Ibid., 76.
42. Ibid., 80.
43. The poem is powerful for others as well. I asked a friend to read my work and offer his criticisms and insights. He reported that "Well" also brought him to tears and caused him some intense spiritual reflection.
44. Studdert Kennedy, *Rough Rhymes of a Padre*, 9–16.

45. G. A. Studdert Kennedy, *More Rough Rhymes of a Padre* (London: Hodder & Stoughton, 1918), 24.
46. Ibid., 58.
47. Ibid., 62.
48. Ibid., 70.
49. Ibid., 76.
50. Ibid., 86–87.
51. Ibid., 89.
52. Jonathan Shay, *Odysseus in America: Combat Trauma and the Trials of Homecoming* (New York: Scribner, 2002), 1–2.
53. G. A. Studdert Kennedy, *Peace Rhymes of a Padre* (London: Hodder & Stoughton, 1920), 14.
54. Ibid., 16.
55. Ibid., 38
56. Ibid., 69.
57. Ibid., 85.
58. Ibid., 91.
59. Ibid., 92–94.
60. Purcell, *Woodbine Willie*, 167.
61. Studdert Kennedy, *Lies*, ix–x.
62. Ibid., 11.
63. Ibid., 10.
64. Ibid., 13.
65. Ibid., 37.
66. Ibid., 69.
67. Ibid., 80.
68. Ibid., 82–83.
69. Ibid., 96.
70. Ibid., 224.
71. Ibid., 235.
72. Ibid., 239.
73. Ibid., 267.
74. Purcell, *Woodbine Willie: A Biography*, 165.
75. G. A. Studdert Kennedy, *Food for the Fed Up* (London: Hodder & Stoughton, 1921), 2.
76. Ibid, 8.
77. Ibid., 54.
78. Ibid., 179.
79. Ibid., 260.
80. Ibid., 178.
81. Ibid., 261.
82. Ibid., 258.
83. Ibid., 186–187.
84. Ibid., 184.
85. Ibid., 63.

86. Ibid., 114–115.
87. Ibid., 64.
88. Ibid., 65.
89. Ibid., 311.
90. Ibid., 312.
91. G. A. Studdert Kennedy. *Democracy and the Dog Collar* (London: Hodder & Stoughton, 1921), 59–60.
92. Ibid., 99.
93. Ibid., 66.
94. Ibid., 56.
95. Ibid., 47–51.
96. Ibid., 206–207.
97. Ibid., 44–45.
98. Ibid., 43–44.
99. Ibid., 92–95.
100. Ibid., 174, 121.
101. G. A. Studdert Kennedy, *Songs of Faith and Doubt* (London: Hodder & Stoughton, 1922), 69.
102. Ibid., 7–8.
103. Ibid., 52–53.
104. Ibid., 53.
105. G. A. Studdert Kennedy, *The Wicket Gate* (London: Hodder & Stoughton, 1923), 13–14.
106. Ibid., 15.
107. Ibid., 24, 27.
108. Ibid., 69.
109. Ibid., 88–89
110. Ibid., 86.
111. Ibid., 69.
112. Ibid., 131–132.
113. Ibid., 226.
114. Ibid., 245.
115. Ibid., 245–246.
116. G. A. Studdert Kennedy, *The Word and the Work* (London: Longmans, Green and Co., 1925), 4.
117. Ibid., 6–7.
118. Ibid., 65.
119. Ibid., 69.
120. Ibid, 6–7.
121. Ibid., 33–34.
122. Ibid., 11.
123. Ibid., 3–4, 9, 28, 55–56.
124. Ibid., 6, 55–56.
125. Ibid., 75.
126. Ibid., 69.

127. Ibid., 57–58.
128. Ibid., 38.
129. Ibid., 46.
130. G. A. Studdert Kennedy, *I Pronounce Them: A Story of Man and Wife* (New York: George H. Doran Company, 1927), 29, 60, 188.
131. Ibid., 266.
132. Ibid., 180–182, 204.
133. Ibid., 123, 183, 217–9, 265.
134. Ibid., 154–155, 157, 181.
135. Ibid., 181, 191.
136. Ibid., 282–283.
137. Ibid., 311–313.
138. Ibid., 16, 70, 278.
139. Ibid., 281.
140. Ibid. 21.
141. Ibid., 228.
142. Ibid, 292, 299–303.
143. Ibid., 292.
144. G. A. Studdert Kennedy, "The Religious Difficulties of the Private Soldier," in *The Church in the Furnace,* ed. F. B. MacNutt (London: Macmillan and Co., 1917), 379.
145. G. A. Studdert Kennedy, *The Warrior, The Woman and the Christ*, (London: Hodder and Stoughton, 1928), 21.
146. Ibid., 119.
147. Studdert Kennedy, *The Word and the Work*, 21.
148. G. A. Studdert Kennedy, *The Warrior, the Woman, and the Christ*, 19–21.
149. Ibid., 15.
150. Ibid., 152.
151. Ibid., 59.
152. Ibid., 311–312.
153. Ibid., 275–276.
154. Ibid., 315.
155. Ibid., 314–315.
156. Ibid., 21.
157. Ibid.
158. Ibid., 203–204.
159. Ibid., 312.
160. Ibid., 103.
161. Ibid., 316.
162. G. A. Studdert Kennedy, "Why Class Hatred?" *John Bull*, Feb. 7, 1925, 13.
163. G. A. Studdert Kennedy, "Modern Dens of Thieves," *John Bull*, April 11, 1925.
164. G. A. Studdert Kennedy, "A Pageant of Truth," *John Bull*, August 1, 1925, 15.
165. Ibid.

166. G. A. Studdert Kennedy, "The Devil's Press Agent," *John Bull*, November 14, 1925.

167. G. A. Studdert Kennedy, "The Great Christmas Sham," *John Bull*, December 19, 1925.

168. G. A. Studdert Kennedy, "Are You a Thief," *John Bull*, February 20, 1926.

169. G. A. Studdert Kennedy, "The Answer's A Lemon," *John Bull*, May 29, 1926, 17.

170. G. A. Studdert Kennedy, "The Answer's a Lemon," *John Bull*, May 19, 1926, 17.

171. G. A. Studdert Kennedy, "The Poisoner of Manhood," *John Bull*, June 26, 1926. 15.

172. G. A. Studdert Kennedy, "The Peer and the Pup," *John Bull*, July 26, 1926, 17.

173. G. A. Studdert Kennedy, "All After the Jam," *John Bull,* September 25, 1926.

174. G. A. Studdert Kennedy, "King Wenceslas Exposed, *John Bull,* December 20, 1926, 20.

175. G. A. Studdert Kennedy, "A Rank, Barefaced Fraud," *John Bull*, April 2, 1927, 15.

176. G. A. Studdert Kennedy, "A Jolly Good Gamble," *John Bull*, July 23, 1927, 15.

177. G. A. Studdert Kennedy, "Come Off It Coward," *John Bull*, Oct. 15, 1927, 17.

178. Ibid.

179. G. A. Studdert Kennedy, "The Accursed Thing," *John Bull*, Nov. 12, 1927, 24.

180. G. A. Studdert Kennedy, "The Woman Who Lost Christmas," *John Bull*, Dec. 24, 1927, 15.

181. G. A. Studdert Kennedy, "Two Terrible Photographs," *John Bull*, April 7, 1928, 13.

182. G. A. Studdert Kennedy, They're at It Again," *John Bull,* February 18, 1928, 22.

183. G. A. Studdert Kennedy, "Plain Talk for Parents," *John Bull*, May 29, 1928, 15.

184. G. A. Studdert Kennedy, "Let the Prince Speak Out," *John Bull*, Feb. 23, 1929, 9.

185. G. A. Studdert Kennedy, "Confound their Politics . . . Woodbine Willie's Last Message," *John Bull*, March 29, 1929, 9.

186. Studdert Kennedy, *Rough Talks by a Padre*, 31–32.

Bibliography

NEWSPAPER ARTICLES

"1000 at City Service, Woodbine Willie and the Power of Money." *Westminster Gazette*, November 11, 1922.[1]

"25,000 Pay Tribute to Dead Padre," *Birmingham Gazette*, March 13, 1929.

"A Cheery St. Fercus Soldier," *The Buchan Observer*, 15 April 1916.

"A Famous Padre: Death of Woodbine Willie," *Gloucester Journal*, March 9, 1929.

"A Momentary Aberration," *Nottingham Journal*, November 12, 1921.

"A Momentary Aberration," *Yorkshire Evening Post*, November 12, 1921.

"A Preacher's Power: Rev. G.A. Studdert Kennedy's Visit to Coventry," *Midland Daily Telegraph*, March 5, 1926.

"Age of Problems: Christianity in Industry," *North Devon Journal*, July 19,1928.

"Alternative to War: The League of Nations." *Sunderland Daily Echo*, Monday May 14, 1923.

"An Ex-Soldier's Complaint." *Sheffield Evening Telegraph*, October 11, 1919.

"Another Worcester Cleric as Chaplain," *Birmingham Daily Post*, December 1, 1915.

"Army Padre on the Right Way to World Peace," *The Leader*, Friday June 23, 1922.

"Asquith Aims at Getting Every Potential Man," *Dundee Evening Courier*, December 21, 1915.

"Bishop's Coal Peace Plan Unacceptable," *Dundee Courier*, August 5, 1926.

"Britain Puts Hope in Fighting Spirit: King's Chaplain, on Visit Here, Says Nation Has Great Task, but Will Solve Problems," *New York Times*, December 23, 1926.

"Broadminded Parson," *The Bioscope*, May 8, 1919.

"Christianity and Industrial Life," *Hastbourne Chronicle*, April 29, 1922.

"Class War is Anti-Christian," *Peterborough Standard*, April 1, 1927.

"Compassion Fatigue is a Set of Symptoms, Not a Disease," www.compassionfa tigue.org, accessed 4 Feb 2021.

"Confusion Worse Confounded," *South Yorkshire Times and Mexborough and Swinton Times,* August 13, 1926.

"Daily Radio Schedule," *Shields Daily News*, April 17, 1925.
"Defense of Bishops' Intervention: Dr. Temple Explains," Staffordshire Sentinel, October 7, 1926.
"Fear of Armistice Day," *Mansfield Reporter and Sutton Times*, November 11, 1927.
"Fight for Right: Mr. Andrew Fisher on Death Better than Dishonour: A New Heaven and a New Earth After the Struggle," *Western Gazette*, March 17, 1916.
"Fruits of Victory, Woodbine Willie's Analysis for Our Times," *Northampton Mercury*, May 12, 1922.
"Futile Victory, Padre's Regret for War Propaganda," *Sheffield Daily Telegraph*, November 28, 1921.
"G. A. Studdert Kennedy Preaches at Palace," *Northern Whig*, March 21, 1927.
"G. A. Studdert Kennedy Preaches at Palace," *Northern Whig*, May 7, 1928.
"Good-bye Old Friend," *John Bull*, March 16, 1929.
"Government Complacence on Unemployment," *Sheffield Independent*, May 29, 1919.
"Industrial Christian Fellowship: Address by Woodbine Willie," *Hastbourne Chronicle*, April 29, 1922.
"Industrial Christian Fellowship: Rev. G.A. "Studdert Kennedy on Socialism," *Gloucester Journal*, Saturday September 24, 1927.
"King's Chaplain Talks to Princeton Classes," *New York Times*, January 14, 1924.
"League of the Church Militant," *The Leicester Daily Post*, October 14, 1919.
"Letters to the Editor: Christianity and War," *Sheffield Daily Telegraph*, December 14, 1921.
"Letters to the Editor: Christianity and War," *Sheffield Daily Telegraph*, December 17, 1921.
"Like Pigs in Hovels," *Yorkshire Evening Post*, March 8, 1928.
"Lloyd George's Policy," *Birmingham Daily Gazette*, "December 11, 1918.
"Lloyd George's Wolverhampton Speech," *Devon and Exeter Daily Gazette*, November 25, 1918.
"Mail: Mustard and Cress," *Hull Daily Mail*, March 31, 1917.
"Modern Voices of Revolt," *Newcastle Journal*, January 27, 1927.
"Moral Injury," https://www.ptsd.va.gov/professional/co-occurring/moral_injury_at_war.asp, accessed 19 Oct 2018.
"Mr. Cook's Two Voices," *Penrith Observer*, August 3, 1926.
"Mr. Lloyd George on British War Aims and Manpower." *Birmingham Gazette*, December 21, 1917.
"No More War Rallies, Hyde Park" *The Scotsman*, July 31, 1922.
"No More War; Today's Call from the Nations; Hyde Park Rally." *Westminster Gazette*, July 29, 1922.
"Not a Fair Deal," *Birmingham Gazette*, December 13, 1926.
"Political Notes," *Middlesex Gazette*, April 9, 1910.
"Premier and an Honorable Peace: Final Emancipation from Reign of Force," *Leicester Daily Post*, November 10, 1915.
"Premier Unfolds His Unemployment Proposals," *Sheffield Independent*, October 20, 1921.

"Prison for Cleric: Posed in Derby as Woodbine Willie," *Derby Daily Telegraph,* September 17, 1923.

"Problems of Society: Rev. Studdert Kennedy's View," *Belfast Telegraph,* February 2, 1929.

"Provision for Rev. G. A. Studdert Kennedy's Widow," *Dundee Evening Telegraph,* February 5, 1930.

"Religion and Social Problems," *Western Morning and Mercury,* November 25, 1924.

"Rev. G. A. Studdert Kennedy: His Coventry Visit," *Coventry Herald,* March 8, 1926.

"Rochester Diocesan Conference," *Tunbridge Wells Courier,* June 4, 1920.

"Ruling Out War: Rev. S. Kennedy on Individual Conscience," *Birmingham Gazette,* April 10, 1924.

"Socialistic Theories Exploded," *Shipley Times and Express,* October 6, 1922.

"Starving Out the Miners," *Daily Herald,* June 3, 1926.

"Studdert Kennedy Appointed as Moorhouse Lecturer," *Newcastle Journal and North Star,* January 27, 1928.

"T.U.C. Invitation to Miners, Church Intervention," *Birmingham Gazette,* July 15, 1926.

"The Center of Unity," *The Advertiser,* May 22, 1926.

"The Hymn Jerusalem," www.prospectmagazine.co.uk/arts-and-books/almost-everything-you-know-about-the-hymn-jerusalem-is-wrong, accessed March 2, 2021.

"The ICF, The Church and Social Service," *Birmingham Gazette,* March 3, 1922.

"The National Mission of Repentance and Hope," www.lambethpalacelibrary.wordpress.com/2016/05/13/the-national-mission-of-repentance-and-hope-1916/, accessed January 15, 2021.

"The Position of Socialism," *Yorkshire Post,* July 17, 1913.

"The Problem of the Churches," *Perthshire Advertiser,* January 19, 1929.

"The Socialism of a King's Chaplain," *Forward,* July 22, 1922.

"Triumph Claimed for Primate," *Nottingham Journal,* February 22, 1927.

"Understanding Post-Traumatic Growth," *Psychology Today.* www.psychologytoday.com/us/basics/post-traumatic-growth accessed March 1, 2021 at 0839.

"Vicar's Remedy for His Parish," *Manchester Evening News,* April 21, 1919.

"Where War Starts." *Yorkshire Evening Post,* September 21, 1922.

"Woodbine Willie" *Hartlepool Northern Daily Mail,* March 26, 1926.

"Woodbine Willie: Arrival at Plymouth from America," *Western Morning News,* March 3, 1924.

"Woodbine Willie at Abertillery: Christ's Social Message." *New South Wales Gazette,* February 5, 1926.

"Woodbine Willie at Hastings: Eloquent Message of Christian Fellowship." *Hastings and St. Leonards Observer,* January 21, 1928.

"Woodbine Willie at Kirkby, Are All Men Equal, Is the World an Unjust Place?" *Mansfield Reporter and Sutton Times,* March 31, 1922.

"Woodbine Willie at Rugby," *Rugby Advertiser,* February 20, 1920.

"Woodbine Willie at Taunton: Ridding the World of Snobbery." *The Courier,* November 4, 1925.

"Woodbine Willie at Tunbridge Wells," *The Courier,* June 1, 1923.

"Woodbine Willie Dead: Famous War Padre," *Belfast Telegraph,* March 8, 1929.
"Woodbine Wille Departs for U.S." *Birmingham Daily Gazette*, October 31, 1923.
"Woodbine Willie: Famous Parson on the Peace Treaty," *Northampton Mercury*, April 23, 1920.
"Woodbine Willie, Famous Parson's racy Address," *Portsmouth Evening News*, January 26, 1922.
"Woodbine Willie Fined," *Northampton Mercury*, June 22, 1928.
"Woodbine Willie Memorial," *Liverpool Echo*, March 25, 1929.
"Woodbine Willie; Powerful Address on the Serious Results of Poverty." *The Advertiser*, October 26, 1928.
"Woodbine Willie's Accident: Preaches For An Hour With a Badly Damaged Foot," *Liverpool Echo,* March 21, 1924.
"World-Wide Demand for No More War." *Daily Herald*, Monday July 30, 1923.
"Woodbine Willie on Playing the Game," *Western Daily Press*, May 11, 1925.

BOOKS AND JOURNALS

Blake, William. "Jerusalem," published in 1807.

Boughton, Harold. "Remembrance of the War," IWM 8667 TS, iwm.org.uk, accessed March 6, 2021.

Brierley, Michael. "Geoffrey Studdert Kennedy: A Brief Life," in *Life after Tragedy: Essays on Faith and the First World War Evoked by Geoffrey Studdert Kennedy*, eds. Michael W. Brierley and Georgina A. Byrne. Eugene, Oregon: Cascade Books, 2017.

Brierley, Michael. "There Ain't No Throne: Geoffrey Studdert Kennedy and the Doctrine of God," in *Life after Tragedy: Essays on Faith and the First World War Evoked by Geoffrey Studdert Kennedy*, eds. Michael W. Brierley and Georgina A. Byrne. Eugene, Oregon: Cascade Books, 2017.

Brierley, Michael W. and Georgina A. Byrne, eds. *Life after Tragedy: Essays on Faith and the First World War Evoked by Geoffrey Studdert Kennedy*. Eugene, Oregon: Cascade Books, 2017.

British Library, "World War 1: The Daily Life of Soldiers." https://www.bl.uk/world-war-one/articles/the-daily-life-of-soldiers#.

Brock, Rita Nakashima and Gabriella Lettini. *Soul Repair: Recovering from Moral Injury after War*. Boston: Beacon Press, 2012.

Carey, D. F., "Studdert Kennedy: War Padre," in *G. A. Studdert Kennedy by His Friends*, ed. J. K. Mozley. London: Hodder & Stoughton, 1929.

Church of England, Articles of Religion. www.churchofengland.org/p accessed January 13, 2021.

Clausewitz, Carl von. *On War*, Eds. and Translators, Michael Howard and Peter Paret. Princeton: Princeton University Press, 1976.

Crafts, Nicholas. "Walking Wounded: The British Economy in the Aftermath of World War 1," https://voxeu.org/article/walking-wounded-british-economy-aftermath-world-war-i, accessed January 19, 2021.

Daunton, Martin. *Wealth and Welfare: An Economic and Social History of Britain 1851–1951*. Oxford: Oxford University Press, 2007.

Drescher, Kent, Mark W. Smith, and David W. Foy. "Spirituality and Readjustment following War Zone Experiences," in *Combat Stress Injury*, eds. Charles R. Figley and William P. Nash. New York: Routledge, 2007.

Ede, W. Moore. "Studdert Kennedy: His Life in Worcester," in *G. A. Studdert Kennedy by His Friends*, ed. J. K. Mozley. London: Hodder & Stoughton, 1929.

Edmonds, James E. *History of the Great War: Military Operations 1916 Vol. I* (London: Macmillan, 1932).

Eichengreen, Barry. "The British Economy Between the Wars" https://eml.berkeley.edu/~eichengr/floudjohnsonchaptersep16–03.pdf accessed December 15, 2020.

Figley, Charles R. and William P. Nash, eds. *Combat Stress Injury: Theory, Research, and Management.* New York: Routledge, 2007.

Grant, Robert. *The Way of the Wound: A Spirituality of Trauma and Transformation.* Oakland: Robert Grant, 1996.

Graubard, Steven Richards. "Military Demobilization in Great Britain Following the First World War," *Journal of Modern History*, December (1947), 19:4, 297–311, Proquest.

Hodgson, Timothy J; Carey, Lindsay B. "Moral Injury and Definitional Clarity: Betrayal, Spirituality and the Role of Chaplains." *Journal of Religion and Health*; New York Vol. 56, Iss. 4 (Aug 2017): 1212–1228, Proquest.

Holden, Wendy. *Shell Shock*. London: Channel 4 Books, 1998.

Kirk, P. T. R. "Studdert Kennedy: I.C.F. Crusader" in *G. A. Studdert Kennedy by His Friends*. London: Hodder & Stoughton, 1929.

Kraft, Heidi Squier. *Rule Number Two*. New York: Little, Brown and Co., 2007.

Litz, Bret T. and Particial K. Kerig, "Introduction to the Special Issue on Moral Injury: Conceptual Challenges, Methodological Issues, and Clinical Applications," *Journal of Traumatic Stress* (June 2019) 32, 341–349. Proquest.

McClenehan, Linda. "Post-traumatic Spiritual Disorder," *Ministry and Liturgy* 40, no. 8 (October 2013): 9–13. Accessed April 1, 2017.

McGrath, Alister E., ed., *The Christian Theology Reader.* West Sussex: John Wiley and Sons Ltd., 2017.

MCTP 3–30E and NTTP 1–15M Combat and Operational Stress Control. Washington D.C.: Department of the Navy, 2016.

Mozley, J. K., *The Impassibility of God: A Survey of Christian Thought.* Cambridge: The University Press, 1926.

Mozley, J. K., ed., *G. A. Studdert Kennedy by His Friends.* London. Hodder & Stoughton, 1929.

Nash, William P. "Combat Operational Stress Adaptations and Injuries," in *Combat Stress Injury*, eds. Charles R. Figley and William P. Nash. New York: Routledge, 2007.

Nash, William P. "The Stressors of War," in *Combat Stress Injury*, eds. Charles R. Figley and William P. Nash. New York: Routledge, 2007.

Nash, William P. and Dewleen Baker, "Competing and Complementary Models of Combat Stress Injury" in *Combat Stress Injury, eds. Charles R. Figley and William P. Nash.* New York: Routledge, 2007.

O'Loughlin, Thomas and Stuart Bell. "G.A. Studdert Kennedy: The Man," https://youtu.be/cnrZ3mgzVj4, accessed Feb 24, 2021.

O'Loughlin, Thomas and Stuart Bell. "Is Studdert Kennedy Relevant to the Twenty-First Century." https://youtu/be/5FjAXPUjBVw.

Parker, Linda. *A Seeker After Truths: The Life and Times of G.A. Studdert Kennedy (Woodbine Willie) 1883–1929.* Solihull, West Midlands: Helion and Company Limited, 2017.

Purcell, William. *Woodbine Willie: A Biography*. London: Hodder & Stoughton, 1962.

Raw, David. *Theodore Bayle Hardy*. Yorkshire: Pen and Sword Books, 2018.

Shay, Jonathan. *Achilles in Vietnam: Combat Trauma and the Undoing of Character*. New York: Touchstone Books, 1994.

Shay, Jonathan. *Odysseus in America: Combat Trauma and the Trials of Coming Home*. New York: Scribner, 2002.

Shay, Jonathan, "Moral Injury," *Psychoanalytic Psychology* 31, no. 2 (2014): 182–191. Proquest.

Sheppard, H. R. L. "Studdert Kennedy: A Friend," in *G. A. Studdert Kennedy by His Friends*, ed. J. K. Mozley. London: Hodder & Stoughton, 1929.

Snape, Michael. *The Royal Army Chaplains' Department: Clergy Under Fire*. Sheffield: The Boydell Press, 2008.

Stanrino, Vincint R., W. Patrick Sullivan, Clyde T. Angel, and Loaunne W. Davis, "Moral Injury, Coherence, and Spiritual Repair," *Mental Health, Religion and Culture* 22, no.1 (2019), 99–114, Proquest.

Stuart, Barbara. "Cognitive Dissonance: A Spiritual Perspective," https://www.mediate.com/articles/stuart.cfm accessed 31 Aug 2018.

Strachan, Hew. *The First World War*. New York: Viking Press, 2003.

Studdert Kennedy, G. A. "The Accursed Thing," *John Bull*, November 12, 1927.

Studdert Kennedy, G. A. "All After the Jam," *John Bull*, September 25, 1926.

Studdert Kennedy, G. A. "A Jolly Good Gamble," *John Bull*, July 23, 1927.

Studdert Kennedy, G. A. "The Answer's a Lemon," *John Bull*, May 19, 1926.

Studdert Kennedy, G. A. "A Pageant of Truth," *John Bull*, August 1, 1925.

Studdert Kennedy, G. A. "A Rank, Barefaced Fraud," *John Bull*, April 2, 1927.

Studdert Kennedy, G. A. "Are You a Thief," *John Bull*, February 20, 1926.

Studdert Kennedy, G. A. "Come Off It Coward," *John Bull*, October 15, 1927.

Studdert Kennedy, G. A. "Confound their Politics . . . Woodbine Willie's Last Message," *John Bull*, March 29, 1929.

Studdert Kennedy, G. A. *Democracy and The Dog Collar*. London: Hodder & Stoughton, 1921.

Studdert Kennedy, G. A. "The Devil's Press Agent," *John Bull*, November 14, 1925.

Studdert Kennedy, G. A. *Dog Collar Democracy*. London: Macmillan Press, 1982.

Studdert Kennedy, G. A. *Food for the Fed Up*. London: Hodder & Stoughton, 1921.

Studdert Kennedy, G. A. "The Great Christmas Sham," *John Bull*, December 19, 1925.

Studdert Kennedy, G. A. *The Hardest Part*. London: Hodder & Stoughton, 1918.
Studdert Kennedy, G. A. *I Pronounce Them: A Story of Man and Wife*. New York: George H. Doran Company, 1927.
Studdert Kennedy, G. A. "King Wenceslas Exposed," *John Bull*, December 20, 1926.
Studdert Kennedy, G. A. "Let the Prince Speak Out," *John Bull*, February 23, 1929.
Studdert Kennedy, G. A. *Lies*. London: Hodder and Stoughton, 1919.
Studdert Kennedy, G. A. "Modern Dens of Thieves," *John Bull*, April 11, 1925.
Studdert Kennedy, G. A. *More Rough Rhymes of a Padre*. London: Hodder & Stoughton, 1919.
Studdert Kennedy, G. A. *The New Man in Christ*. London: Hodder & Stoughton, 1932.
Studdert Kennedy, G. A. "The Peer and the Pup," *John Bull*, July 26, 1926.
Studdert Kennedy, G. A. "Plain Talk for Parents," *John Bull*, May 29, 1928.
Studdert Kennedy, G. A. "The Poisoner of Manhood," *John Bull*, June 26, 1926.
Studdert Kennedy, G. A. "The Religious Difficulties of the Private Soldier," in *The Church in the Furnace*, ed. F. B. Macnutt. London: Macmillan and Co., 1917.
Studdert Kennedy, G. A. *Rough Talks by a Padre*. London: Hodder & Stoughton, 1918.
Studdert Kennedy, G. A. *Rough Rhymes of a Padre*. London: Hodder & Stoughton, 1918.
Studdert Kennedy, G. A. *Songs of Faith and Doubt*. London: Hodder & Stoughton, 1922.
Studdert Kennedy, G. A. "They're At It Again," *John Bull*, February 18, 1928.
Studdert Kennedy, G. A. "Two Terrible Photographs," *John Bull*, April 7, 1928.
Studdert Kennedy, G. A. *The Warrior, The Woman, and the Christ*. London: Hodder & Stoughton, 1928.
Studdert Kennedy, G. A. "Why Class Hatred?" *John Bull*, February 7, 1925.
Studdert Kennedy, G. A. *The Wicket Gate*. London: Hodder & Stoughton, 1923.
Studdert Kennedy, G. A. "The Woman Who Lost Christmas," *John Bull*, December 24, 1927.
Studdert-Kennedy, G. A. "Woodbine Willie: Religion and Politics After the Great War," *History Today*; Dec 1, 1986; 36, 12; 40.
Studdert Kennedy, G. A. *The Word and the Work*. London: Hodder & Stoughton, 1925.
Walker, Simon Herold, "Saving Bodies and Souls: Army Chaplains and Medical care in the First World War," *Postgraduate Journal of Medical Humanities*, 3 (2016): 24–38. https://humanities.exeter.ac.uk/media/universityofexeter/collegeofhumanities/history/researchcentres/centreformedicalhistory/pdfsanddocs/2_-_Army_Chaplains_and_Medical_Care_in_the_First_World_War.pdf accessed December 1, 2018.

NOTE

1. All newspaper articles were sourced through the British Newspaper Archive. https://www.britishnewspaperarchive.co.uk.

Index

About the Author

Dayne Nix has taught for the Naval War College since 2001. He has taught Joint Maritime Operations since 2009 and was promoted to full professor in 2018. He also taught National Security Decision Making from 2007 to 2009 and taught "Faith and Force" in the War College's elective program from 2001 to 2004.

He holds a BA degree from the University of Colorado in international affairs, the MDiv from Denver Seminary, the ThM degree from Duke University, the MA degree from the Naval War College (with distinction) in national security affairs, and the PhD in the Humanities from Salve Regina University.

CDR Nix is a retired U.S. Navy chaplain and previously served in the U.S. Marine Corps as a communications officer. He has received numerous military awards, including four Meritorious Service Medals.

He is the author of, *The Integration of Philosophy, Politics, and Conservative Islam in the Thought of Muhammad Iqbal* (Mellen Press) and "American Civil-Military Relations: Samuel P. Huntington and the Political Dimensions of Military Professionalism" (*Naval War College Review*, Spring 2012) as well as other articles and conference papers.

Between 2011 and 2013 he facilitated the development and delivery of "Religion and Security in World Affairs," a conference jointly hosted by Georgetown University's Berkeley Center for Religion, Peace and World Affairs and the NPS Center for Stabilization and Reconstruction Studies in Monterey. He maintains a continuing interest in the role of religion in national security affairs as well as the role and experience of chaplains in the military.

Professor Nix has been married to Linda K. Nix (Page) for fifty years. They share four children and ten grandchildren.

www.ingramcontent.com/pod-product-compliance
Lightning Source LLC
LaVergne TN
LVHW091529200926
848483LV00002B/343
* 9 7 8 1 6 6 6 9 0 8 6 5 7 *